COMPUTERS AND CLASSROOM CULTURE

Janet Ward Schofield

University of Pittsburgh

CAMBRIDGE
UNIVERSITY PRESS

Published by the Press Syndicate of the University of Cambridge
The Pitt Building, Trumpington Street, Cambridge CB2 1RP
40 West 20th Street, New York, NY 10011-4211, USA
10 Stamford Road, Oakleigh, Melbourne 3166, Australia

First published 1995

Printed in the United States of America

Library of Congress Cataloging-in-Publication Data
Schofield, Janet Ward.
Computers and classroom culture / Janet Ward Schofield.
p. cm.
Includes bibliographical references and index.
ISBN 0-521-47368-3 (hardback) – ISBN 0-521-47924-X (pbk.)
1. Education – Data processing. 2. Computer-assisted instruction.
3. Computer science – Study and teaching. 4. Computers – Social
aspects. 5. sex roles   I. Title.
LB1028.43.S34   1995
371.3'34 – dc20   95-1624
                                                   CIP

A catalog record for this book is available from the British Library.

ISBN 0-521-47368-3 Hardback
ISBN 0-521-47924-X Paperback

To my family
with love and hope for the future

and to Laurie
a friend who has made so much possible

CONTENTS

ACKNOWLEDGMENTS

THE PLACEMENT OF THESE ACKNOWLEDGMENTS NEAR THE beginning of this book is appropriate because it symbolizes the important role that others have played in making it possible. Chief among these individuals is Brad Huber, who, over the course of two years while a postdoctoral fellow working with me at the University of Pittsburgh, was a tremendous help in assisting in the design of this research, as well as in very capably conducting hundreds of hours of observation and countless interviews. Also important to this research over several years were Debra Evans-Rhodes, then a graduate student in social psychology, who played a significant role in gathering observational data, and Van Yasek, a graduate student in anthropology. The care and patience that they demonstrated in working on the analysis of the interview data made a significant contribution to this project. The able assistance of David Verban, another graduate student in social psychology, was also of great value during the first year of the project. Anthropology graduate students Bernie Harrigan and Mike Rasmussen also made a substantial contribution to this research by conducting dozens of student interviews. Finally, I would like to thank social psychology graduate students Cheri Britt and Rebecca Eurich-Fulcer for their assistance in certain aspects of the data analysis as well as postdoctoral fellow Gail Futoran for her helpful comments on this manuscript and her very useful work on a closely related research project.

Lucille Jarzinka and, at a later point, Debbie Connell were responsible for the daunting job of transcribing the literally thousands of pages of dictated field notes and taped interviews on which this book is based. They both approached this task with care, patience, and intelligence, which I deeply appreciate. In addition, Debbie Connell had major responsibility for organizing this massive data set to prepare it for analysis and for assisting in the preparation of this manuscript. The infinite patience she evidenced in her work and her remarkable organizational skills saved me hundreds of hours of work and managed to keep things moving when gridlock seemed close to inevitable. For this, as well as for her unfailing good nature, I am profoundly grateful.

A number of undergraduates at the University of Pittsburgh contributed to this project by assisting in the analysis of the interview data. Important in this respect were Bozena Ali, Valerie Balavage, Leslie Gedman, Tammy Kirkpatrick, Hillary Konowal, Donna Liggon, Erin Mamros, Maureen McKissick, Diane Miller, Valerie Morzyellowski, James Omslaer, Saundra Saylor, Amy Schultz, and Amy Woodbury-Webber. I would like to extend a special word of thanks to Haruna Isa, an undergraduate, who during the several years he worked on this project made an unusually fine contribution to many phases of the work.

I would also like to express my appreciation to John Anderson of Carnegie Mellon University and his associates, especially Franklin Boyle, for their willingness to let us observe the field test of the artificially intelligent tutor they developed, as well as meetings of their research group. Their conduct in allowing my research team such unfettered access when they had no prior personal experience with us exemplified scientific ideals of openness and cooperation in the pursuit of knowledge.

I would like to thank Lauren Resnick and Bob Glaser, codirectors of the Learning Research and Development Center, for providing a very supportive environment for my work. Sara Kiesler also deserves a note of thanks for organizing, with the support of the Markle Foundation and the Social Science Research Council, two very fine interdisciplinary conferences that contributed significantly to my thinking in writing Chapter 7.

This book would not have been possible without the cooperation of the teachers and students at the school studied. My deepest thanks to all the teachers who had the courage to open their classrooms day after day to me and the other members of the research team when initially we could tell them little more than that our goal was to see what was happening there and to try to understand the role that technology played in it. It is only a concern about confidentiality that keeps me from singling out for special recognition the teachers who made a special contribution to this study through their long-term cooperation with our observational work. The willingness of teachers and other school staff members to talk with us about their experiences in both formal interviews and informal conversations was also invaluable, and I am grateful to the large number of individuals who cooperated in this manner. The students who participated in interviews also deserve thanks for taking the time to talk with us so openly. Thanks also to the school district personnel and the parents whose cooperation was essential to the conduct of this research.

My sincere thanks also go to my family: to my mother, Sarah Ellis Ward, and my late father, William Ward, for providing a supportive home environment that valued intellect, excellence, and service to others; to my husband, Douglas, and my daughters, Alanya, Heather, and Emily, for enriching my life by being such good companions when the solitary work of writing is done and we are able to share the day's experiences, take a ride on our bicycles or in a canoe, or set off on journeys to new places. Finally, these acknowledgments would not be complete without thanks to Laurie Sallows, whose friendship over the years and extraordinary helpfulness in so many regards contributed in important ways to creating an environment that made this work possible.

The research reported here was funded by the Office of Naval Research (Contract No. N00014-K-85-0664). I would like to express my appreciation to Susan Chipman, the project monitor, for her insightful comments and unfailing helpfulness. Some of the work that made Chapter 7 possible was funded by a contract with the National Science Foundation (Contract No. RED-9253452). However, all opinions expressed herein are solely those of the author, and no endorsement of the conclusions by the ONR or NSF is implied or intended.

Portions of this book have appeared previously in the articles and book chapters cited here. The material is reprinted with the permission of the publishers indicated:
Schofield, J. W. (1994). Barriers to computer usage in secondary school teaching. In C. W. Huff & T. Finholt (Eds.), *Social issues in*

computing: Putting computing in its place (pp. 547–580). New York: McGraw-Hill.

Schofield, J. W., Eurich-Fulcer, R., & Britt, C. L. (1994). Teachers, computer tutors, and teaching: The artificially intelligent tutor as an agent for classroom change. *American Educational Research Journal, 31*(3), 579–607.

Schofield, J. W., Evans-Rhodes, D., & Huber, B. (1990). Artificial intelligence in the classroom. *Social Science Computer Review, 8*(1), 24–41.

1

INTRODUCTION

CHANGES IN COMPUTER TECHNOLOGY DURING THE PAST several decades have been extraordinary in both their magnitude and rapidity. Ten years ago Lepper pointed out that portable personal computers costing less than $1,000.00 were available that had more computational power than could have been delivered 30 years before that by a $10 million machine the size of an average living room (Lepper, 1985), and the cost per unit of computational power has continued to decline dramatically. An even more striking way of illustrating the pace of change is to compare the computer and automobile industries. As Lepper notes, if the automobile industry had obtained increases in efficiency and reductions in cost comparable to those occurring in the computer industry, a Rolls-Royce would cost less than $2.75. Furthermore, it would get almost 3,000,000 miles per gallon and be capable of towing an aircraft carrier.

These remarkable increases in computational power have been accompanied by rapid proliferation in the uses to which computers can be put. Computers now play an important roll in manufacturing, sales, transportation, entertainment, and finance and are found in consumer products ranging from automobiles to toys for preschool children. Developments in computer networking now allow individuals to communicate with others around the globe with extraordinary speed and ease. Advances in both computer and laser optical storage technologies have led to the development of videodiscs, which enable the user to interact freely with complex multimedia programs in ways virtually undreamed of only a few decades ago.

The likely social and economic consequences of this technological revolution are a subject of considerable controversy (Burnham, 1983; DeSola Poole, 1977; Dunlop & Kling, 1991; Hiltz & Turoff, 1978; Kling, 1991; Toffler, 1980; Zuboff, 1988). Some scholars pre-

1

sent an almost utopian vision of the potential embodied in these developments (Feigenbaum & McCorduck, 1983; Papert, 1980; Straub & Wetherbe, 1989). Others have a profoundly different view, emphasizing actual or likely negative consequences (Braverman, 1974; Buesmans & Wieckert, 1989; Mowshowitz, 1986; Reinecke, 1984; Weizenbaum, 1976). However, most proponents of these diametrically opposed schools of thought generally agree on one thing – that change has been and will continue to be major in both size and scope.

Much attention has been paid to the impact of computer technology on work, perhaps because changes in this realm have been so far-reaching. Training for a wide variety of civilian and military jobs, ranging from Federal Express delivery personnel to tank gunners, has been profoundly influenced by the advent of computer-controlled videodisc systems (Garfinkel, 1989). Developments in robotics have substantially altered the nature and number of blue-collar workers needed in many industries. Advances in other sorts of computer technology have changed many white-collar and professional jobs in important ways (Bikson, Gutek, & Mankin, 1981; Buesmans & Wieckert, 1989; Derfler, 1989; Folk, 1977; Hiltz, 1982, 1988; Kuhn, 1989; Lipinski, Lipinski, & Randolph, 1972; Mowshowitz, 1986; Shaiken, 1986; Strassman, 1985; Straub & Wetherbe, 1989; Wood, 1989). Opinions differ sharply about whether these changes are to be welcomed, but the existence of change is rarely denied.

The impact of computer technology has not, of course, been limited to the workplace. For example, popular press reports suggest that computers can facilitate romance as individuals utilizing electronic networks become acquainted with each other and then engage in electronic courtships. On the other hand, the term, *computer widow*, has been coined to describe the situation of wives whose husbands seem to prefer interacting with their home computers to interacting with their spouses. Computer-based "virtual reality" experiences attract thousands of vacationers in cities such as Las Vegas. The extent to which computer technology has changed leisure time activities is highlighted by the growing incidence of "video-wrist," an ailment found among adolescents who spend

2

long hours, and large sums of money, playing video games. The medical community is also faced with learning how best to treat numerous other stress-related injuries stemming from the increasing use of computers in the workplace (Horowitz, 1992). In sum, the broad scope and significance of the changes that computer technology appears to foster suggest that Herbert Simon and others who contend that the computer is not just the invention of the century but a "one-in-several-centuries" innovation (Simon cited in Lesgold & Reif, 1983) are correct.

One important domain of life that appears likely to be influenced by advances in computer technology is that of education. Here again there is controversy about the probable effects. Some scholars make rather startling claims about the computer's revolutionary potential. For example, Derrick Walker (1984, p. 30) contends that "the potential of computers for improving education is greater than that of any prior invention, including books and writing." In 1984 Seymour Papert (quoted in Cuban, 1986, p. 72), the developer of LOGO and a well-known proponent of the benefits of educational computing, claimed, "There won't be any schools in the future. . . . The computer will blow up the school."

Others take a much more restrained view. For example, Cohen (1988) points to the often glacial pace of change at the core of our educational system and concludes that if computer technology does become widely used in ordinary school settings, it will be for standard and relatively undemanding activities such as drill and practice. He calls for stepping back from the rush to acquire computers for schools to ask both value questions about how one should learn and teach, as well as hard-headed financial questions about cost-effectiveness. Cuban (1986) reminds us that at one time people held what, in retrospect, seem to be almost ludicrously exaggerated expectations about the potential impact of other technological innovations such as radio, film strips, and television on the educational system and cautions against the heedless adoption of computers by schools merely because they are widely used elsewhere. Other scholars have even argued that computer use can exacerbate problems in our educational system. For example, since schools serving affluent children tend to have more computer

3

equipment than those serving less affluent children, the long-standing achievement gap between the rich and the poor is likely to grow even wider if computers do contribute importantly to children's education.

In spite of such divergence of opinion within the scholarly community, there is a widely shared expectation in the general public that the use of computers will somehow enhance education. Thus, it is common for PTAs and other parent groups to engage in fundraising drives to procure computers for their children's schools. Apple Computer's "Apple for the Students" program, which gives computers to schools in exchange for students bringing in receipts for purchases from local merchants, has received widespread community support. Further, there is concern that children who do not become familiar with computers during their years in school will be left behind in an increasingly technological society. Such concerns are reinforced by government reports, such as the report of the Secretary's Commission on Achieving Necessary Skills (U.S. Department of Labor, 1991), which indicates that the ability to use technology is one of the five broad competencies required for effective participation in today's workplace.

These two factors have contributed importantly to an extraordinary increase in the number of computers in schools in the past 15 years. For example, between 1981 and 1987 the proportion of U.S. schools with one or more computers intended for instruction more than quintupled from 18% to 95% (Office of Technology Assessment, 1988). Furthermore, the average number of computers available in schools that have computers also rose dramatically, increasing nearly tenfold in the 4 years between 1981 and 1985 according to some estimates (Staff, 1985). Although the rate of change has recently slowed somewhat, the number of computers in schools is still increasing at over 10% a year (Quality Education Data, 1992). Current expenditures for computer hardware and software for pre-college education total almost $1 billion a year (Anderson, 1993). Furthermore, as Levin and Meister (1984) point out, such figures significantly understate real costs since substantial training and maintenance expenses are also incurred when computers are used.

In spite of the rapid proliferation of microcomputers and related

4

technology in schools, and the very significant amount of money spent on them, many schools and school systems appear to have given relatively little thought to how to utilize these machines once they have them. Further, when such thought has occurred it has often been focused narrowly on issues such as what software to purchase or how to keep the machines from being physically damaged or stolen. These issues are undoubtedly very important. Obviously, if the software is poorly designed or the computers are lost or broken little of educational value will result from their purchase. However, I would argue that equally fundamental to realizing the potential of computer technology to improve education is an awareness of schools and classrooms as social organizations that both influence the way in which any new technology will be adopted and are influenced by that technology in sometimes unanticipated ways.

A long history of research on change in educational settings suggests the importance of an awareness of the ways in which the structural and organizational aspects of educational systems influence the adoption and adaptation of innovations (Crandall & Loucks, 1983; Fullan, 1982; Gross, Giaquinta, & Bernstein, 1971; Huberman & Miles, 1984; Oettinger, 1969; Sarason, 1971; Schofield, 1982; Smith & Keith, 1971; Sussman, 1977; Van den Berg, Van Velzen, Miles, Ekholm, & Hameyer, 1986). There is little reason to think that things will be different with computers, as Cohen (1988) and Cuban (1986) have suggested. In fact, although little research has focused on this sort of issue, that which does exist highlights the influence of social and organizational factors on computer usage in schools. Thus, in thinking about likely consequences, one needs to recognize that computer systems are "complex social objects constrained by their context, infrastructure and history" (Kling & Scacchi, 1982, quoted in Kling, 1991, p. 358). A particular combination of hardware and software may be utilized in very different ways in different contexts with very different results. For example, Becker (1984) found that the amount and type of computer utilization in elementary school classrooms is related to the relative importance of different actors (teachers, principals, or other administrators) in the acquisition of those machines. Another part of the same study demonstrated a linkage between the type of individuals heavily involved in the acquisition process and teachers' reports of the impact of these computers on both cognitive and noncognitive student outcomes. Similarly, a paper based on a series of case studies of microcomputer usage concludes that "the effects of microcomputers on education will depend, to a large extent, on the social and educational contexts within which they are embedded" (Sheingold, Kane, & Endreweit, 1983, p. 431).

Although the ways in which computers are utilized are undoubtedly influenced by the ongoing context into which they are introduced, it is also reasonable to expect that their use will in turn influence that context, again often in unanticipated ways. For example, Hativa, Swisa, and Lesgold (1992) studied two contrasting computer-assisted instruction (CAI) systems used in schools and concluded that both influenced classroom competition in ways unanticipated by their designers. Similarly, several studies have suggested that using computers in the classroom leads to changes in the teachers' role, such as a decrease in teacher-centered activities or a shift from an emphasis on lecture and recitation to more individualized coaching (Gearhart, Herman, Baker, Novak, & Whittier, 1994; Kerr, 1991; Linn, 1992; Office of Technology Assessment, 1988). In light of all the attention given to the possible improvement of student learning as a consequence of computer use, it is both fascinating and somewhat ironic that some studies find that teachers are quick to observe changes in student enthusiasm, peer social processes, and student–teacher relations after the introduction of computers into their classrooms even when they do not see much change in student learning (Becker, 1983; Sheingold et al., 1983).

There are many indications that changes in classroom structure and social processes often follow the introduction of computers (Brod, 1972; Collins, 1991; Hawkins, Sheingold, Gearhart, & Berger, 1982; Kerr, 1991; Levin & Kareev, 1980), as discussed earlier. However, their widespread use in schools is so recent and research relating to their social impact in educational settings is so sparse that few generalizations seem warranted. One thing does seem clear – though computer use in and of itself is hardly a concep-

6

tually satisfying variable likely to have consistent and predictable results. Factors such as the purposes for which the computers are used (drill and practice, simulations, tutoring, communication, etc.), the specific hardware and software chosen to achieve these ends, the ratio of students to computers, and the physical location of the computers (classrooms vs. school libraries or computer labs) all seem likely to influence social and academic outcomes profoundly. To take an obvious example, it is unrealistic to expect measurable academic consequences of computer usage when students do not work on the machines for more than 10 or 15 minutes a week, as is frequently the case. On the other hand, intensive use might be expected to shape both the amount and the nature of what students learn.

Just as the kind and amount of computer use have obvious implications for the likelihood of various academic outcomes, so too they have implications for social outcomes. For example, drill and practice programs that do little more than serve as electronic workbooks may pose relatively little challenge to standard operating procedures or traditional teacher–student relationships. However, artificially intelligent computer-based tutors or wide-area computer networks may pose a much more profound challenge to existing classroom practices and roles. For example, artificially intelligent tutors could well influence authority relations in the classroom by reducing students' dependence on the teacher for achievement of their learning goals. Similarly, wide-area computer networks have the potential to reduce students' dependence on their teachers by giving them relatively easy access to a wide variety of individuals with expertise greater than their teachers' in specific content areas. In addition, such networks make possible close and ongoing collaboration between students from widely separated geographic areas that just was not feasible before.

THE RESEARCH QUESTIONS

The perspective developed in the preceding section, which is very consistent with a viewpoint Kling (1990, 1991) and his colleagues have dubbed "the web model," influenced the research reported in this book in two fundamental ways. First, it led to the dual focus on how computer usage changes classroom social processes and on how the social context shapes computer usage. Second, it led to a methodological decision that will be discussed shortly.

The dual focus of the research reported in the following chapters can best be captured by indicating the two general questions that underlie the work. The first is, "What is the effect of the instructional use of computer technology on students and on classroom social processes?" Since classroom social processes are of great potential significance, both for their effect on academic achievement and for their impact on students' conceptions of learning and attitudes toward school, it is important to take the possibility of such impact seriously and to explore the extent to which it is a reality. Chapters 2 and 3 detail some of the ways in which computer use does indeed appear to affect students and teachers, as well as the classrooms in which they function.

The second question that underlies this research is, "How does the social context in which computers are used for instruction shape their use?" When beginning the study, I expected that classroom processes were likely to be changed by computer usage in ways that were anticipated neither by those who developed the technology nor by the decisionmakers who were responsible for the computers' presence in the classroom. Initially, this second question was seen as secondary. It quickly emerged as a very important focus of the research as work during the first months of this project again and again suggested the crucial and pervasive effects of context on computer use. Chapters 4, 5, and 6 deal with this issue.

With regard to methodology, the belief in the likely importance of context led to the decision to undertake an intensive qualitative study of computer usage at one high school so that it would be possible to delineate the context studied in rich detail. It seemed as if this strategy would be fruitful in suggesting linkages that might not be readily apparent otherwise, given that very little is known about what these context effects might be. However, awareness of the highly varied nature of computer applications and of the likelihood that different applications might both have different effects and be affected in different ways by context factors led to a decision to explore a wide variety of applications within this school. Thus, following Sheingold, Hawkins, and Char's (1984, p. 51) exhortation to "ask questions about particular uses of . . . technology in order to begin to understand its relation to the social life of classrooms," the study reported here examined virtually every case in the school in which computers were available for use. This led to the exploration of situations as varied as geometry classes in which college-bound students used artificially intelligent computer-based tutors to learn how to construct proofs and business classes in which vocational students learned basic word processing skills.

Having given the reader a sense of the questions that the research was designed to illuminate, as well as of the general approach taken, I will briefly lay out the structure of the rest of this chapter. First, I describe Whitmore High School,[1] the site at which this study was conducted, and discuss why it was selected. Then, I briefly outline the historical and policy context of computer usage there. Next, I turn to a description of the methods used in gathering and analyzing the data upon which this book is based.

RESEARCH SITE

Data gathering took place during a 2-year period, from September of 1985 to June of 1987 in Whitmore High School, a large urban high school that serves approximately 1,300 students from extremely varied socioeconomic backgrounds in the Waterford school district. Although the data were gathered some time ago, my continuing research on computer use in several schools in Waterford (Schofield, Futoran, & Eurich-Fulcer, 1994a; Schofield, Futoran, & Eurich-Fulcer, 1994b) clearly suggests that the issues raised in this book are still very pertinent. Whitmore's student body was about 55% African American and 40% white. Most of the remaining students were

---

[1] Pseudonyms are used for all individuals, institutions, and places in order to protect the confidentiality of those participating in this research.

Asian Americans. Whitmore's student body roughly mirrored the racial and ethnic composition of the students enrolled in the school district in which the school was located, although it had a slightly higher proportion of African Americans than the district as a whole.

As is the case in a great many urban high schools, the kind of student body found at Whitmore changed materially during the 1970s and 1980s. In the early 1970s, whites constituted over two-thirds of the student body. Many of these students came from well-educated and reasonably affluent families living in a neighborhood that was widely considered one of the most desirable residential areas within the city. Another substantial group of students came from Italian and Irish ethnic working-class communities. Fifteen years later a markedly increased proportion of the students were African Americans from economically disadvantaged neighborhoods with relatively high drug abuse and crime rates. The turnover rate in the predominantly African American community immediately adjacent to the school exceeded that of any other community within the city, posing to the school the challenge of working effectively with numerous transient students. Whitmore continued to enroll many students, both African American and white, from working-class and middle-class backgrounds. However, the proportion of students from such backgrounds dropped sharply, whereas the proportion of students whose families routinely had to deal with marked economic hardship increased markedly.

The school's faculty was about 80% white and 20% African American. African American teachers were distributed relatively evenly throughout the school's 10 departments, with the notable exception of the foreign language and science departments, which were entirely white. Roughly half of the school's 88 teachers were women. However, the gender composition of the different departments varied dramatically in ways that one might expect given traditional gender roles. So, for example, about 70% of the mathematics teachers were men compared with about 30% of the English teachers. Also consistent with traditional staffing patterns was the fact that the school's principal was a white male.

The very large majority of the school's faculty were middle-aged, and many of them had been at the school for one or even two decades, thus personally experiencing the changes mentioned earlier. It was not uncommon for these teachers to contrast the current student body unfavorably with the earlier one making observations similar to those reported in the following field notes:

> Mr. Davidson [a white middle-aged teacher] went on at considerable length about the way in which the student body has, as he sees it, deteriorated over time. . . . His basic thesis is that 10 or 15 years ago the students here were very bright. [He says] most of them were white and Jewish, and many were extremely interested and motivated. Now the student body has changed [in ways he finds discouraging].

Some of the dismay about changes in the student body was most likely a reflection of the negative racial attitudes that permeate our society. For example, the teacher just quoted ended up being sanctioned by the district for using the word *nigger* in a derogatory way in the classroom, and before this occurred a researcher from this study noted that he tended to address his remarks to the section of his classroom in which the white students sat. However, it is clear that the changed nature of the student body posed a challenge for teachers no matter what their racial attitudes. For example, conversations with the school's African American librarian and an inspection of checkout records of classic books clearly suggested that the students' propensity to read the kind of material available in the library had declined rather dramatically. Teachers in the vocational courses especially had to deal with students who clearly did not want to be in school. Explaining why he let only about 60% of the students in a vocational course he taught use the computer in his room, Mr. Powers said in an interview:

> I would have to say that maybe 60% [of the students] I would let use it [the computer]. The other 40% don't attend school anyway or they are the type of kid [who] would probably scratch the glass [on the monitor] or something like that. You got to realize I don't get no scholars in here [*sic*]. A lot of the kids I have, have either been in jail or are serving active probation. Whitmore's a beautiful school, a good school, but it just happens that this is one

of the courses that attracts the lower elements. . . . They don't care. They don't even want to be here anyways. . . . I've had kids come up to me and say, "I'm here because the judge says I have to attend or go back to jail, one or the other. He didn't say I have to [do my school] work, though. He just said I had to attend. . . ." They down and out refuse to do anything.

In spite of such problems, Whitmore was generally perceived within the community as a solid, reasonably well-functioning institution, clearly neither the very best nor the very worst of the high schools in the city. The results of the California Achievement Tests routinely administered by the school district during the 2 years of the study suggest that this image had a basis in reality. For example, in both years almost exactly 50% of Whitmore's students who took the test scored at or above the national norm on the reading section of the test (51% in the study's first year and 48% in the study's second year). Comparable figures for other schools in the district ranged from a high of 74% to a low of 29%. Although acknowledging a serious attendance problem, a fairly high suspension rate, and some concern about the need for more security personnel, a report from the Visiting Committee of the Commission on Secondary Schools of the Middle States Association of Colleges and Secondary Schools wrote in its evaluation of the school a few years before the beginning of this study, "The students . . . are respectful, sincere, and appreciative of the services provided. . . . The vast majority . . . have maintained a sound focus on the value of education and their personal responsibilities."

There were several factors that made Whitmore attractive as the site for this research. First, the school's relatively diverse student body made it possible to observe the reactions to computer use of a much broader range of students than would have been possible in a more homogeneous school. Second, as mentioned earlier, the achievement level of the school's students, as indicated on standardized tests, was close to average for the nation as a whole. This fact by no means warrants blithe generalization from Whitmore to some hypothetical "average" school in the United States. However, it does

12

make it likely that the observations stemming from this study will have broader applicability than if it had been conducted in a school with either unusually strong or weak students. Third, Whitmore had computers available for use with a rather common set of applications including business classes emphasizing word processing and computer science classes emphasizing programming. At the beginning of the study, Whitmore had roughly one computer for every 27 students. This ratio meant that it fell roughly in the middle of the district's 10 high schools in terms of the ratio of students to computers. Statistics on the distribution of computers in high schools nationally suggest that the average number of computers per 30 students at the beginning of the study was 0.8 (Office of Technology Assessment, 1988). The comparable figure at Whitmore was 1.1, suggesting that it had somewhat, though not dramatically, more computers per student than average. The number increased notably both nationally and at Whitmore during the course of the study.

Another major important consideration in the decision to conduct this research at Whitmore was that it was the site of a field test for the Geometry Proofs Tutor, an artificially intelligent computer-based tutor designed to help teach students geometry proofs. The developers of the Geometry Proofs Tutor, which is usually referred to as the GPTutor, selected Whitmore as a field test site for several reasons. First, and perhaps most important, it was relatively close to the university where the tutor's developers were located. They weighted this factor heavily to minimize travel time since one or even two research team members in addition to the cooperating teacher were often in the field test classrooms, helping out when students encountered bugs in the software and informally observing students' reactions to it. Second, the physical layout of the school enabled it to provide a relatively high level of security for the computers on which the tutor ran. This was vital since the field test used computers with an aggregate value near a half million dollars. (The software has since been modified so that it operates on much less expensive machines.) Third, the school had an adequate power supply to run the machines and an air-conditioning system good enough to keep them at an acceptable temperature.

13

Fourth, the school's principal was quite positive about having the project located in his school.

HISTORICAL AND POLICY CONTEXT OF COMPUTER USE AT THE RESEARCH SITE

Although Whitmore was very unusual in serving as the field test site for the GPTutor, in most ways the computers it had available for students reflected standard district policies and practices relating to computer usage at the high school level at the time the study was conducted. Specifically, the district in which Whitmore was located had decided in the late 1970s and early 1980s that it was important to provide high school students with the opportunity to learn programming. Early in this period students in various high schools, including Whitmore, utilized teletype machines linked up to a central mainframe computer. But practical difficulties with this approach, such as the wasted time when the computer "crashed," as it frequently did, and the advent of affordable personal computers led the district to switch over to computer labs utilizing Tandy personal computers. Thus, by 1984 the district had equipment worth almost a quarter of a million dollars in the labs for computer science classes, substantially more than the sum expended on computer equipment for any other single instructional purpose.

Consistent with the district's emphasis on computer programming at the high school level was the fact that the computer science lab at Whitmore constituted the area containing the largest single concentration of computer equipment at the beginning of this study and that the equipment in that room was expanded and upgraded substantially during the study. In its emphasis on using computers for programming, Whitmore reflected a pattern common in the United States throughout the 1980s (Bulkeley, 1988; Educational Testing Service, 1988). Although the emphasis on programming has clearly declined in recent years, it is still a component in the majority of high school classes designed to teach students about computers (Becker, 1993).

14

Another substantial expenditure, roughly $125,000, was made on computer equipment for gifted students in the district in the early 1980s. However, this expenditure reflected less of a policy decision and a subsequent financial commitment than a willingness to take advantage of what one district administrator termed a "financial windfall," since a state program for the education of gifted children covered most of the cost. The equipment purchased through this program was gathered together in a lab that will be described in more detail later.

The district also purchased equipment for various vocational programs, especially business education. Thus, Whitmore, like most other high schools in the district at the beginning of this study, had several computers available for use in business classes and a few computers located one to a room for Visual Communication and Power and Energy classes. During the course of this study, the number of computers available to business classes expanded substantially as the district's decision to place a moratorium on the purchase of typewriters and to increase the availability of computers in business classes was implemented. Whitmore, like the large majority of the district's high schools, did not use CAI programs. Such programs, which are generally used for drill and practice in basic skills, were present only at the two district high schools whose students had the lowest scores on standardized achievement tests.

The 5-year technology use plan prepared for the district shortly before the beginning of this study listed five goals, including the maintenance and expansion of the existing computer science curriculum offerings. Some of these goals, such as giving students access to computers starting in elementary school, were, generally speaking, met. However, others proved harder to accomplish. For example, one of the goals was to "provide computer literacy for all students." As defined in the report, computer literacy included providing students with information on topics such as computer-related careers, how computers work, what they can and cannot do, how to use computers, and how they influence society. The district explored the idea of meeting this goal by developing a required course for ninth graders. However, this idea was not

15

implemented at Whitmore or elsewhere in the system due to what one district administrator called "scheduling difficulties." The nub of the problem appeared to be that unless one were to expand the school day or cut the time allotted for each class period, neither of which was seriously considered, adding a computer literacy course meant that students had to drop something else. State requirements for graduation, requirements for college admission, long-held ideas about the courses students should take in high school, as well as the political and financial costs inherent in dropping a particular course when the district had a highly tenured and unionized faculty, made it hard to find room in students' schedules for such a course.

A second goal proved rather elusive both at Whitmore and in district high schools more generally, as it has nationally (Becker, 1993). This was to "provide for increased use of the computer as an instructional tool in all instructional areas. . . . (e.g., math, reading, remedial and gifted, vocational, business, English, etc.)." Certainly some movement in this direction occurred. For example, labs were set up in middle schools for use in language arts. However, attainment of this goal at the high school level was stymied by numerous factors, some of which will be discussed in considerable detail in Chapter 4. It will suffice here to point out that this goal was not a high enough priority to be allocated the very substantial amount of money for equipment, curriculum development, new staff, and training of existing staff that would have been needed to achieve it. Planning documents prepared by those interested in technology contained strong statements about the importance of exposing all students to computers to prepare them to live and work in a world in which technology will play an increasing central role, and many in the district took these statements seriously. However, given that voters were very resistant to tax increases, spending money on new computer equipment or staff training programs meant decreasing resources available for other activities. Thus, once certain basic and obviously needed equipment, like computers for programming and business classes, had been purchased, it became increasingly difficult to get additional money allocated for computer technology or its support.

METHODOLOGY

The way the study on which this book is based was conducted is of real importance for readers since it has direct and important implications for how seriously they should take the observations and conclusions contained herein. Because I believe methodology is so important, I have included a more lengthy description of the methods used for data gathering and analysis than is typical of most books using a similar approach. However, I recognize that some readers may have neither the desire to wade through the fine details of how the data were gathered and analyzed nor the training needed to make that an interesting and productive enterprise. Thus, I have decided to briefly describe the approach taken in this work here and to place a much more detailed discussion of methodological issues in the Appendix. I would strongly encourage readers to read the Appendix, since it explores issues ranging from procedures taken to minimize reactivity and bias to details on the number and nature of the classes that were observed. However, for those who prefer not to read it, or who would rather read it after looking at the chapters dealing with the study's substantive conclusions, I have written the brief methodological overview that follows.

The two major methods of data gathering utilized in this 2-year study were intensive qualitative classroom observations and repeated semistructured interviews with teachers and students. The extensive handwritten notes taken during classroom observations were later audiotaped for transcription and analysis. Similarly, all interviews were audiotaped and transcribed. During the 2 years of the study, the research team observed roughly 30 different classes, including 8 classes of students using the artificially intelligent GPTutor and 7 control and comparison classes that learned geometry the traditional way; 7 different computer science classes taught by 5 different teachers; and 4 business classes each taught by a different teacher. In addition to conducting almost 400 hours of observations, the research team carried out over 250 interviews with students randomly selected from classes that were observed. These interviews were constructed to explore issues that the existing literature or the ongoing classroom observation suggested were important. To supplement our frequent informal conversations with teachers, almost two dozen formal interviews were conducted both with teachers who used computers in the classes we observed and with those who had the opportunity to use computers in their classrooms but chose not to.

To analyze the thousands of pages of data in a careful and systematic way was a major undertaking. All field notes were coded using procedures similar to those described in Strauss (1987) and Strauss and Corbin (1990). Basically, this consists of an iterative process that begins long before data gathering is completed. This process involves reading the notes numerous times, coding them by topic and theme; studying, comparing, and contrasting the notes falling under any given code; and finally looking for patterns and themes that bring together separate codes into a coherent analysis of the situation. An important aspect of this process is that specific efforts are made to check whether the developing understanding of the situation is warranted, which includes undertaking further data gathering designed both to fill gaps in the emerging analysis and to bring to light weaknesses or errors in it.

The interviews were also coded, although in a different way than the field notes. Typically, interviews were analyzed using the kinds of procedures traditionally employed in content analysis (Holsti, 1968). Specifically, answers to each question were grouped together, coding categories appropriate to the question were constructed, and responses were then categorized by two coders individually. In drawing conclusions, care was taken to integrate information from the observations and the interviews, as well as any other existing data sources, such as archival material and informal conversations with teachers and students.

Overview of the Book

The majority of this book is organized as a series of interrelated case studies that explore the two issues mentioned earlier. Chapters 2 and 3 focus on the impact of computer use on classroom social functioning. Chapters 4, 5, and 6 emphasize investigation of

18

the impact of the social context in which the computers are used on patterns of use. Chapters 2 and 3 discuss two very different kinds of computer applications, which appear to have both common and unique effects on classroom social processes. Chapter 2 looks at the impact of an artificially intelligent tutor designed to help students in three different college-bound tracks (regular, advanced, and one for gifted students) learn to do geometry proofs. It concludes that use of the tutor brought about a substantial number of important and unanticipated changes in both students' and teachers' behaviors, including things as varied as changes in teachers' grading practices and in students' interest and effort. Chapter 3 focuses on introductory computer science classes. Specifically, it compares students' reactions to learning about computers in the classroom with their reactions to working with computers in the lab as they develop their programming skills. It concludes that students both preferred the latter to the former and worked much harder in the lab than in the classroom. Furthermore, it explores a variety of differences in the social functioning of the two milieus that appeared to contribute substantially to the students' increased interest and effort while working with the computers in the lab.

Chapter 4 introduces consideration of this book's second focus, the impact of the social milieu on computer use, by investigating the question of why so many teachers at Whitmore failed to make substantial use of the computer technology available to them. Factors discussed range from problems with the support infrastructure to more subtle issues such as teachers' concerns about using a tool they are less knowledgeable about than some of their students. Chapters 5 and 6 deal with the impact of gender on computer use. Specifically, Chapter 5 explores gender-linked patterns of use in the computer lab set aside for gifted students, exploring how it came to pass that the lab functioned virtually as a club for white boys in a school that was so heterogeneous. Chapter 6 starts with the finding that although male and female enrollments in Computer Science 1 classes showed only a minor disparity, favoring males, the more advanced classes were predominately male, as is so often the case. It discusses the factors that led to this situation and closely examines the experiences of the very few female students who did choose to enroll in such courses. It concludes that these students were generally very isolated and, even worse, that some of them experienced gender-linked teasing, taunting, and even sexual harassment that were far in excess of the level of such behaviors experienced in most other classrooms at Whitmore.

Finally, Chapter 7 integrates material from the case studies preceding it and from the existing research literature to draw conclusions about the likely consequences of computer use on classroom social functioning. In addition, this chapter discusses the extent to which computer use is likely to change education, exploring both the transformative potential inherent in it and the factors likely to influence whether this potential will be realized.

2

THE GPTutor
Artificial Intelligence
in the Classroom

T HIS CHAPTER ADDRESSES THE IMPACT OF ONE UNUSUAL but potentially very important use of microcomputers – their use as intelligent tutors – on classroom structure and functioning. Specifically, it discusses the impact of an artificially intelligent tutor on both teachers' and students' behavior. Ideally, intelligent computer-based tutors are designed to follow what a student is trying to do, diagnose the difficulties the student is experiencing, and present instruction relevant to those difficulties, providing individually tailored learning experiences that proceed at a pace determined by the student's capabilities (Anderson, 1984). Thus, the use of intelligent tutors seems to hold real promise for improving schooling as we know it today. The cost of the development of such software is high, and some of it currently requires rather expensive hardware to operate. However, there is reason to believe that within the relatively near future the cost of artificially intelligent tutors for educational purposes will no longer be prohibitive (Lesgold & Lesgold, 1984). Thus, intelligent tutoring is a potentially revolutionary educational innovation that may well become a practical reality from a technical and a fiscal perspective in the foreseeable future.

Some of the very characteristics that make the artificially intelligent tutor an innovation with real promise also make it likely to bring about important changes in traditional classroom relationships and practices. For example, teachers whose students are using an artificially intelligent tutor, like teachers whose students have access to wide-area computer networks such as the Internet, need to adjust to the fact that their classrooms now contain another source of expertise, which students may choose to turn to before consulting them. However, unlike textbooks or standard reference materials that are routinely available to students as sources of information, computer-based tutors are designed to interact with students and to be responsive to them as individuals. Thus, it seems likely that intelligent tutors will produce greater change than many more commonly used software applications such as drill and practice programs that function as sophisticated electronic workbooks and fit much more readily into established classroom roles and routines.

Unfortunately, we know little about what the changes associated with the use of artificially intelligent tutors might actually be. Given the speed with which computers are becoming commonplace in U.S. schools, and the continuing development of artificially intelligent tutors in areas ranging from electric circuiting to computer programming to algebra (Anderson, Boyle, & Reiser, 1985; Bierman, Breuker, & Sandberg, 1989; Lawler & Yazdani, 1987; Office of Technology Assessment, 1988), such knowledge seems important for two reasons. First, it may identify unintended side effects of tutor usage so that the full ramifications of decisions about whether and how to use them will be more apparent. Second, it may be helpful to those attempting to prepare teachers to use such tutors in their classrooms in a maximally effective way. Before proceeding to discuss the impact on teachers and students of the specific computer-tutor studied, I will briefly describe both the tutor itself and the classes in which it was used.

THE GEOMETRY PROOFS TUTOR (GPTutor)

The GPTutor is a sophisticated artificially intelligent tutor developed by John R. Anderson and C. Franklin Boyle at Carnegie Mellon University. This tutor is designed to teach geometry students how to do proofs. Like most other artificially intelligent tutors, the GPTutor consists of three parts. The first is the Expert, an expert system (Brady, 1986) that contains the knowledge necessary for constructing a wide variety of geometry proofs. The Expert contains over 300 "if–then" rules that embody the definitions, axioms, and theorems necessary to solve the 192 proof problems presented by the GPTutor. Many of these rules are accompanied by what are called heuristics, which indicate the kinds of situations in which such rules are likely to be of use. Given the premises a proof problem starts with, a diagram representing the problem, and the conclusion toward which the student is working, the Expert uses the rules and heuristics to construct a solution file that contains most of the common proofs to the problem (Wertheimer, 1990). The Expert also contains information about "bugs," that is, mistakes that students often make.

The second part of the GPTutor is the Tutor itself. The Tutor uses information from both the Expert and the student (via the Interface) to help guide the student's proof construction. Specifically, it provides both solicited and unsolicited help. Students who are lost can ask to review material or request a hint. In the former case, they are presented with a window on their video screen that typically contains a diagram and basic review material on the requested topic. If students ask for a hint, they are given a strategic hint appropriate to their current situation. Such hints often direct students to focus on certain aspects of the diagram or help them use the other information already on the screen to move forward on the proof. Hints can be tailored to the proof path any particular student is on because, in essence, the GPTutor matches the student's past steps to one of the various proof paths produced by the Expert and uses this, in addition to information about common bugs, as a basis for determining what the most productive next step would be. Unsolicited help is supplied when a student has made two consecutive logical errors while working on a single inference in their proof.

The third part of this software is the Interface, which allows students to communicate with the computer using a keyboard, a mouse, or a combination of the two. The Interface is designed to allow minimal use of the keyboard for students who wish to use the mouse extensively. Specifically, students have available a menu that contains all the symbols necessary to enter geometric statements using the mouse. Short standardized descriptive rule names (such as *def-bisector* for definition of a bisector) are used for referring to every theorem, axiom, or definition when the student uses the keyboard. This Interface contains a spelling checker and other features designed to prevent problems in communication between the student and the GPTutor. One distinctive and potentially important aspect of the GPTutor's Interface is the way in which the proofs are presented. The givens of the proof appear at the bottom of the screen and the statement to be proved appears at the top, along with a diagram of the problem. The student's job is to create a "proof graph" that shows how the givens can yield the statement to be proved (Wertheimer, 1990). Each step between the givens and the statement to be proved is treated as an inference involving a set of premises, a reason, and a conclusion. For example, the student can select the premises for each step by pointing to them with the mouse, proceed to type in the reason, and then point to or type in the conclusion. The proof-graph approach was utilized because it makes visually apparent the way in which the steps of the proof fit together. Furthermore, the GPTutor developers felt that this approach highlights the fact that one can reason either forward from the premises or backward from the conclusion and that choice points exist where one must decide which of the many inference rules are most appropriately used (Anderson, Boyle, & Yost, 1985).

Due to the underlying philosophy and goals of its developers, the GPTutor was constructed to interact in a businesslike way with the students. Thus, it lacks the gamelike or "humanizing" elements of many pieces of educational software. For example, it does not use color or graphics, above and beyond very straightforward diagrams, to catch the students' interest as many pieces of software do. It does, however, indicate success on a proof with a brief sound as well as a screen message, SUCCESS!!. The tutor was designed for use by individual students, and the large majority of the time it was used that way at Whitmore. However, as discussed in more detail in the Appendix, in two classes students worked in pairs rather than individually.

At the time this study was conducted, the GPTutor could only be used on a very expensive artificially intelligent work station, the Xerox 1108. However, since that time it has been rewritten (with-

24

out changing the features just described) so that it will run on an Apple Macintosh 512. Further description of the tutor can be found in Anderson, Boyle, and Reiser (1985), as well as in Wertheimer (1990).

Utilization of the GPTutor appeared to result in a number of important changes in both teachers' and students' behavior. However, before proceeding to discuss these changes, I will briefly describe the way in which geometry classrooms at Whitmore normally functioned. This description, and the conclusions about the impact of the GPTutor presented in this chapter, are based on the observations and interviews described in the Appendix. As discussed in more detail there, we observed eight different classes in which the GPTutor was used before, during, and after the period of tutor use. As additional points of comparison, we also observed two classes taught by the same teachers without the tutors and three classes taught by the remaining two geometry teachers. The former will be referred to as control classes, whereas the latter will be called comparison classes.

GEOMETRY CLASSES AT WHITMORE

Generally speaking, the four geometry teachers at Whitmore, all of whom were men, took a quite traditional approach to instruction very similar to that described in large-scale studies of schools in the United States like Goodlad (1984). So, for example, when the GPTutor was not in use (either because it was never used in these classrooms or because it did not happen to be in use that day in a classroom that did use it on other occasions), classes generally began with a review of the previous night's homework. This review was led by the teacher, normally standing at the front of the class, who either worked the problems at the board with some assistance from students or selected students to write their solutions to the problems at the board and then led the class through those problems. Typically, the teacher then introduced new material or reviewed previously covered material using a lecture format. The lecture was punctuated by the teacher's calling on stu-

25

dents to answer questions related to the material being presented. Students were allowed to pose questions during the lecture. However, such questions were usually answered by the teacher rather than being used to stimulate discussion and participation by other students. Next, the teacher typically presented students with a set of problems related to the material just covered to work on at their seats. As students did this, the teacher would either sit at his desk or circulate, inspecting students' work and commenting on it in a voice often clearly audible throughout the entire classroom.

Although there was some degree of individual variation among teachers and classes, the teaching of geometry at Whitmore was clearly characterized by all four of the classroom elements that Goodlad (1984) found so common in his sample of over 1,000 classrooms in the United States. First, as exemplified by the emphasis on lecture and working problems at the board, the primary focus for teaching and learning was the entire group. All students in a classroom were expected to be working on the same material at any given point in time, regardless of their particular level of competence. They were virtually never asked to work in small cooperative groups.

Second, the teachers all functioned as what Goodlad (1984, p. 108) calls "the strategic pivotal figure in the group." Specifically, they controlled relatively firmly what, when, and how material was presented, as well as the kind of learning activities in which students engaged. Teachers did give students some choice, such as frequently asking which homework problems they wanted to go over or whether they wanted an additional example worked on the board. However, this choice was within clear limits and was offered within a framework for the day's work set by the teacher.

Third, the norms governing students' behavior were consistent with the teachers' maintaining the kind of control over the classroom described earlier. So, for example, students were expected to obtain permission before addressing the class, to listen quietly when the teacher gave instructions, and to take notes when the teacher lectured. Task-oriented discussion between students was not generally encouraged, although it was tolerated at the end of class while students worked on their homework as long as it was not noisy and did not involve students moving far from their seats. Social conversations were actively discouraged, especially if they were at all noisy, except at the very end of class when teachers tended not to enforce the norms against such activity very strongly.

Fourth, as was the case in the classrooms observed in Goodlad's study, the emotional tone in the classrooms we observed was relatively flat, rather than being either strikingly hostile or warm and upbeat. The classrooms observed in this study varied more on this dimension than on the others discussed here, with one of the comparison teachers using sarcasm more than his colleagues, and Mr. Adams, one of the teachers using the GPTutor, bringing a level of obvious enthusiasm to his teaching that was not consistently evident elsewhere. In spite of these differences, all four of Whitmore's geometry teachers had much in common, and no one teacher stood out as taking a markedly different approach from the others with regard either to the content covered or to pedagogical practice.

This chapter will now turn to its major focus – the kinds of changes that use of the GPTutor appeared to induce in the eight classes observed using it. Although some of the patterns to be described were stronger in some classes than others, the following discussion centers on those changes that were relatively reliable, appearing to at least some degree in class after class. Although teachers' and students' behaviors are no doubt interdependent, for heuristic purposes changes in the teachers' behaviors will be discussed first followed by a discussion of changes in students' behaviors.

CHANGES IN THE TEACHERS' BEHAVIOR

A Shift in the Amount of Attention Devoted to Different Types of Students

The introduction of the computer tutors appeared to change the relative amount of attention given to students of different ability levels. More specifically, it increased the amount of time devoted to those having problems by Mr. Adams and Mr. Brice, the two teachers who used the GPTutor. As indicated earlier in this chapter, before the arrival of the tutors, and in the control and comparison classes, teachers often had students work through geometry problems and proofs on the board. (Recall that *control classroom* is the term used to designate classes taught without the GPTutor by the two teachers who used the GPTutor in their other classes, whereas *comparison classroom* refers to geometry classes taught by teachers who did not use the GPTutor at all.) Another commonly used teaching method was to work through problems by having students who were seated volunteer answers to the teacher's questions. Not surprisingly, in these situations teachers tended to call disproportionately on the more advanced students, as previous research has suggested is often the case (Bossert, 1979). This saved considerable time, raised the probability of a correct answer, and saved the poorer students the embarrassment of making mistakes in public. The problems posed by waiting for a slower student to supply an answer that other students have already figured out are made clear in the following excerpt from the field notes from a geometry class in which two able students challenge the fairness of Mr. Adams's usual behavior:

> Mr. Adams says, "Ready? Okay, What's the answer? . . . " Tim answers the question correctly. Mr. Adams says to Tim, "You get the extra credit!" . . . Ida says heatedly, "That's unfair! You always call on Tim for extra credit. . . . He gets all the credit." Allie chimes in complaining too. Mr. Adams . . . assigns another extra credit problem and says, "Ida will choose who answers this time." Allie and Pete finish first. They have their hands up. Mr. Adams says, "Okay. Choose." Ida replies . . . "I want to call on one of those," pointing over to Debbie and Katy, clearly the two slowest students in the class. Both of these girls have their heads bent over their papers, still working. Debbie says to Mr. Adams, "Can I ask a question?" He answers it. She continues to work . . . Ida says, "Are you ready Katy?" [Katy is not.] Mr. Adams says "The bell is going to ring any minute and no one will get the credit. . . . Time is going. . . ." Mr. Adams says in a loud voice, close to a shout, *"Would you please call on someone so I can give the credit out!"* Ida hesitates and calls on Debbie. Debbie gets seven angles right, but the eighth [the most difficult, which was the real

point of the example] is wrong. Pete volunteers the correct answer. Mr. Adams lets him show the class how he got to his answer, saying "This is the one you all missed, so I want you to watch . . . . " As the class files out [but is still within earshot], Mr. Adams says in a very biting tone to Ida, "A wonderful teacher you'd make!" Ida defends herself saying heatedly, "Sometimes it's not having the right answer. It's having a chance. If you give her a chance . . . " Mr. Adams interrupts saying, "Here are people having difficulty. You . . . focus all the attention on them. Isn't that embarrassing? It puts them in a corner." Ida says, "Okay; Okay. But why don't you even call on them?" Mr. Adams replies, "You need to learn something about people. They get it wrong. They make bad subtraction errors."

When using the GPTutor, in contrast, the slower students often received considerably more attention than the brighter ones. Mr. Adams's comments in an interview suggest that he was well aware of this change:

Interviewer: Have you noticed that [when using the computer tutors] you're giving [more] attention to certain sorts of students versus other ones? Or does it pretty well even out?

Mr. Adams: No, I would say in general I give much more help to students that are much slower and need the help. . . . I'm giving more help to them than I ever was able to in the past. . . . A lot more time . . . [the computer] frees you up for individualized attention . . . knowing that the rest of the class is doing something constructive.

Such attention was not likely to be embarrassing because students working on their computers were often unaware of exactly which student the teacher was working with. In addition, as Mr. Adams pointed out, the GPTutor provided a substantial amount of help so the teacher's work with the slower students did not impede the rest of the students, who could continue to progress without interruption. It is worth noting that the team developing the GPTutor ended up concluding on the basis of pre- and posttests that average and lower than average students who had little confidence in their math skills (along with underachieving gifted students) benefited the most from the tutor (Wertheimer, 1990). It seems reasonable to speculate that part of the gain in skills that these students evidenced stemmed from their increased opportunity for direct and extended interaction with their teacher.

A Shift in the Teachers' Role Toward Becoming a Collaborator. A second shift in the teachers' role behavior was also apparent in the computer-tutor classrooms. Specifically, the teachers functioned less as authoritative experts and more as collaborators than they had previously. This shift was beautifully captured by the words of one student who was asked in an interview about whether using the computer-tutor had changed his teacher's behavior. He replied, "He doesn't teach us any more. He just helps us."

What is this distinction between teaching and helping? The teaching role as it often appears to be defined in high school consists of rather formally imparting a body of facts to less knowledgeable individuals through lectures and very structured class participation. The teacher's separate and superior status is well symbolized by his or her physical position – typically standing above and in front of students who are expected to be watching and listening carefully. In the control and comparison classrooms, the teacher's authoritative position was made clear by the common practice of calling upon students to answer questions or work problems at the board. In doing this, the teachers exercised control over the class not only by choosing between students who indicated a desire to participate, but also, less commonly, by calling on students who would have preferred not to become the focus of the class's attention.

In contrast, in the GPTutor classes, as in the computer science labs that are discussed in Chapter 3, the teacher functioned more as a collaborator than was typical under other circumstances. Specifically, rather than addressing the entire class in a relatively formal manner, the teacher tended to work on an individual basis with students. Just as important, in the computer-using classes the teachers were less likely to initiate teacher–student interactions. Rather, they were often kept busy responding to student requests for assistance, thus shifting control for initiating interactions into the hands of the students.

A Change in the Content and Context of Help Giving. One clear difference foreshadowed earlier between classrooms using the GPTutor and those that did not was the sharp contrast in the degree to which the teachers' help was individualized. Although students in classrooms not using the GPTutor received some individualized help, they did not receive as much as students using the computer-tutor. Furthermore, it is important to consider the nature of this apparently individualized help, which was often given in public contexts, such as when the student was working a problem on the board at the front of the classroom. While such help was often useful to its intended recipient, it was not likely to be especially useful to other students unless they were having the same or a very similar problem. There were at least two consequences to this. First, understandably, it was not unusual for other students to "tune out" while a classmate received help, starting social conversations, daydreaming, and the like. This, of course, decreased their time on the task and slowed their rate of progress. Second, as mentioned earlier, teachers recognized this problem and were sometimes loath to "waste" too much time explaining something to one student that most students already understood. This sometimes made it difficult for those at the bottom of the class to get the help they needed, especially since these students tended to need more time than others to assimilate the teacher's explanations. Similar concerns also inhibited teachers from elaborating on certain complicated points with the most advanced students, since this was also likely to lose the rest of the class.

In an important sense, much of the helping of individuals in the traditional classroom situation has a dual purpose – it is undertaken both to help the particular member of the class ostensibly being helped and to provide a forum for discussion of points of which the teacher wants others to be aware. Thus, the length and elaboration of a teacher's reply appeared to be dependent not only on the needs of the particular student whose work raised the issue,

31

but also on the teacher's perceptions of the needs of other students. Although this is an efficient and sensible approach in classes that have large numbers of students, it means that "individualized" help in the whole class situation may not be nearly as individualized as it seems at first glance.

In contrast, the teacher's help to students using the GPTutor was more fully individualized. The teachers moved around the classroom to check on whether students working at the computers needed help just as they circulated in the traditional classrooms when students did seat work, but differences in their helping behavior were quite apparent. Most obviously, the teachers tended to speak in a lower tone, audible only to the student with whom they were dealing and those quite close by, rather than in tones clearly audible throughout the classroom. This fact reflected the clear shift in the intended audience for the advice from that student and his or her classmates to that student alone. In addition, since their help was no longer on display for the whole class, it was possible for the teachers to attend to a particular student's need during a helping interaction irrespective of whether this was useful to others. In fact, when writing about his experiences in a journal for other mathematics teachers, one of the teachers whose classes we observed wrote:

> Individualizing my instruction was the greatest difference in my teaching style [while using the computer-tutors]. With students who had poor spatial abilities I was able to use manipulatives. . . . I had time to challenge exceptional students with harder problems and to supply them with resources, usually books, that would be helpful. These opportunities are limited in typical classroom interactions. (Wertheimer, 1990, p. 315)

Not only did the teacher's help become more fully individualized while the computer-tutors were in use; the social situation surrounding that help changed quite markedly in at least two respects – the extent to which students could control the kind and amount of help they received from the teacher changed markedly as did the likelihood that help was received in a private rather than a public situation.

In geometry classes not using the computer-tutor, there appeared to be three common situations in which students received help. First, they were often able to ask for it, most typically but not exclusively at the beginning of class when the teacher went over homework problems. Second, teachers often supplied unsolicited help, or asked peers to do so, when a student had made a public mistake working a problem on the chalkboard. Finally, some teachers circulated through the class offering help as they noticed mistakes in problems students were working on while in their seats. Typically such advice was offered in tones loud enough so that it was clearly audible throughout the classroom, supporting the idea mentioned earlier that certain kinds of apparently individualized help are often aimed in reality at a much broader audience than the apparent one.

Although in the first case students could avoid the teacher's assistance if they so desired by not asking for help with troublesome problems, they did so at the cost of continuing to be unable to handle the work expected of them. In the other two kinds of situations, the teacher, not the student, typically initiated and controlled helping episodes. For a student to reject such help or even to seem overtly uninterested was clearly counternormative. The teacher's control over helping is part and parcel of his or her broader control of the class through mechanisms such as requiring note taking and deciding which students would be required or allowed to speak. Overall, this created a rather passive role for students and one with little control of the pace and content of their activities.

In contrast, students working on the computer-based tutors were somewhat freer to decide how much help they would receive as well as to determine its source. Some students strove to be very independent, doing all they possibly could do on their own, without even the GPTutor's help:

Interviewer: The tutor had a number of windows designed to help you. . . . How often did you use them?

Sharon: At the beginning I didn't use them at all. I tried to figure everything out on my own. But then, toward the end, when the problems became more and more difficult, I started

to use it more. I seldom used the one where the computer selected for you [i.e., gave you the next step], but I used the one
that would tell you the rules you could use.

More often students preferred to get frequent and repeated assistance from the tutor:

Interviewer: The computer had a number of windows designed
to help you. . . . How often did you use them?

Katy: *A lot!* The review list showed all the rules that we learned.
You could click it if you forgot. It'll give you a quick review
of the rule. The applicable rules were helpful because instead
of giving you the long list, they gave you only the rules you
could use for a particular problem. . . . They were helpful in
solving the proofs 'cause without them I don't think we
would have solved them as easily.

Very few preferred to get help from the teacher before even
trying to get it from the computer-based tutor, although there were
a few exceptions to this generalization, as suggested by the following exchange:

Interviewer: The tutor had a number of windows designed to
help you. . . . How often did you use them?

Anna: Hardly ever. . . . Sometimes I couldn't get the teacher's
attention so I just used the windows.

Finally, after the GPTutors were introduced into their classrooms, teachers seemed to spend longer periods of time helping
individual students. Contributing to this phenomenon may have
been a recognition that other students would not generally be held
back by an extended helping episode with one student since they
could continue to work on their computers. Taken together, these
factors meant that the teachers did less routine hovering and
checking of most students' work. Instead, their advice seemed to
come proportionately more frequently than it did in the traditional
classroom situation as a result of a student's expressed desire for
such assistance. Thus, students assumed a considerably more au-
tonomous and active role in the computer-tutor classrooms than
they had previously.

An Increased Emphasis on Effort in Grading

The use of the GPTutor also led to potentially important changes in the teachers' grading practices. Mr. Adams and Mr. Brice, like the other geometry teachers, usually based the grades they gave on some formal criteria involving relatively objective measures of performance on homework assignments, quizzes, tests, and the like. However, when using the computer-tutor they both made a change. Specifically, both decided independently to emphasize effort more than they had previously:

Interviewer: Did having the computers change the basis on which you assigned grades at all?

Mr. Brice: Well, I did give them a grade for the lab [computer] work they did. The control class didn't get a grade for the lab work because there wasn't any lab to work in.

Interviewer: Was it how much they accomplished, or how hard they worked, or some combination?

Mr. Brice: Probably how much they stayed on task . . . Breaks here and there would affect their lab time. It was how much time they spent on task, not necessarily how much they learned.

Since one of the major advantages of the GPTutor was that it allowed students to work at their own pace, grading everyone against the same standard of accomplishment no longer seemed consistent with the way the class was structured. It is particularly noteworthy that Mr. Adams adjusted his grading system to reflect effort even though he was philosophically opposed to this:

Interviewer: How has the introduction of the computer tutors changed the basis on which you assign grades?

Mr. Adams: *This is a problem!* . . . I've had to develop a policy. . . . Effort meant a lot more this time [i.e., when using the GPTutor compared to when not using it]. It had to. See, I'll be honest with you. . . . I just don't buy effort. It just doesn't mean much to me. It doesn't. . . . I'm a geometry teacher. . . . A college is going to assess a student's ability according to that grade. . . . So, I just can't give a B for effort. . . . This is my philosophy. . . . So that's why this is a little unusual, because effort is going to count.

Interestingly, the chairman of the math department mentioned to a research team member that he could not evaluate the teachers using the GPTutors very well since those classes were run so differently from ordinary ones and different teaching skills were needed. Thus, the utilization of the tutor raised questions about both teacher and student evaluation.

CHANGES IN THE STUDENTS' BEHAVIOR

Given that the GPTutor was field-tested in three different kinds of classes (regular, advanced, and ones for gifted students) in a coeducational and racially mixed public high school, it was tempting to try to assess differences in the reactions of different kinds of students to it. However, in general this was extremely difficult to do in any systematic way, the main reason being that gender, race, and the kind of class were seriously confounded. So, for example, white males outnumbered all other groups in geometry classes for gifted students and were markedly underrepresented in all but one of the four regular classes using the GPTutor. Thus, when differences did occur between tracks it was not clear whether they were due to the student's level of ability, to factors such as race or gender, or to other factors. Furthermore, it was not uncommon for students, especially girls, who officially belonged in one of the advanced tracks to actually end up in a lower track for geometry due to scheduling considerations or personal preferences. It was difficult to know how to treat such students for purposes of analysis since their tested ability level placed them with one group whereas they actually functioned as part of a different group. Thus, with one exception, I have chosen to describe modal reactions to using the GPTutor rather than to discuss differences related to students' background characteristics. The exception, which involved a difference in male and female students' reactions to the competition engendered by the GPTutor, was the one instance in which the

36

reactions of students seemed consistently enough influenced by racial, gender, or academic track membership to warrant making such comparisons.

Increased Motivation

One of the most striking changes in the classrooms using the GPTutor was the increase in student involvement and effort. This change was evidenced by markedly increased time on task and clear increases in the apparent level of involvement and concentration. High levels of effort and involvement, even in the face of difficulty, capture the sense of what both numerous psychological theories (Beck, 1990; Reeve, 1992; Smith, 1969) and everyday parlance subsume under the concept of motivation. Thus, the clearest change in the students' behavior associated with the use of the GPTutor was an increase in their apparent level of motivation. Before discussing the origins of this change, I will present some of the evidence on which this assertion is based.

With regard to level of effort, the heart of the concept of motivation, both students and teachers remarked in interviews on the change associated with the use of the GPTutor. Specifically, when asked in the post-use interviews how using the computer-tutor influenced their behavior, students most commonly mentioned an increase in their level of effort. Both of the teachers using the GPTutor also spontaneously mentioned in their interviews this increase in student effort.

Before the arrival of the computer-tutors, and in the control and comparison classes, it usually took the teacher a few minutes to get the class settled down and ready for work. Mr. Adams generally started his classes more promptly and continued them right up to the closing bell more than the other geometry teachers we observed. However, even students in his classes made it difficult to use all of the 45-minute class period productively when they were not using the GPTutor, as is evident from the following excerpt from project field notes:

I [the observer] arrive before the bell [which indicates the start of class] rings. Kathy, Tim, and Debbie are in their seats already.

37

The two girls are consulting about their homework. . . . The bell rings. Karen saunters in and takes her seat. Ida comes in after Mr. Adams begins to ask for homework saying, "Pass it in if you've got it . . . . " Rachel strolls in while Mr. Adams puts the first problem on the board. He ignores her. Karen says, "Are we almost done with these circle problems? I hate them." Ida is looking at a postcard that Karen has shown her. Mr. Adams says, "Ida, put that thing away and pay attention." Ida looks at the postcard for another 15 seconds or so and then hands it back to Karen who holds it to her nose and inhales happily before putting it away. Katy complains, "It's so hot in here today." Mr. Adams gives the students a problem to work on. Ida and Rachael remove their jackets.

In many of the control and comparison classes it was not unusual for the last 5 or 10 minutes to be devoted to socializing. Sometimes the teacher had simply covered all he wanted to and judged that it did not make sense to start something new in the time remaining. Another common practice that contributed greatly to lost instructional time was giving out a "homework" assignment well before the end of the class period and asking students to work on it in class. Although the rationale for this practice was that the teacher could help students with any difficulties they might encounter, many students chose to chat with friends for 10 or 15 minutes rather than doing this work in class. Thus, in many classes that did not use the computer-tutors it was common for numerous students to spend a total of 10 to 15 minutes a period chatting about sports, clothes, teachers, or other nonacademic topics. This accounted for a substantial proportion of the 45-minute class period.

Almost immediately after beginning to use the GPTutor, many students began working on their proofs well before the starting bell, a situation rarely observed in the control and comparison classes. In addition, students frequently continued working after the closing bell, also very atypical behavior in other geometry classrooms. In one extreme case, a fistfight nearly broke out between one student staying after his class was over to try to finish a proof and another who arrived early for the next class and wanted to get started on the same machine. An excerpt from the project's field notes illustrates the unusually prompt start of the classes using the computer tutor:

> By the time the bell to start class rings, three-fourths of the students in class today have problems on the screen and are working on them. The others [have all logged on and] appear to be waiting for their problems to appear. . . . I'm struck by the fact that the students have started their work without a word from the substitute teacher who is in charge of class today.

In addition to starting work more promptly and working through the last minutes of the period, students using the GPTutor also appeared to be more engrossed in their work than those in the traditional classes. Of course, in observational work it is difficult if not impossible to get a precise measure of whether students are concentrating since those skilled in the art of classroom behavior may find ways to appear to be working when in reality letting their attention wander. Yet all indications were that the level of concentration rose. Students often spontaneously mentioned this change in interviews:

Interviewer: How did using the computers change the way you behaved in class?

Diane: Well, we didn't talk as much. On the computer you really concentrated on the screen – didn't have time to talk to the person next to you.

The fact that students made much quicker progress on the proofs than either the teachers or the tutor's developers anticipated suggests that the students were indeed focusing their attention on the proofs. This increased focus is apparent from field notes like the following, as well as student and teacher interviews:

> The room is extremely quiet now [as students continue to work at the computers]. There are just little beeps [from the machines] every minute or two. Except for one brief interchange between two white boys there has literally been no student to student talk in the 15 minutes of class so far.

Factors Contributing to the Increase in Motivation. Since several sources of evidence all converged to suggest that use of the computer-tutor enhanced student motivation, an obvious question that arises is, Why? The data suggest several complementary reasons for the change, including an increase both in friendly competition between classmates and in the students' enjoyment of their work.

As discussed earlier and consistent with other research (Hawkins & Sheingold, 1986), a change in grading practices followed introduction of the computer-tutors. Specifically, both teachers using the GPTutor began to count effort more than they had, in spite of the fact that one of them was philosophically opposed to this practice. One possibility is that this accounted for the students' increased effort. Yet the evidence suggests that this was not a major contributing factor. Specifically, only 2 of the over 70 students interviewed about how using the GPTutor influenced their grades said they thought their level of effort on the computer contributed to their grades. A few additional students remarked that persistent and unnecessary use of a software feature called "system select," which could be used to essentially present the student with the problem's solution, would be viewed negatively by their teacher, although they did not specifically indicate that it would hurt their grades. Fewer than 10% of the GPTutor students who were asked why the computer-tutor kept track of all their work (which was done primarily for research purposes) believed that this record might be used in grading. Instead, they typically said it would be used to isolate areas in which students needed more help or to see if students were using the system select feature so much that they would not learn anything. Thus, overall, the change in the teachers' grading practices does not seem to be a major factor accounting for the widespread and striking increase in the students' effort and involvement. In fact, it is worth noting that in both years of the study students using the GPTutor rated their desire to pass the course and their desire to get good grades, both extrinsic sources of motivation, as influencing their behavior in geometry significantly less at the end of the year than at the beginning. In contrast, the randomly selected groups of control students from other geometry classes indicated an increase in the importance of grades as a motivation in the course of the study's first year and no change over time in the importance of grades as a motivation on the study's second year (Eurich-Fulcer & Britt, 1990).

Increased Sense of Competition and Personal Challenge. A more tenable explanation for the students' increased effort and involvement was the unusually high level of friendly competition that developed between them. Although the extent of this increase varied somewhat from class to class, it was apparent in all the GPTutor classes, especially among the boys. In the classrooms in which this increase was most apparent, a high proportion of the relatively infrequent student conversations concerned a comparison of how many of the available problems the students had completed.

The teachers, students, and observers all noticed the change in the level of competition. Both Mr. Adams and Mr. Brice remarked on it in interviews:

Mr. Adams: Just listen to them. Just watch them as they're waiting for a problem to come up. They say, "What problem are you on? Where are you at? Oh, you're only there. Oh, I was there two days ago!" That kind of stuff.

One student, Kathy, responded to a question about whether the introduction of the GPTutor changed the level of competition in her class this way:

It seemed more competitive because we were all competing to get done. . . . I don't think anybody was planning to compete. It just happened. . . . When the computers came . . . everybody's competing. We were all saying, "Well what number are you on?" trying to . . . pass everybody up.

When the students were asked in the post–computer use interviews why they had started getting to class early after the arrival of the computer-tutors, roughly 40% spontaneously indicated that it was because of the competition. In addition, when asked directly whether the introduction of the tutors had changed the level of competition in the classroom students overwhelmingly responded in the affirmative. Close to three-quarters of the GPTutor-using students perceived increased competition when using the tutors. Exchanges like the following were common:

Interviewer: Did geometry class seem more or less competitive when you were using the computer-tutors?

Mike: It was more competitive. We went at each other. . . . It was like we were having a race – who would get to the end of each chapter in the book through the computer. I won . . . because I knew it!

Rather ironically, the very fact that the tutors were designed to let students progress at their own pace created a situation that fostered competition between students. In traditionally taught geometry classes, students never have the chance to get far ahead of or behind each other in the way they can in a class using computer-tutors. As indicated earlier, all of the geometry teachers we observed typically began with a brief lecture or a discussion of specific geometry problems, either new ones or ones from the preceding night's homework. Some students were able to do these problems faster or more accurately than others, and in that sense the potential for competition existed. However, since the teachers normally kept the class focused on a particular problem or set of problems until they felt most of the class understood what was happening, the stronger students were not able to move through the curriculum faster than their peers. They could differ from their peers in the quality of their work, but they could not get substantially ahead. Similarly, although the slower students sometimes got lost on a particular problem, they were soon presented with a different one, which they had at least some chance of solving. Thus, the daily situation was not conducive to intense competition about the speed with which students could progress since the opportunity for pulling dramatically ahead of their peers was not there.

In contrast, when students used the computer-tutors, some students were able to progress much faster than others. The faster students were not held back by their teacher's desire or need to teach to the class as a whole. Neither could the slower students skip over the problems that gave them difficulty in one area and

42

hope to do better in another, for the software was organized into a series of problems that were to be solved in a specified order. The fact that the problems were numbered and that students were seated close enough to each other that they could talk without shouting also encouraged the development of competition because it made it easy for them to communicate simply and clearly about their relative progress. The kind of interchange illustrated in the following field notes from Mr. Brice's class was common:

> Dan says to Val, who is at the computer next to him, "What number are you on?" Val replies "Fifty-two." Dan says "Shit, we're on 41."

This kind of competition was considerably more noticeable in the study's first year, when students worked on all the problems in one large block, than in the second year, when tutor use was alternated with regular classroom activities, suggesting yet another factor that shaped the impact the GPTutor had on classroom functioning. Nonetheless, even in the second year of the study two-thirds of the students reported that using the GPTutor made their class more competitive.

In general, students reacted very positively to this increase in competition. In both years of the study, a clear majority of the students said in interviews that they thought the competition had a positive effect on learning, and this response was especially strong and consistent in the regular track classes. Exchanges like the following were very common in the student interviews:

Interviewer: How did this competition affect the students involved?

Michael: It didn't make us act any differently toward each other. I think it made us learn more because we were trying to think and beat the other person out. . . . The more we thought the more we learned and the faster we got done. . . . I thought it was fun.

Similarly, in both years of the study, relatively few students reported a negative effect of this competition (3% and 14%, respectively). Rather, they spoke of the competition as creating a sense of fun and excitement, a desire to excel, and even, rather ironically, an atmosphere in which students helped each other more.

Students often spontaneously characterized the competition generated by the tutors with positive terms like *good competition* or *friendly competition* as illustrated in the following excerpt from an interview:

Interviewer: Did geometry class seem more or less competitive after the introduction of the computer-tutors?

Iris: More competitive . . . I mean, when we did the book who cares if you did your homework that day? Who cares if you answer all the questions. . . . We just want to get out of there. But now, it's good competition, it makes you want to work more. . . . If the person next to me is . . . two or three problems ahead, I'll work faster.

At first the conclusion that students enjoyed the competition and were motivated by it seems to fly in the face of much recent work that emphasizes the positive impact of cooperation on both learning and motivation and the potentially negative consequences of competition (Johnson & Johnson, 1974; Johnson & Johnson, 1992; Johnson, Maruyama, Johnson, Nelson, & Skon, 1981). However, it is important to recognize that neither the classroom task structure (whether students work as individuals or with others as part of a group) nor its formal reward structure (the basis on which grades or other classroom rewards are assigned) actually became more competitive with the introduction of the GPTutor. Specifically, the task structure in both the GPTutor classes and in the control and comparison classes was typically individualized, with students generally working by themselves. Similarly, the use of the GPTutor did not create a competitive zero-sum situation in which one individual's achievement undermined others' learning or grades. If anything, as discussed earlier, the explicit expectation that students would work at their own pace on the GPTutor and the increased emphasis on effort created a less competitive reward structure.

The fact that the competition to complete problems had no marked impact on students' grades may have been very important

44

in keeping it friendly and good-natured. Students seemed to experience it as a game rather than as a struggle with serious consequences, as suggested by the following comments:

Mark: It was like a fun competition. It wasn't that really serious. We would help each other.

Nancy: It was . . . a big joke. It wasn't really anything serious. We just did it to be silly. We just had fun doing it. . . . It got us into it – sort of a goal.

Typically individuals at roughly the same place in the set of problems tended to trade information on who was pulling ahead at a particular point in time. Comments about relative pace were usually, although not always, phrased in a way that praised the faster student rather than denigrating the slower one (e.g., "I'm really whipping through these," rather than "You are sure dumb"). As one student, Darlene, put it:

The people in my class are really nice and everything. They don't tease each other like, "Ah ha, I'm ahead of you," or nothing because they know that everybody learns at a different pace.

Yet another factor contributing to the generally positive reaction to the competition may have been the fact that students had at least some control over whether they joined in it or not In contrast to the situation in which a teacher puts all students into a competitive situation by creating a competitive reward structure, students in the GPTutor classes could decide for themselves whether to initiate competitive exchanges, whether to respond to the competitive overtures directed toward them, and to whom they would direct their competitive remarks. Not too surprisingly, there was some tendency for the stronger students to compete more, as a substantial number of students noted in interviews.

Although none of the students mentioned in their interviews that boys were somewhat more likely to compete than girls, this did, in fact, seem to be the case. For example, examination of all field notes taken in the GPTutor classes revealed that obvious instances of competition were almost three times more frequent for boys than for girls, although overall the number of boys and girls in the classes observed did not differ markedly. This figure is not presented as a precise estimate of the actual ratio, since some instances of such talk may have been missed when recording the field notes. However, the magnitude of the difference does suggest that the phenomenon is real, especially since the increase in competition following the introduction of the GPTutor was so immediate and clear that research team members paid close attention to trying to understand how competition manifested itself when gathering field notes from very early on in the study.

Other evidence also supports the conclusion that the competition was especially evident among the boys. For example, when students spontaneously mentioned in interviews the names of those who competed a great deal they were more likely to mention boys than girls. In addition, when answering questions on this subject, students frequently asserted that students who seemed competitive by nature were the ones who were especially likely to compete on the tutor. As will be discussed in Chapter 5, boys were more likely to exhibit overt competitive behaviors in many situations than were girls and thus, perhaps, were more likely to appear to their peers as competitive by nature.

Although students did, generally speaking, have some control over whether they got involved in the competition stimulated by use of the GPTutor, it is undeniably true that students who preferred not to compete were occasionally put in an awkward situation by peers who persisted in asking in a competitive way for information that students did not wish to share. One student, Mary, explained how she got pushed into competing by boys in her class:

> I was never competitive before. . . . I mean I don't like it. . . . I thought it was sort of stupid to compete. But then Daniel [whom she previously described as competitive whether or not he was on the GPTutor] just kept [saying], "I'm going to beat you." So, then [I said to myself], "We'll see!"

Similarly, just hearing how far ahead others were could be discouraging to students who were not progressing as rapidly as their peers. In spite of the widely shared view that the competition was all in good fun, a few students reacted negatively to it. The strongest indictment of it came from an African American girl in one of the advanced classes:

Interviewer: How did this competition affect the students involved?

Rena: Well, I think it got on everyone's nerves. A lot. Certain people were just being total jerks about it. . . . Some people are actually struggling. . . . They think they are bad at math. They think there is no way that they could compete. . . . They know that they're behind, so they're just going to let that idiot go on their merry way.

Thus, it should be noted that the competitive interchanges that so many students enjoyed and found motivating were discouraging and aversive to at least a few of their peers.

Increased Enjoyment. Students may have been motivated to work harder when using the GPTutor simply because they enjoyed using it. The majority of students indicated in interviews that using the GPTutor was more fun than learning geometry conventionally, and some specifically linked this increased enjoyment to an increase in motivation. Prior theory and research (Malone & Lepper, 1987) suggest the kind of linkage between enjoyment and motivation implied by the following exchange:

Interviewer: What do you think are the major advantages of using a computer to help you learn geometry?

Paul: If it's fun, it makes you want to learn something! It's fun!

The students' increased enjoyment of geometry when using the computer-tutors had numerous sources. In addition to the generally positive reaction to competition just discussed, use of the GPTutor increased students' sense of control, a feeling that has clearly been linked by prior research to increased motivation as well as positive attitudes toward school (Henderson & Dweck, 1990; Lepper & Chabay, 1985). Recall that students using the GPTutor gained a considerable amount of control over when, whether, and how they received help from their teacher. Although the

GPTutor became very directive after a student had made two successive errors, as long as the student progressed along a path that could potentially lead to a viable proof it let them proceed, even if they were on a suboptimal route. This sense of control over their work may have been particularly rewarding for these students since, as adolescents, they were at a period in their lives in which issues of autonomy are particularly salient (Steinberg, 1985). Many students did indeed express pleasure at their relative independence from direct adult control when working on the computer in interviews about their experiences in the GPTutor classrooms.

Furthermore, there was a strong link in many students' minds between computers and playing games, which predisposed them favorably to working on computers and led many of them to work in a productive but playful manner (e.g., seeing who could take the most steps to complete a proof successfully) in spite of the competition:

> Mr. Brice looks next at Ben and Marcus at the computer next to Andy. He says, "Whoa, guys. What are you doing there?" Mark says, "We're making a road map," referring to the very complicated proof graph on their screen which has resulted in a large array of lines. Mr. Brice . . . asks them what they are trying to prove and comments, "Well, you've taken a roundabout way." Marcus says, "Well, we like to get a lot a steps in there!"

One feature of the software that may have contributed to this sense of playing while working was a "success sound" that occurred when students completed a proof.

Considerably more important than the success sound in making work on the computer-tutor pleasurable and in motivating students appeared to be the sense of personal challenge that students felt. Challenge, like competition, is characteristic of many games. Numerous students remarked on this sense of challenge in their interviews. A student named Alice described this sense particularly vividly:

> It was . . . brain against software, because the computer does . . . challenge you. You feel like, "Well this computer knows it all, and if I can get through this computer, I've got to be the great-

48

est. . . . I've got to know . . . *geometry* pretty dag gone well if I can get this all by myself," . . . especially at the end of the program. That was really challenging. It's the problem versus you. Like they [the problems] are there and they sort of say, "Well come and get me!" . . . And you sit there and you say, "I bet I can get done with that. I bet I can get that problem done." When you get done, you feel real happy, like you just beat up somebody that you really hated and you go, "*Yeah! Ha, ha, ha, ha!*"

Although other students used somewhat less bellicose similes to describe their feelings, the sense of challenge and of pleasure in striving to meet the challenge in Alice's remarks was common.

Although Alice's comments can be interpreted as taking note of how she compares with her peers ("If I can get though this computer, I've got to be the greatest"), there is also evident a very deep sense of engagement with the problems and a desire to master them ("And you sit there and you say, 'I bet I can get that problem done'"). Numerous theorists have pointed out the importance of this kind of focus on mastering material for students' enjoyment of their work and their motivation to persist at it (Ames, 1990; Ames & Ames, 1989; Ames & Archer, 1988; Henderson & Dweck, 1990; Lepper & Chabay, 1985; Nicholls, Patashnick, Cheung, Thorkildsen, & Lauer, 1989). For example, Ames and Archer (1988) argue that when students see their classes as emphasizing mastery, they are more likely to report using effective learning strategies, to believe that effort is likely to lead to success, and to enjoy their classes. They argue that a focus on mastery is fostered by a classroom climate that, among other things, defines progress as success and evaluates students on the basis of their progress. The explicit expectation that students would progress at their own pace and the presentation of the success sound and message when students finished problems, even if they were well behind others, were certainly consistent with this. Also encouraging an orientation toward mastery was the fact that the software was constructed so that students could not progress until they had successfully dealt with the problem at hand, a situation rather different from the regular classroom situation where the teacher might decide to move on before every single student had mastered a given problem.

49

There is no doubt that many elements of the GPTutor class-rooms, especially the widespread competition between students, were not conducive to an exclusive focus on mastery. However, as the work of both Ames and Archer (1988) and Jagacinski and Nicholls (1987) suggests, the positive effects of a mastery-oriented learning environment on students' motivation and enjoyment are not necessarily canceled out by the simultaneous presence of factors conducive to an emphasis on one's performance relative to others. Rather, the positive effects of elements encouraging mastery appear to persist even when students also perceive that their performance relative to peers is important too.

Increased Ability to Express Negative Affect. In addition to enjoying the emphasis on challenge and mastery stimulated by use of the GPTutor, rather ironically, students responded positively to the computer-tutors because they felt free to express frustration and anger to them in a way they could not with a teacher without violating strong norms. Often the expression of anger and frustration had a rather playful feeling to it, just as the competition described earlier did. That is to say, students were not deeply upset or profoundly angered by their interactions with the computer-tutors. Rather, when they were momentarily frustrated they were able to express this feeling in a way that gave them satisfaction. Thus, it was fairly common for students to tell the computer to shut up, to call it names like "stupid fool," or even to swear at it. In fact, in one class one girl swore at the computer so regularly that her teacher joked about wiring the computer so that it would shock her every time she did so. Sometimes, though not often, students would hit or shake the computer or slap the mouse down very hard in spite of the teachers' emphatic instructions when the computers were introduced about the importance of properly treating the equipment.

In sharp contrast, direct verbal and physical venting of frustration and anger through name-calling, swearing, or physical assault was virtually nonexistent in interactions directed from students to teachers at this school. (Not surprisingly, such behavior was explicitly forbidden in the *Student Handbook*.) Students clearly felt able to speak much more freely when dealing with the computer-based tutors than with their teachers, and teachers generally let the verbal abuse of the computer pass as a kind of amusing expression of emotion. The difference in what is acceptable when students are dealing with the computer and with an adult in a position of authority is made clear in the following field notes:

> Tara says, "This computer should be shot." Mr. Adams squats down and begins explaining the problem to her. Bob says, "Shit," to his computer. Ms. Donavon [who as part of the staff involved with the field testing of the computer assists students with bugs in the program or hardware failures] overhears him and thinks he said, "Sh," possibly to her since she's standing nearby talking to one of his classmates. She says, looking at Bob, "What was that?" The blood rushes to his face and he doesn't answer. She says to him, "Why are you turning every shade of red?" Then the light dawns and she says, "It wasn't 'sh.' It was . . . . " She then gives a small laugh, and Bob looks down at his terminal and types away industriously.

Decreased Fear of Embarrassment. Another factor contributing to students' involvement with work on the computer and their feeling that it was fun was a sense of being more comfortable in the GPTutor classrooms because of a decreased fear of embarrassment. Students generally agreed that working on the computer-tutors was less likely to be embarrassing than doing geometry the more traditional way. Thus, working on the tutors was likely to lessen the emphasis on learning as a public performance in which one's value is either affirmed or undermined, a perspective that many theorists have argued is detrimental to learning (Ames, 1990; Ames & Ames, 1989; Ames & Archer, 1988; Henderson & Dweck, 1990; Lepper & Chabay, 1985; Nicholls et al., 1989). The following exchange is typical of the students' responses to questions about this issue:

Interviewer: Was it more or less embarrassing to make a geometry mistake when you were using the computers than it was before?

Alice: I think it was less because you were working all by your-

51

self. If you were answering a question [in a traditionally structured class] and you answered it wrong, the whole class would know. When you were working with the computer, nobody really knows.

As indicated earlier, in traditionally structured geometry classes students are often called upon to perform before others, as the teacher has them do board work, answer questions at their seats, and the like. This can be embarrassing for the students who are behind or just plain lost since their difficulties become very public. Even seat work can be embarrassing because teachers commonly comment on it in a tone clearly audible to the rest of the class, as is apparent in the following field notes taken by an observer seated in the back of the classroom:

> Students begin working quietly at their seats. Mr. Adams walks around. . . . He says, "Good," to Sally when he sees her work. He says, "Wait a minute," to Irene and, "No, No, No!" to Linda after looking at her work. He then goes back over and looks at Sally's work again and says, "Wait a minute. Wait a minute, Sally. What's 180 plus 4?"

Mistakes on the GPTutor were more likely to be private. First, the computers were placed so that students could not see each other's screens. Second, although the teachers did circulate and make comments as students' at their computers worked, the fact that students were facing different directions, working on different problems, and were not expected to be attending to the teacher when he was helping other students made it less likely that others were monitoring these comments. Third, the fact that the tutor had a number of help functions that let students privately request a review of previous material or hints on how to do a problem meant that those who were particularly sensitive about appearing to need assistance had a readily available nonhuman source of help. It is interesting to note, and consistent with my argument, that one of the few features of the computer that drew frequent criticism from the students was the use of a beeping sound to indicate a mistake. However, there are two reasons why this beeping may not have been overly inhibiting. First, beeping could be triggered by things other than student errors. Second, even when a student made an error other students were often unaware of whose computer had beeped. Thus, students were freed to continue working on the computers even when they were not sure they were correct, rather than stopping out of fear of making a mistake that would result in an embarrassing beep.

CHANGES IN THE GPTutor

This book focuses on two major issues – the ways in which the use of technology influences classroom functioning and the ways in which the existing social context in the classroom and school influence technology use. Before closing this chapter, which has focused on the first of these two questions, I would like to turn to a very brief discussion of a topic related to the second – the evolution of the GPTutor during the 2 years it was being field-tested at Whitmore. Understanding something about the changes made in the tutor in response to students' reactions to it helps shed light on possible areas of mismatch and friction between the assumptions embedded in software and the students who use it or the environments in which they function.

Since the focus of this chapter is on the social aspects of utilizing an artificially intelligent tutor, this discussion will not dwell on changes such as the addition of more explanatory dialogue, the clarification of explanations, and the addition of a requirement that students start the proof by typing in the goal in order to help make the point toward which they were working more salient, all of which were implemented with specific cognitive goals in mind. Rather, it will concentrate on changes connected in some reasonably direct way to the students' functioning as social beings with affective responses to their learning experiences and to their classroom environment.

One of the first changes of this sort was the addition of a success sound, a rapid, repeated beep automatically emitted by the computer upon the students' completion of each problem. Originally, the GPTutor had just one very low-key way of recognizing a student's successful completion of a problem – the word *success* flashed briefly on the screen. In less than two weeks after the tutors were first used, student complaints about the paucity of tangible rewards for success led to the supplementing of this written recognition of their success with an auditory one. This allayed student complaints, although some students still indicated they would have preferred more reward for completion of a problem, including ego-building messages like "You're smart" or enjoyable experiences such as the presentation of a cartoon. In fact, many students found ways to magnify the reinforcement provided by the GPTutor, most frequently by repeating the word *success* out loud when it appeared on the screen:

> The students work through the proof. "Success" appears on the screen. They smile at each other and raise their arms as if they have just won a race. Melvin repeats, "Success, success."

Sometimes this repetition of the word *success* was done in quiet tones as if the students were speaking to themselves. Other times the word was repeated in loud, jubilant tones that clearly called the student's completion of the problem to the attention of all his or her classmates.

A second change in the GPTutor was the replacement of a feature called "system select" by sets of dialogue with increasingly strong and directive hints. The system select feature was initially created to provide the next step in a proof for students who were so lost that the various help and review windows were not enough to set them on a viable proof path. However, one problem with this feature of the software was that if a student repeatedly used it, the tutor itself would proceed to complete the proof without any real input from the student. Students were specifically instructed to avoid using this feature unless they were completely confused. Most did so. In fact, many chose not to use system select when it might have been helpful in moving them forward:

Interviewer: Was it difficult to get students to use the system select feature judiciously?

Mr. Adams: Oh no. No, no, no. If I were to make a generalization I would say they didn't like to use it. . . . They were proud . . . very proud. I'm talking about 75% to 80% of the students . . . [who] want to do it on their own.

However, there were some students who abused the feature by using it very liberally rather than working to solve the problems on their own first. A few of the slowest students used system select a lot when they got substantially behind their peers, thus suggesting one negative result of a focus on how their accomplishments compared with those of their classmates. It is of interest that this same situation, getting substantially behind one's peers, also evoked the same behavior in one or two of the most accomplished students on the rare occasions they got behind, as Mr. Adams's remarks indicate:

> One of our brightest students used it [system select] for the first 3 days she was on the computer because she missed the first week and was 10 or 20 problems behind everybody. She couldn't stand the peer pressure . . . so she let the computer do the first 20 problems and then never used it again. . . . She doesn't like to be behind everybody. It's not just peer pressure, it's a self-imposed pressure [too].

A third change made in the GPTutor was an increase in the number of student errors the tutor would tolerate before intervening unilaterally to redirect the student along a more productive path. Initially, the tutor was programmed to allow students to continue on circuitous or suboptimal routes as long as they did not make a clear error. However, as soon as the student had made two consecutive errors the tutor unilaterally intervened. One of the implications of Anderson's theory of cognitive skill acquisition on which the tutor is based is that it is wasteful to let learners wander around trying out incorrect solutions. Thus, the GPTutor was designed to help students over hurdles that delayed successful completion of the proof.

However, many students strongly objected to the automatic assistance feature, saying that the tutor often took over before they had a chance to fully explore the routes they wanted to follow. Often they were forced to leave the path on which they were working and moved to a correct path without being convinced that they had been irretrievably wrong, even when this was the case. The students' negative reactions to this feature of the tutor were no doubt intensified by the fact that initially the tutor was not able to distinguish effectively between errors that were the result of typing mistakes or momentary inattentiveness and those that reflected a serious lack of understanding. In addition, the students disliked the fact that the help was generally quite restrictive. For example, rather than helping students proceed along a suboptimal but workable path on which they had made errors, once the tutor intervened it unilaterally moved the student to a more direct path. Finally, the students' frustration was no doubt increased by the fact that the tutor did not have the capability of explaining in a global way why the new path was better than the one on which the student had been working. All in all, students did not willingly transfer control of their activities from their teacher to the computer-based tutor. They objected strongly enough to the initially very controlling setup of the tutor that the software's designers made changes that somewhat reduced the frequency with which the tutor "took over" and compelled students to work on what it had determined was the best approach to the problem. Some students still chaffed at the degree of control exerted by the tutor. However, the developers decided not to relax this control further because of their concern that this would lead to less effective instruction.

These clashes between the tutor's initial design and students' preferences made it evident that undergirding the GPTutor, and in fact any piece of software, is a set of assumptions, both implicit and explicit, about the user and the context in which the use will occur that may or may not be correct. (See Lepper & Chabay, 1985, for an interesting discussion of these issues.) First, as mentioned earlier, the GPTutor was designed for individual use, rather than for use by pairs or larger groups. Although students actually did use the tutor in pairs in two classrooms because of the interest of one of the research's sponsors in the possibility of joint usage, no one connected with the project saw this experiment as a success.

Not only was the GPTutor designed to be used by an individual, but seeing the tutor in use made it clear that, initially, it was designed with a certain kind of individual in mind, implicitly if not explicitly. This person could be characterized as a "model student," or a "straight arrow," that is, as a highly motivated student genuinely interested in learning. The design of the GPTutor assumes that its users are willing to work independently without a great deal of human supervision, to ask for help when it is needed, and to accept unsolicited and very directive help when the tutor presents it. Unlike many gamelike pieces of educational software that seem designed for more reluctant learners, the GPTutor does not try to disguise its pedagogical intent or to seduce students into learning through colorful graphics, fantasy, or exciting adventure themes. Rather, it seems to assume that the student using the tutor actively wants to learn and thus will review material and ask for and utilize help as needed. The original version, with the system select feature, showed great trust in the learner's intrinsic motivation and self-reliance. It assumed, for many students correctly, that the feature would be used to help out when an impasse was reached, rather than to complete the proofs automatically without effort but also without learning. It had no built-in mechanism to prevent near constant use of this feature by students uninterested in learning or feeling pressured by being behind. The initial design of the software ignored the sensitivity of students to their social context, which led some students to complain about the beeps that signaled errors and others to overuse the system select feature.

The tutor was designed on the basis of a theory that focused on the cognitive processes of learners. The affective and social needs of students and, for that matter, a substantial number of pedagogical issues received little if any systematic consideration in the initial design of the tutor. Thus, it is ironic that the preceding analysis of changes in student behavior concludes that many of the factors that contributed to students' positive reactions to the tutor were affective and social in nature. In cases in which the tutor's design created obvious problems relating to these needs, its developers were generally quick to make changes on an ad hoc basis, such as the addition of a success sound. However, as a general rule, it seems likely that more systematic attention to affective, social, and pedagogical factors is likely to increase the effectiveness of instructional software.

SUMMARY AND CONCLUSIONS

In summary, both teachers' and students' behaviors appeared to be influenced in important ways by the utilization of the artificially intelligent computer-tutors. Teachers began to devote more time to the slower students. They also began to act in a somewhat more collegial fashion and to provide more individualized help. In addition, they weighted effort more heavily when computing students' grades. Students changed too, showing a marked increase in task-related effort and involvement that appeared to be due to the confluence of several factors including a major increase in the amount of good-natured peer competition, an enhanced sense of challenge, and greater enjoyment of their geometry classes. It seems reasonable to suggest that these factors may have contributed to the positive impact of the computer-tutor on many students' ability to do geometry proofs, which is discussed elsewhere (Wertheimer, 1990).

Since artificially intelligent tutors are clearly the exception rather than the rule in present-day classrooms, many readers may wonder about the implications of this study for understanding the likely impact of more common kinds of educational software, such as educational games or drill and practice packages. Because educational software is so varied, and much of it differs in many ways from the software studied here, it is hard to draw any certain conclusions on this topic. However, this chapter does have some implications for those interested in more traditional kinds of CAI.

On the issue of whether CAI programs are likely to produce the specific kinds of changes documented in the classroom using the GPTutor, the likelihood of similar changes is most probably related to the similarity of the software along certain crucial dimensions. Consider for a moment the issue of increased student motivation, which this chapter has suggested was one of the important outcomes of use of the GPTutor. Lepper, Woolverton, Mumme, and

Gurtner (1993) argue on the basis of studies of human tutors and the literature on motivation that four factors are especially important in encouraging the development and maintenance of intrinsic motivation in students, one of the changes that the use of the GPTutor seemed to stimulate. These are a sense of challenge, self-confidence, curiosity, and personal control. Lepper and his colleagues then offer specific suggestions about how instructors, be they human or computer-based, can foster these factors. The GPTutor embodied a surprising number of these suggestions, given that its developers did not base their design decisions on such analyses. For example, Lepper et al. (1993) suggest several specific things that can be done to increase a sense of personal control, many of which were built into the operation of the GPTutor. To increase objective control one can, like the GPTutor, offer choices about how much help the students receive, as well as give them instructionally irrelevant choices such as whether to type in material or use the mouse instead. In addition, a subjective sense of control can also be increased by things such as using an indirect type of feedback (e.g., giving hints rather than answers), as the GPTutor often did. This chapter suggests some additional factors, such as the decrease in the likelihood of public embarrassment and an increase in the sense of enjoyment and the ability to express frustration in satisfying ways, which also seemed conducive to encouraging students to want to work at learning. If such analyses are correct, one could judge the likely impact of computer use and other educational innovations on students' motivation by judging the extent to which they are likely to foster such conditions.

One very practical implication of this chapter for users and developers of educational software, be it traditional CAI, more advanced intelligent CAI software, or other innovative uses of computers in instruction, is the importance of looking beyond the obvious question of its likely cognitive impact. Specifically, much more attention needs to be given to assessing the impact of computer use on a broad array of factors ranging from teacher and student behaviors to structural changes within schools or school systems. For example, the developers of the GPTutor had no idea that the self-pacing feature would influence teachers' grading practices. Neither, to our knowledge, has there been much consideration of this possibility by most school systems adopting CAI for classroom use. Yet if the self-pacing characteristic of many popular CAI programs influences teachers' grading practices, this is an outcome of considerable importance.

It is becoming clear that students may use both traditional CAI software and the kind of software studied here in rather different ways than its creators intended. For example, no one anticipated the playful elaboration of unnecessarily complicated solutions to proofs that some students engaged in when using the GPTutor. Although this kind of deviation from expected usage was constructive, not all deviations were. For example, in the computer room reserved for gifted students at Whitmore, which is discussed in detail in Chapter 5, students were observed using a computer-based educational game that was supposed to encourage them to learn through using a variety of reference tools. They played this game for months before actually using even one of these tools, since they were too excited and involved in the game to interrupt their play and consult these sources (Schofield, 1989b). A study by Hativa, Swisa, and Lesgold (1989) also demonstrates the discrepancy between developers' expectations and actual practice in CAI software. Specifically, this study demonstrated how a widely used piece of CAI software designed to encourage students to learn mathematics in an individualized and noncompetitive manner actually appeared to encourage competition. In a very different study of the impact of computer technology on social processes within schools, Newman (1990) reports that a local-area network set up to encourage collaborative work in science unexpectedly also provided a mechanism that teachers in other subjects used to facilitate group work. Thus, this chapter is part of an emerging literature that suggests the importance of conducting classroom-based field tests of educational software that are sensitive to the unexpected.

In conclusion, it should be emphasized that I do not contend that all the changes discussed in this chapter will necessarily follow the introduction of artificially intelligent tutors, or even the GPTutor itself, into any and all classroom environments. Indeed, recent papers have pointed out the dangers of thinking of classroom computer usage as if it were a conceptually satisfying independent variable (Lepper & Gurtner, 1989; Schofield & Verban, 1988). As indicated in Chapter 1, the effect of computer usage is likely to depend on a plethora of factors including the kind of software used (e.g., drill and practice, simulations, networking, tutoring), the kind of students using the software, the social and physical context of the computer use, and prior classroom practices. This chapter has focused on the changes that occurred in the classrooms studied to indicate that important and often unplanned changes in student and teacher behavior are likely to occur when new technology is introduced and to suggest that greater attention needs to be devoted to understanding precisely what these changes are likely to be.

3

COMPUTER SCIENCE 1
The Classroom and the Lab as Contrasting Learning Environments

WHITMORE OFFERED STUDENTS A SEQUENCE OF TWO classes devoted primarily to programming. The first of these classes, called Computer Science 1, introduced students to the BASIC programming language. In the second course, Computer Science 2, students continued their study of BASIC and were also introduced to PASCAL. A few students who were really interested in programming and who had performed well in Computer Science 2 were allowed to take a more advanced course called Computer Science 5, which consisted of participating in Computer Science 2 classes a second time in order to do more advanced projects. The kind of programming tasks students worked on are described later in this chapter. They ranged from programs to alphabetize lists or compute simple payrolls to those involving relatively complicated graphics and sound.

Computer science courses were quite popular at Whitmore, so that the computer science room and the adjacent lab were used for virtually every one of the seven class periods in the school day during both years of the study. Each year there were 5 or 6 Computer Science 1 classes and 1 Computer Science 2 class. The 11 Computer Science 1 classes taught during the 2 years of this study ranged in size from 8 to 20 students. The 2 Computer Science 2 classes had no more than a dozen students each. As described in more detail in the Appendix, weekly observations were conducted during a 2-year period in the Computer Science 2 classes. Six Computer Science 1 classes taught by five of the six computer science teachers were also observed extensively.

Most of the students enrolled in computer science courses were in the regular or mainstream group of students who intended to continue their education at technical schools, community colleges, or other institutions of higher learning after completing high school. The students in the gifted and advanced groups, in general, did not take computer science since their schedules were often very full with advanced placement and other accelerated courses. Roughly 55% of the students in Computer Science 1 were boys. A similar proportion were African American. Although the proportion of African American students taking Computer Science 2 was virtually identical to the proportion taking Computer Science 1, the proportion of female students dropped rather precipitously, as will be discussed at length in Chapter 6. Although district policies did not allow any formal prerequisites for enrollment, there was a de facto requirement that students must have completed Algebra 1. The rationale given for this requirement was that programming involved mathematics. Thus, students taking the more rudimentary general math sequence were rarely able to enroll. The majority of students in computer science classes were juniors and seniors, due to the fact that more advanced students were given preference in enrollment.

Students enrolled in computer science at Whitmore were typically enthusiastic about it. For example, when asked whether they were glad to be taking the course over 90% of the students in both Computer Science 1 and Computer Science 2 replied affirmatively, and most were quite enthusiastic. Yet observation of these classes and more differentiated questions about reactions to the courses revealed that computer science courses were conducted in two very different kinds of settings, the classroom and the computer lab, and that students' attitudes toward learning in these two different settings varied dramatically. This chapter briefly describes the way in which computer science courses were organized at Whitmore. Then, it documents the students' differential reactions to the two different class settings and explores why students' reactions to the two complementary parts of the course varied so radically. It concludes that the use of computers in the lab led to often inadvertent changes in the way class was conducted that were highly motivating to students.

THE CLASSROOM AND THE LABORATORY

The facilities for teaching computer science at Whitmore consisted of a regular-sized classroom and a similar adjoining room in which the computers and printers were located. The classroom was equipped, as were most other classrooms at Whitmore, with a blackboard across the front wall, a teacher's desk in front of the blackboard, and rows of chairs with writing arms attached lined up facing the blackboard and the teacher's desk. Most of the top half of the wall separating the class from the room housing the computers, which was frequently referred to as "the lab," was made of glass to allow simultaneous visual surveillance of both rooms. A door through the side wall of these rooms allowed easy movement from one to the other. Although the lab had blackboards on the front wall as well as one side wall, there was no special desk for the teacher. The computers were arrayed on four parallel rows of tables, one against the wall separating the classroom and the lab, two adjacent rows down the middle of the room, and one final row abutting the wall farthest from the classroom. One chair was placed near each computer, and the computer tables were large enough so that students had space for books or papers. In all but the largest classes, there were more computers than students. Although there was a door directly connecting the lab to the hallway, it was rarely used since students normally exited through the classroom.

All of the five computer science teachers observed at Whitmore made use of both rooms, although they differed markedly, as will be discussed later, in the proportion of time spent in these two locations. Not surprisingly, rather different kinds of activities were carried out in the two settings. The social context of learning also varied dramatically in the two settings. As indicated earlier, the students had very different reactions to the two different milieus, and the reasons for this are the main focus of this chapter.

The classroom was used for five major purposes. First, teachers lectured students about topics such as the history of computers, the past and current uses of computers, and the various kinds of programming languages and their uses. Second, class time was sometimes used simply for reading. Students were not allowed to take their computer science textbooks home with them. (I was told this policy had been adopted because the $35 books were too expensive to have one for each of the students in the five or six sections of Computer Science 1 taught each year.) Thus, to the extent that a teacher wanted students to use the textbooks at all it was necessary to do so during class time. Third, the classroom was the location in which tests and quizzes were administered. These tests often focused on the material presented in the lectures and/or the book. Fourth, teachers provided students with specific information about the programming language they were studying. So, for example, the first-year students learned about READ statements in BASIC in the classroom. This kind of information was generally presented in relatively small chunks immediately before students received an assignment utilizing it in a program. Fifth, students were sometimes instructed to write programs they would later try out on the computers in the laboratory. With the exception of work on constructing programs, these kinds of activities were virtually never conducted in the room housing the computers.

In the classroom, the teacher's approach was similar to that traditionally found in academic classes at Whitmore. Thus, lectures were the primary vehicle of instruction. In addition, the teachers often posed questions and then selected the students who were allowed or required to try to supply the answers. The approved way to learn in such situations was to attend closely to the teacher and be responsive to his or her directions about taking notes, supplying answers, and the like. These classroom practices are very consistent with those found in a wide variety of high school classrooms in large-scale national studies (Goodlad, 1984; National Science Foundation, 1978; Sirotnik, 1981).

In contrast to the classroom, the lab was used for working *with* the computers rather than learning *about* them. Typically, the students' task in the lab was to create, debug, improve, and elaborate programs. Students generally sat in front of their computers working on a programming project assigned by the teacher. Different teachers varied somewhat in the tasks assigned. However, in the very beginning of the year it was common for teachers to have students write programs to perform fairly straightforward mathematical calculations, such as converting Fahrenheit temperatures to centigrade or computing simple payrolls. Quite soon students progressed to writing somewhat more complicated programs incorporating a greater variety of commands. They frequently had a week or more to complete these tasks. It was common for teachers to require that these programs have certain characteristics that demonstrated competence with specific commands or programming skills, but to leave the precise nature of the program up to each student. So, for example, the teacher might tell students to do a program incorporating loops but leave the function the program performed up to the students, as is apparent from the following excerpt from an interview with one of the computer science teachers, Mr. Edwards:

Interviewer: How much choice do students have? . . . Let's say you wanted the students to learn to do certain types of statements. Could they embed it in a structure of their own choice?

Mr. Edwards: They were completely on their own. What I would do is say, "What you're going to do this week is make a database program. I don't want anybody's to be the same. I want everybody's to be different. You can make it perform anything that you want it to do and in any fashion you want to do. I wanted it to be formatted on the screen. I want it to go to the disc and I want you to be able to retrieve it back again and add more information to it." How they went about that was completely up to them.

In the computer lab teachers rarely tried to instruct the class as a whole. Just as the teachers of students using the GPTutors circulated and dealt with students' problems individually, so too the computer science teachers went from student to student in the lab as the need arose. This occurred quite spontaneously since different students had problems with different parts of their programs. Thus, as was the case in classrooms using the GPTutor, it would have been not only unnecessary but also cumbersome and inefficient to try to ensure that every student listened to the teacher's interactions with all other students.

STUDENTS' PREFERENCE FOR THE LAB

Students' strong preference for working *with* the computers in the laboratory rather than learning *about* them was obvious in their everyday behavior. For example, they would frequently ask the teacher if they could go to the lab and would make negative comments if told that the class was not going there. Requests to stay in the classroom to work were extremely rare. The students' clear preference for the lab is illustrated in the following field notes:

> He [a substitute teacher named Mr. Wilborn] says, "Who wants to go to the lab?" Hands shoot up around the classroom. Almost all of the students have raised their hands. A couple of cries like "Yeah!" and "Let's go" emanate from the back of the room. The teacher says, "All right. Let's get started." The students literally surge out of their seats into the lab. . . . Within 1 minute they are all seated in the lab with the computers on.

> John [who is in the classroom with his classmates] is . . . cursing Mr. Erie [his teacher] under his breath. . . . John says to Mr. Erie that the class should go to the lab, that being in the classroom is very, very boring. John then says, "It's been shown in a national survey that students in classrooms of one color are bored." Mr. Erie replies, "You're making this up John. You don't know what you're talking about and you never do." John replies, "It's just boring being in here."

This same preference was evident in the interviews. When asked whether they preferred to spend their time in the computer science lab or the classroom, over 80% of the students interviewed in both

Computer Science 1 and 2 classes stated a clear preference for the lab. Not a single student reported preferring the classroom. Exchanges like the following were common:

Interviewer: Do students act differently in the classroom and the lab?

Tim: They're bored in the classroom. They love it in the lab.

Consistent with their obvious preference for the lab, students often evidenced an enthusiasm for and interest in their work in the lab rarely apparent in the classroom. Thus, for example, it was common for students to put their heads down on their desks in the classroom to rest, whereas such behavior was extremely rare in the lab. Note the striking difference between that kind of evident boredom and the atmosphere in the lab:

Celia [who is working in the lab] calls out to no one in particular, "There's five minutes left." Someone replies, "That clock must have a new battery. Time is going so fast!"

In interviews students also frequently made spontaneous distinctions between their reactions to the two settings, as is evident in this exchange:

Interviewer: Can you tell me how computer science is different from your other classes?

Renata: There's no class I'd rather be in . . . I could stay all day, as long as we're in the lab.

Ms. Patrick, one of the computer science teachers, commented about students' reaction to the computer lab: "It's . . . like playing. The kids are in there before the bell rings and after the bell rings you have to kick them out." Although most students, in fact, left the lab quite willingly when the bell rang, they did generally appear to enjoy it a great deal. Mr. Brice, who taught both computer science and geometry, noted that students known as troublemakers by teachers in other classes were not problems in his computer science classes, especially in the lab. "Their personalities change," he asserted. It is worth noting that these findings are very consistent with those of a similar study conducted in a middle school serving very poor urban minority students. Specifically, that study concluded that students were on-task over 90% of the time in the computer lab compared with 56% of the time in class and that disciplinary incidents were practically nonexistent in the lab in clear contrast to the class setting (Sills, 1992).

Of course, the fact that the students at Whitmore preferred the lab to the classroom is not in and of itself evidence that the lab is necessarily a better environment for learning. It is certainly possible to learn without enjoying the process and to enjoy oneself without learning. Thus, my goal here is not to argue that computer science should be taught exclusively in a laboratory setting because students enjoyed it more. Rather, it is to examine why the laboratory was, relatively speaking, so attractive to students and what the implications of the differences in the settings were for students' involvement with and attitude toward their work. I will argue that the students' preference for the lab was not just a result of a preference for programming over learning about computers or the other activities conducted in the classroom, although that is undoubtedly a part of the explanation. Rather, the two different milieus were very different contexts for learning. Specifically, the students' relationship with their teacher changed as they moved from one setting to another, as did their relationships with their peers. In addition, the relation between the students and their work underwent a major shift. I will argue that most of these changes had a very positive effect on students' motivation.

THE BASIS FOR STUDENTS' PREFERENCE FOR THE LAB

A Changed Relationship Between Students and Their Teachers

The students' relations with the teacher changed as they moved from the classroom to the lab. The shift in their relationship paralleled the change in teacher–student relationships described in Chapter 2 when geometry students shifted from whole class instruction to work on the GPTutor. Specifically, in the computer lab the teachers functioned less as expert authority figures and more as skilled collaborators or coaches than they had previously. Students often remarked on this change. For example, when asked a very general question about how computer science classes were different from their other classes over two-thirds of the students in both Computer Science 1 and 2 classes mentioned that their relation with their teacher was different, most commonly describing it as less of an authority relationship or as more friendly. One student put it this way in responding to another question about whether his relationship with his computer science teacher was different from his relationship with other teachers:

> He don't treat us like we're students and he's the teacher . . . Most teachers think, "I'm the teacher. You have to listen to me." Sometimes that irks people because they try to tell you how to do everything and some people don't like to be bossed around.

A large number of the students also characterized computer science teachers as more helpful than other teachers, echoing the observations of the student in the GPTutor classes quoted in Chapter 2 who said of his teacher, "He doesn't teach us any more. He just helps us." As one computer science student put it:

> Usually he's helping people. Whereas most teachers stand up and talk at us, he comes around and actually sits down with you and tries to help you with your program, like individual help as much as he can. Most classes the teacher stands there and talks to you and you do your work and you hand it in and they give it back to you and that's it.

This shift in the teacher's role occurred for many of the same reasons in the computer lab as it did when the GPTutors were in use and the geometry students experienced a similar shift from lecture-based whole class instruction to more individualized interactions with the teacher. As indicated earlier, a lecture format focuses attention on the teacher's superior knowledge since the lecture generally consists of information the teacher already knows that students are supposed to learn. Teachers exert a great deal of control over the topics to be covered in lectures and, not surprisingly, tend to emphasize things they know a great deal about and avoid areas in which their knowledge is less complete. Thus, in the classroom the teacher can generally provide a consistent display of knowledge superior to that of the students and apparently sufficient to the task at hand. This was not possible to such an extent in the lab for reasons to be discussed shortly. In addition, since questions posed by the teacher during lectures generally concerned specific facts, such as "What does the word *binary* mean?" or "What does the acronym ASCII stand for?" teachers were continually in the position of telling students whether they were right or wrong. Tests constituted yet another occasion in which the teacher's authority as arbiter of what is true was reinforced in the classroom.

Because the class constitutes an audience whose attention the teacher needs to direct and retain in order to achieve his or her goals during a lecture, the threat of distraction or disruption is a serious one. Thus, rules against speaking without permission or moving out of one's seat are promulgated. Even the posing of too many unprompted questions by students may be discouraged if it interrupts the flow of the material planned by the teacher. Formal mechanisms for signaling a student's desire to speak, such as the raising of a hand, allow the teacher to accommodate students' queries and comments without disrupting the ongoing sequence of teacher-led activity. All in all, whole class instruction through lecturing creates a situation in which the teacher needs to maintain quite strict control over students' behavior. Attempts to achieve this control often involve threats of disciplinary action or grade reduction. Thus, the authority that the teacher has solely by virtue of his or her position as teacher is often made quite salient.

The situation in the lab was quite different. There, the students' attention was not typically directed toward a teacher standing at the front of the room supplying them with information they were expected to learn. Rather, the student's task was to create working programs using whatever resources were available, including their own, their peers', and their teacher's knowledge, as well as programming manuals located in the room. Students worked on their programs as individuals, requesting the teacher's assistance when they felt they needed it.

In the lab, teacher–student interactions were less likely to be

71

authority-initiated demands for attention or information than in the classroom and more likely to be student-initiated requests for assistance. It was relatively uncommon there for the teachers to approach students and offer unsolicited advice. Rather, the need for assistance was frequently so great relative to the time the teacher had available that he or she was kept busy responding to student-initiated requests for help. When teachers had a temporary respite they tended to take care of paper work, work on their own programs, or even play computer games rather than circulate offering unsolicited help. Computer Science 2 classes were much smaller than the introductory course. However, the teacher in charge of them, Mr. Brice, acted much as he and the other teachers did in Computer Science 1, partly because he felt that advanced students should be encouraged to work independently and partly because he enjoyed improving his programming skills by working on difficult problems himself.

In the lab, even very knowledgeable teachers were often presented with problems that they had to think about deeply. In fact, teachers could commonly be observed consulting programming manuals for information or struggling to figure out how to solve a problem, behaviors that were much less common in the classroom. Teachers could decide what programs to have students work on in the lab in a way that reflected their own areas of expertise, just as they were free in the class to emphasize the topics with which they were most familiar. For example, teachers who had more experience with graphics than others assigned more graphics programs. However, many students were sufficiently interested in the work that they went beyond the assignment's minimum requirements in ways that were not always easily predicted. In addition, there were a few students, generally white boys, for whom computers were a hobby of great personal interest. These students entered the computer science courses with a great deal of programming experience and were highly motivated to create rather elaborate programs, well beyond what was required. Thus, it was not uncommon for students to ask questions or present programming problems that constituted a real challenge to their teachers. All this combined to create a rather different image of the teacher in the lab than in the classroom. Rather than being seen as a repository of an endless store of facts, the teacher was seen as a sometimes fallible individual trying to apply and extend his or her knowledge, much as the students were.

In the lab students also had a way of judging the quality of their work that was much less dependent on the teacher's authority than it typically was in the classroom. Specifically, they could try their programs out and see if they functioned as they were intended to. The fact that they did so was independent confirmation that the programs worked. Their failure to do so was an objective indicator of the program's deficiencies. This tended to undercut the authority of the teacher as the final arbiter of "right" and "wrong" and "good" and "bad." Students could see for themselves if their program functioned and whether the results were impressive or not. Thus, students received clear and immediate feedback without having to depend on the teacher's judgment. Interestingly, one negative consequence of this shift in the standard that students used for judging their work was the frequent lack of interest shown in their teacher's advice on how to make the structure of a program more elegant or efficient. Idiosyncratic ways of doing things, which might be dysfunctional in the long run, were accepted as unproblematic by students, even though their teachers might try to point out ways that were better:

Mr. Brice: I have a kid named Jim Chiu, whose father is at the university . . . Jim has his own brand of looping, which is very unique to him. When he helps other students it doesn't mesh into their programs very well. So, I kind of discourage other kids from accepting, point blank, his solutions to a problem . . . Occasionally I have to say, "Jim, don't help these people anymore, because you're not teaching them the way I would like them to be taught . . . " If they were in Computer Science 2 I would be able to explain it to them, but right now they think, "If it works, it works." They don't see why it would be nice if it had a nice running pattern to it. As long as it works, they figure it's good.

73

In fact, the acid test of whether or not a program would work was applied not only to students' efforts but also to the teachers'. Thus, the teachers' skill in solving the problems students brought to them was constantly on trial. If a program would not run after a student followed a teacher's advice, it was clear that the advice was deficient in some regard.

In cases where the teacher was knowledgeable, a very clear sense of colleagueship arose between students and the teacher. This kind of relationship was perhaps most evident between Mr. Brice and his students and appeared to be felt by teacher and student alike. Speaking about one of the computer hobbyists, Mr. Brice said:

> I have a student . . . who is very talented in programming. If I had any problems or challenges I could give them to him and he could work them out. Between the two of us one would come up with a solution for it.

Students' remarks about Mr. Brice also reflect this sense of colleagueship and mutual exploration of their subject:

Interviewer: Compared with other classes, how important is the teacher in helping you learn in computer science?

Sarah: When they share with you what they are learning it's important. He shares what we're learning because he learns from us too. We depend on him but he learns from us. Other teachers know everything. You can't argue with them. About dates, for example, they know! Mr. Brice is like "I don't know. I'll look in the book." Then if you're wrong, you're wrong. He listens to what you have to say.

The contrast between the teacher's role as a somewhat distant repository of authoritative information in the classroom and as a coach or skilled collaborator in the lab was apparent in all of the computer science classes observed. However, there were clear variations on this theme that depended heavily on the teacher's level of skill as a pedagogue, disciplinarian, and programmer. For example, although Mr. Davidson knew much about many aspects of programming, he had great difficulty controlling the students, especially in the classroom. He greatly preferred teaching evening classes at a local community college and conducting a consulting business – both settings in which his demands for quiet attentiveness were more likely to be met. The high levels of tension and disrespect apparent in his classrooms were not conducive to the development of an easy colleagueship in the lab. Mr. Davidson often offered individualized assistance to students in the lab, working cooperatively with them to solve problems that arose. However, he was also prone to withdraw from them, even sitting out in the classroom catching up on paper work, including the grading of tests. In fact, on several days during which his class was observed working in the lab Mr. Davidson spoke to no more than two or three students during the entire period, except for making an announcement at the beginning that students should go to the lab to work on programs.

In contrast, a number of other teachers' computer skills were too weak for them to provide consistently useful guidance when students faced difficult programming problems in the lab. This was hardly surprising since they had been pressed into service because teachers were needed in spite of the fact that they had little background in computer science. A declining student population and a tight budget meant that rather than hiring new teachers with strong computer skills, Whitmore tended to use faculty from the math or science departments to teach computer science. Most of these individuals did not meet the district standards for certification as computer science teachers, and their skills were often not adequate to the challenge of solving unexpected programming problems. One of these teachers said emphatically during an interview, "I hate computers and I hate not being able to help the students." Students were well aware of this lack of programming skill, using words like "quack" to describe such teachers.

One strategy for handling the dilemma of teaching something they really did not know very well was for teachers to spend a higher proportion of their time in the classroom, where, as has already been discussed, their lack of a strong working knowledge of programming was not such a handicap. Others avoided the lab in more unconventional ways, going on occasion as far as showing slides of a summer trip to far flung parts of the United States. Although students' lack of respect for such teachers was evident in interviews, they were generally reasonably compliant in the classroom, which allowed the teachers to play out a fairly traditional role there. Typically such teachers adopted a more collegial manner in the lab. However, they were not dependably able to solve relatively straightforward problems, which the better students could often handle:

> Linda shows the teacher the listing of her program and he says, "Well it looks good to me; I don't know why it isn't working." He walks away. Mark [an average student] leans over to look at Linda's program. He points to one thing that is evidently wrong. Linda makes a change and then runs the program . . . She says to the teacher, "Hey, it works now."

Students reacted negatively to teachers who were frequently unable to solve routine problems, thus suggesting that although they valued the sense of learning together with their teacher they experienced in the lab, they, not surprisingly, desired a teacher who could act as a knowledgeable guide or skilled colleague in the joint search for solutions rather than as a relatively uninformed peer.

A Changed Relationship with Peers

One factor that undoubtedly contributed to the shift in the relationship between students and teachers as they moved from the classroom to the lab is that teachers did not enforce as many rules restricting students' freedom in the lab as they did in the classroom. In the classroom setting, where the students are an audience, it is distracting, even disruptive, for students to leave their seats or talk among themselves. Such behaviors make it hard for others to see and hear as they need to in order to follow the teacher's lesson. Teachers recognize this and use their authority to prevent or at least minimize these behaviors. In sharp contrast, the teachers' work in the lab, providing assistance to individuals who need it, is not likely to be hampered by other students leaving their seats or

76

talking quietly. Thus, all of the computer science teachers appeared more tolerant of such behaviors in the lab setting, mitigating the distinction between teachers, who can move and speak as they please, and students, who cannot.

The easing of such restrictions was clearly noted by students, who enjoyed the comparative freedom of the lab. Many took advantage of it to do a considerable amount of socializing. For boys, this often meant discussing sports. For girls, this was more likely to entail talking about other students, both male and female, and family members. For both groups, but especially the boys, it also meant playing games on the computer when they could. However, students also took advantage of their freedom to move about and talk with others to obtain help with their work. In fact, over three-quarters of the students interviewed said that classmates in computer science helped their peers more than students in other classes did. Students found this a very positive feature of working in the computer science lab, often making enthusiastic comments as in the following interview:

Interviewer: What is the best thing about taking computer science?

Carol: The students help each other. It's like teamwork. In other classes we don't get to do that . . . People have fun. They help each other out and I think that's great!

Many of the students explicitly linked the comparatively high rate of helping to the unusual degree of freedom in the lab to talk or move about:

Rich: They help each other more because they have the freedom to talk . . .

Interviewer: More than in other classes like English or geometry?

Rich: Yeah, because in most of the other classes they frown on people talking to each other. The teachers want total silence.

Of course, the fact that students were free to move and talk in a way that made it possible for them to get help from other students without resorting to subterfuge and breaking class rules does not mean that they would necessarily do so. In fact, a small number of students chose to work in an almost completely solitary fashion. Yet the large majority did seek and receive help from their peers frequently and seemed to feel quite positive about it. A number of factors seemed to be conducive to this development. First, it was a clear fact of life in the computer science lab that the teacher was often busy with other students. Thus, when the need for help arose students often had to wait quite a while if they insisted on making the teacher their only source of advice. Seeking help from a peer was often the more efficient way to proceed:

Ron: There should be more than one Mr. Brice. There should be two or three of him. He's always running around to a different person helping him out. He can't always get to a person [who needs help]. . . . But if the person beside you knows what he's doing, it's all right.

Second, most students were sufficiently interested in their programs to want to get help when they were stuck rather than using the teacher's inability to help them immediately as an excuse for doing nothing or socializing for long periods of time. The words of one student clearly convey this widely shared feeling:

You really have ambition to work in there [in the computer lab]. In other classes you just do what you have to do, but in here you want to make everything better. You don't just want to pass. You want to get an A+ on everything.

In most classrooms one major disadvantage of turning to peers rather than the teacher for help is that it is often hard to know how much credence to give their advice. For example, a peer can misspell a word, give one the incorrect formula for the area of a circle, or give bad advice on the organization of an essay. The student who needs help is often not in a good position to evaluate the quality of the advice received. However, in computer science students used a quick and efficient mechanism to evaluate advice on programming – to try it and see if it worked.

There were two common patterns of peer help, reciprocal help between friends and help given by unusually knowledgeable students to a wide variety of others. With regard to the first pattern, it was common for friends or acquaintances to help each other, often as part of a reciprocal relationship in which help was sometimes given and sometimes received. One boy answered a question about which students work together in the following way:

> People who have stuff in common work together. Me, Dick, Bill, and Don are all athletes. We're all interested in football and baseball and we're always talking about everything. We just work together. And John too. Renata I've never worked with. Tonya, only a little bit.

Since patterns of social interaction within the school were heavily influenced by race and gender, such exchanges of assistance typically, though not always, occurred between students of the same sex and/or race. Often the giving and receiving of help was embedded in an ongoing interaction that rapidly switched back and forth between casual socializing and a more task-oriented focus:

> Bill, who is white, is working on a game program. He asks Mark, who is also white, to help him finish it. They are joined by Doug and Martin, both of whom are African American. Part of the time the boys collaborate on the program, often yelling loudly about whose statements are right. [In general this is good-natured with the students kidding each other about the particular way they go about solving programming problems.] They also discuss the dance that is scheduled for tonight and football.

A number of classes contained students known as "wizards," who were widely recognized as being unusually talented or experienced in computer programming. Such students, invariably male and usually white, often provided a great deal of assistance to students who knew less than they did. In many cases there seemed to be a tacit exchange of social acceptance for information received. As one student put it talking about a slightly built white male wizard:

First when we found out Ned was good, people was [sic] kind of jealous . . . and talked about him. They got real upset just because he knows what he's talking about. Now it's okay since he's helping everybody. They thought he was going to be selfish about it.

Another student, who talked in an interview about the consequences of the fact that he and his friend were considered wizards, said:

They ask us how to do this or what you do in this case. . . . They ask a lot of questions. . . . Some students are really upset because we're in that class. . . . But when they need help they're all real nice and friendly.

Sometimes the wizard's special competence allowed an ego-gratifying display of superiority. Such displays were not appreciated, but they were generally tolerated as the price one had to pay for expertise:

Bill [a white wizard] says to Don [who is black], "You got a problem," when Don's chemistry program says that water is a poison. Don lists his program and looks at it intently for a few minutes. Then he turns to Bill and says, "What's the matter here?" Bill says, "Okay. Let's see." . . . Bill starts troubleshooting, listing out the program, typing in changes, and the like. At one point Don tries to type something in on his keyboard and Bill says in an irritated tone, "Hold on a minute. Hold on a minute!" He then continues to study the program. . . . He points to one section of it and says in a voice loud enough for the whole class to hear, "This is why. You don't have the locate statement like you should." Don says a bit sarcastically, "Well, sorry!" Bill replies in a cool tone, "You have to be intellectual about it."

The wizards were consistently able to bolster their self-esteem by helping others and generally did not boldly resort to rubbing in their superior capability as Bill did. The sense of accomplishment inherent in solving the problem and the admiration of their prowess by the other students normally seemed to suffice. Of note is the fact that even less capable students often had the gratifying experience of solving a problem that stumped a peer. No doubt the frequency of this experience was increased by the fact that students often helped friends who tended to be at a roughly similar academic level. In addition, student's programs often failed to run because some minor convention, which could be spotted even by a relatively unskilled programmer, had been violated. As one student put it poignantly:

> Even the kid in the class who doesn't know anything knows something others don't know. It has happened to me [and] I'm the dumbest [in our class].

Although helping between students was a widespread phenomenon in the lab, generally accepted by students and teachers alike, there were some norms that regulated it. Teachers' attitudes toward specific instances of such helping varied, depending to a large extent on whether they felt assistance was really needed. Furthermore, teachers disapproved of cases in which more advanced students literally took over and wrote major sections of programs for other students, rather than providing assistance with specific problems. Students saw nothing wrong with getting help from other students, including copying part of a program, when they were stuck. But they objected to "byting," copying part of someone's program without asking permission and/or acknowledging the assistance. They also objected to students who didn't honor the unwritten rules about reciprocity, which required those who received help to return it if they could:

Roberta: Dick . . . doesn't like sharing with Charlie because Charlie . . . just takes the examples. . . . He doesn't give the input. He just takes the output.

Occasionally friction arose when the teacher or a student felt such norms were being violated. However, in general, helping interactions among peers were positive in tone and contributed substantially to students' enjoyment of the lab as well as to the development of their programs.

These helping interactions contributed to learning in at least three important ways. First, a request for assistance from a peer, often from a friend, provided substantial motivation to try to solve a problem. Students seemed to want to avoid letting their peers

81

down in such situations. Thus, they generally worked fairly hard at solving problems brought to their attention. This provided a good opportunity for practicing their debugging skills and gaining new knowledge through trying out ideas or consulting a manual. Second, peers seemed to feel very free to discuss and evaluate each others' suggestions as they worked on solving problems. Sometimes this generated quite heated discussions. The process of formulating and defending their ideas in discussions with peers seemed likely to help solidify a student's knowledge and clarify mistaken beliefs. Furthermore, even though their relationship with the teacher in the lab was collegial relative to the classroom, some students were inclined to accept a teacher's advice as likely to be right until proven otherwise. In contrast, peers' advice was often subjected to more serious scrutiny, which called for more thinking and consideration of alternatives since the students felt freer to reject it. One student captured this sense of freedom when discussing peer helping by saying:

> They can help when the teacher is trying to get around. . . . You can ask questions and they'll tell you. If you don't like it you can do it another way.

When rushed or too interested in their own programs or social conversations to want to converse at length, students did sometimes just allow others to copy from their programs without discussion or explanation. However, most students seemed aware that merely letting a friend copy was not conducive to learning and thus in the long run was not doing their friend a favor. At least some could articulate a conscious strategy of trying to get their peers to think. One student who helped others a great deal explained his approach to helping with the programming of math problems this way:

> When I help another student, I don't give him the answer. I'll write down the formula and ask him what he wanted to do . . . and then I'll tell him to try and figure out what is in the formula. If they get it wrong, I'll tell them what they have to figure out.

Finally, some students asserted that they preferred help from peers rather than from teachers since they could understand it better coming from someone with a level of knowledge or manner of speaking nearer their own.

In sum, students' freedom to interact more with their peers in the lab was a by-product of the fact that the teachers did not lecture there. The individualized mode of instruction common in the lab made it unnecessary to forbid or strictly control student interaction. Indeed, the fact that the students' need for assistance often could not be met promptly by the teacher encouraged teachers to allow students to help each other. Students used this freedom both to socialize and to help each other. The socializing added an element of fun to their time in the lab that was not readily available in many other classroom settings. Although many students spent a substantial amount of time that could have been devoted to their work socializing, most also showed a level of interest in their work in the lab that was not so readily apparent in the classroom. The giving and receiving of help often appeared to be quite effective both in encouraging students to think about what they were doing and in creating a positive attitude about the class:

Interviewer: What's the best thing about computer science?

Donna: That it's not so strict. You learn a lot more in a social environment with other students helping you out instead of just the teacher. I've learned a lot from other students. . . . That's the best part.

It is worth noting that other studies of environments in which computers were readily available for classroom use have suggested that this spontaneous helping of peers is likely to emerge if permitted by the teacher (Baker, Gearhart, & Herman, 1989, 1990, 1991).

A Changed Relationship Between Students and Their Work

Lab Work More Connected to Students' Career Goals. Computer science is an elective course at Whitmore. Although some students reported enrolling in it primarily because it fit into their schedules or because of intrinsic interest in the subject matter, the most common reason given for enrolling in computer science was the belief that it would be of direct use in later education or in students' careers. A large number of students planned careers in fields such as secretarial work, computer programming, and architecture in which the need for various kinds of computer skills is obvious. Many others, who were undecided about specific careers, were nonetheless confident that a knowledge of computers would be helpful in almost any field, as illustrated in the following excerpt from a student interview:

Interviewer: Why did you decide to take Computer Science 1?
Charlie: Well, for a lot of reasons. Computers is [sic] a growing industry and I figure if I take it now . . . I'll have a head start on whatever I want to do later.

Students' preference for working in the lab was linked to the fact that many of them believed that gaining experience with computers by learning programming would ultimately be more useful to them than most of the things they did in the classroom. For example, some students felt that learning about the history of the development of computers was irrelevant to their goals in taking the course. However, this explanation is far from complete. Students needed to learn the kind of information about BASIC and PASCAL commands conveyed in the lectures if they were going to be able to program. They clearly recognized this, as evidenced by the fact that over 80% believed that these lectures were helpful to them in their later lab work. As one student put it in an interview:

Students get mad when they have to go into the classroom because they want to get on the computers. . . . But when Mr. Brice gives an assignment they're happy they was [sic] over there because they know what to do when they get on the computers.

Yet students were often very inattentive and restive during such lectures. In some classrooms, this restlessness sometimes progressed to open insolence when students were supposed to be reading the textbook or engaging in other particularly unpopular activities:

The class is extremely rowdy now, with relatively few students reading [as they were instructed to do]. . . . I [the observer] get hit by a flying spitball that was apparently intended for Ernie who is sitting near me. Mr. Davidson asks the students to be quiet saying, "There's only five minutes left. Let's get some work done." He then says to Ernie, who is talking quietly but audibly, "Did I ask you to be quiet?" Ernie says, "Sorry." Five or six [repetitions of] "sorry" echo through the room. Such echoing happens frequently in this class. For example, a few minutes ago Mr. Davidson explained something to a student and then said, "Do you understand? Are you following?" and around the room I heard four or five echoes of the same phrases. . . . A male voice calls out loudly from the far side of the room, "Close those legs!" and giggles and laughs circulate around the room. Ernie is beet red in the face in what appears to be an effort to control the volume of his giggles. Mr. Davidson says repressively, "There's been a lot of unnecessary talking today."

Such behavior was much less common in the lab.

Lab Work More Connected to Students' Personal Interests. In the classroom students were presented with facts to learn, as was often true in many of their other academic classes. Although many of these facts, such as information about the hexadecimal system, were basic to understanding how computers actually work, students tended to find them relatively uninteresting in comparison with programming in the lab, as is clear from the following excerpt from a student interview:

The teacher said at the beginning, "You're going to learn about the computer." I was like, "I don't want to learn *about* the computer. I just want to use it!"

One major attraction of lab work, compared with classroom work, was the degree to which students could link the work to their own personal interests and fantasies. As one student put it:

You gotta do what he says. You gotta do the program he wants you to do, but . . . you can write things that are your creativity. . . . You can put in parts that are from you. In other classes you don't have that freedom.

This freedom to "put in parts that are from you" was highly motivating to students. For some students, generally boys, this meant creating programs that kept track of information on sports teams or raced cars across the screen. Reflecting traditional sex roles to a striking degree, girls were much more likely to create programs that dealt with personal relationships. For example, a number of girls seemed fascinated by endless variations on a program constructed to flash their own and their boyfriends' names on the screen like the one described next:

Marta: I made this cute little thing and it asked for your name and your boyfriend's name. Then it prints little hearts. I did that. . . . I did that and I'm so happy about it!

The kind of material covered in the classroom was less readily melded with personal nonacademic concerns and fantasies. Thus, it was far less appealing to most students. In addition, students were motivated by the sense of freedom and control that the ability to link work in the lab to their interests gave them, relative to many other school settings, including the computer science classroom, where they experienced much less of a sense of control over their environment. This feeling of control and the resultant personalization or ownership of the product is apparent in the following excerpt from an interview with a student:

Interviewer: Are you glad you are taking Computer Science 1 or not?

Sara: I'm glad. It's fun. You can make your computer do what you want to do. You can put what you want to put on it. You have your own disc and your own computer. It's fun.

Lab Work Requires Active Experimentation Rather Than Passive Assimilation. When asked how being in the lab differed from being in the classroom, over 80% of the students spontaneously mentioned the contrast between the passive assimilation of knowledge characteristic of the classroom and the active involvement in learning typical of the lab. They overwhelmingly preferred a sense of active involvement in learning. As one student put it pithily, explaining why he liked the lab better, "You ain't got to listen to the teacher talk." Other students complained that taking notes on the teacher's lecture or reading the text was just plain boring. In contrast, working on the computer to develop and debug programs was generally seen as much more enjoyable and exciting. Exchanges like the following about computer science, especially about the lab, were common:

Interviewer: How would you rate what you learned in computer science compared with what you learned in other classes?

Eric: I think I learned more in computer science 'cause it was different. Instead of just reading something out of a book and remembering it – that's what you normally do in other classes – in computer science you just work on it until you know it.

Another student expressed a similar sentiment in this extract from an interview:

Interviewer: How is computer science different from your other classes?

Elsie: A lot of people are used to the chalkboard method where the teacher writes something on the board and you just take it from there. But this course requires you to think things out for yourself.

Interviewer: Is that difficult?

Elsie: When I first got here it was, but now I'm learning. I got used to it.

One major difference between learning in the computer lab and learning in the computer science classroom and other similar settings was the extent to which students learn through active trial and error. More than 85% of the students interviewed mentioned this as a distinguishing feature of computer science, and the lab was clearly the setting in which this kind of activity occurred.

87

Students' fundamental task in the lab was to figure out how to make their programs accomplish certain goals. Even fairly simple programs often failed to work on the first try. Not surprising, more complicated ones generally required considerable debugging. Once programs worked, students were prone to try to improve or elaborate them, thus creating another cycle of improvement through trial and error:

Charlie: I like the satisfaction of doing something that I feel was the best I could do. . . . I can make it [the program] look nicer or do something more – put more extras on it. . . . I enjoy that.

This process of trial and error required an active engagement on the part of the students that tapped their intellect and imagination in a way they felt other classes generally did not. Student interviews were filled with favorable comments such as the following:

It's different from every other class. [In other classes] you just sit at a desk and you have to do as you are told. Here you do what you are told but you can create things.

The class is fun, but it requires a lot of thinking. I would encourage [others] to take it.

I learn new things everyday. I love it. It's a challenge and I love challenges.

One might expect that working by trial and error would be discouraging to students, especially those who faced error very frequently. However, generally speaking, this did not seem to be the case for a number of reasons. First, it was clear to students that the fact that a program did not work the first time was not some kind of fatal indictment of their skill. Students understood that debugging was a normal part of the creation of a program. Students could observe for themselves that everyone, including the teacher and any wizards in their classrooms, often had to struggle to create programs that functioned as they were intended. Second, students generally discovered their own errors when they tried out their programs rather than having someone else point them out to them. This, combined with the fact that errors generally did not have negative consequences for students' grades, made errors a signal of a problem to be dealt with rather than an embarrassing failure:

Ned: On the computer if you mess up you can always go back and change a line or fix it. In other classes [like art] once you're done and they grade it if it's wrong it's wrong. . . . You might be able to figure out what you did wrong, but it's too late after that. But in computer science you can every so often run the program and see what's wrong and fix it before the teacher grades it. So trial and error is pretty important. It helps you learn what you're doing wrong. It helps you figure out how to fix things up and how to make them . . . right.

Since students were responsible for marshalling the resources necessary to fix their errors, for many students programming was experienced as a series of personal challenges. This sense of active personal challenge was very motivating to many students:

Sam: They [students] know they are not doing it [programming] for the teacher really. They are doing it for themselves, seeing the effects of what they put in come back out on the screen and work. They're doing it . . . to try to better themselves. Each program gets better and better.

If students had difficulty in meeting these challenges by themselves, help was readily available, from peers if not always from the teacher, so few students remained stuck on a particular problem for so long that it became really frustrating or created a debilitating sense of failure.

SUMMARY AND CONCLUSIONS

The learning environment in the lab embodied a number of the features called for by many scholars who have written recently about the need for educational reform. Such writings have been heavily influenced by the constructivist perspective on knowledge

89

development (Von Glasersfeld, 1989), which owes a great deal to relatively recent research in cognitive science. This viewpoint starts with the premise that all knowledge is created as individuals make sense of their experiences rather than being passively received from others, including authoritative sources. Such a viewpoint challenges the emphasis in current practice on didactic teaching and stresses the importance of encouraging students to build on their existing knowledge, to be actively involved with learning rather than to see their task as the assimilation of an expert's knowledge, and to have the opportunity to reflect on and discuss their work with others (Simon, 1993).

Students' preference for working *with* computers in the lab rather than learning *about* them in the classroom was clear. There is no doubt that some of the material covered in the classroom lectures was crucial in helping them achieve their goals in the lab. However, in general, work in that environment was perceived as boring. Students were often inattentive, sometimes even insolent, and showed relatively little interest in or enthusiasm for their work in the classroom setting. In contrast, the large majority of students enjoyed their time in the lab and evidenced much more involvement in their work there.

This increase in enjoyment and motivation was due to many factors. Relations between students and teachers became much more collegial when the students worked on the computers, a change very consistent with the constructivist emphasis on the primary importance of the learner's active thought in an environment that is designed to challenge his or her existing notions in ways that will foster the development of even more viable ones (Simon, 1993). In sharp contrast to the GPTutor classes, students interacted with each other much more in the lab than during whole class instruction. Although much of this interaction was purely social, and hence potentially distracting, task-oriented helping interactions were also very common. The freedom to exchange help served many positive functions, as might be expected from the constructivists' emphasis on the important role others can play in stimulating cognitive reorganization (Von Glasersfeld, 1992), as well as the substantial literature on peer helping (Webb, 1982). In the lab, students were more readily able to link their work to their own interests and goals than in the classroom, which has been demonstrated in experimental work to enhance both learning and students' attitudes toward their work (Anand & Ross, 1987). In addition, the sense of personal challenge created by the active involvement in trial-and-error learning created an atmosphere conducive to active thinking rather than passive assimilation of knowledge.

This enjoyment of, and preference for, working with computers rather than in a more traditional classroom situation was quite parallel to the reaction of students using the GPTutor to study geometry, as was the increase in student motivation. This should not be too surprising, for although the specific kinds of computers and software that students used in the two situations varied dramatically, there are some clear parallels in the changes in the students' experiences. In both cases, the use of computers was accompanied by a marked shift in the role of the teacher. Specifically, in both cases, when students used computers the teacher's role shifted from that of the expert who presented knowledge to be assimilated to that of a coach or tutor who individually assisted students with problem solving. In both situations this meant that help was more likely to be received at a juncture when the student needed and wanted it and that it was more likely to be given in private rather than in public. Furthermore, in both situations students working on the computer could generally keep their mistakes private while they struggled with them for long periods of time if they so desired. In addition, students became somewhat less dependent on their teacher since they had an alternative and perhaps less threatening source of help they could turn to before the teacher if they so desired (the GPTutor in the first case and their peers in the second case). In both cases, they were freed from certain preexisting classroom norms that were sometimes galling (the prohibition against showing anger in the GPTutor case and the rules forbidding conversation and physical movement in the computer science classroom). Also, in both cases, students often experienced a clear sense of challenge while working on the computers.

In spite of all these similarities, it must be pointed out that the changes in students' classroom experiences brought about in these two cases by shifting from the environment in which computers were not used to those in which they were used were definitely not identical. In fact, in one important regard they were markedly different. Whereas there was a striking increase in competition when students used the GPTutors, students clearly cooperated more in the computer lab than in the computer classroom. It should be noted that neither of these changes was absolutely predetermined by the technology being used. Although the GPTutor was really designed for individual work, there is no inherent barrier to students using it cooperatively. In fact, in two classes the teacher required pairs of students to work together at the strong urging of one of the agencies that funded the computer-based tutor project. Although the developer and teachers using the tutor concluded that it was better used by individuals than by pairs of students, it would be possible to require or permit students to work jointly with the software and hence make it likely that the GPTutor would lead to increased cooperation, just as it would be possible to require students in the computer science lab to work in pairs or to prohibit them from doing so. Nonetheless, the GPTutor has features that make it less likely to engender cooperation than using computers for programming does. The most obvious one is that the GPTutor is designed to supply help. Thus, the students' need for additional help should decrease as a function of the tutor's ability to perform its stated function. In sharp contrast, it seems likely that as a group of computer science students work on individual programming projects, they will need more help than the teacher is able to supply without long delays. Thus, the situation is ripe for an increase in peer cooperation, although it does not absolutely require it.

Readers may have noted an apparent inconsistency in the arguments presented in this and the preceding chapter. In the former, the competition that developed between many of the students in the GPTutor classes was said to contribute to their enjoyment of computer use and their interest in their work, whereas in this chapter it was argued that cooperation between students contributed to these same outcomes. It is possible, of course, that the analysis presented in one or both of these chapters is mistaken. However, I would suggest that this is not the case. Rather, I would argue that both of these are possible and, without repeating the preceding analysis here, try to indicate why that might be the case. In the first place, the competition that occurred in the GPTutor classes and the cooperation that occurred in the computer labs had something very important in common – they were the result of peer interactions rather than interactions directed by or toward the teacher. Adolescents are at a developmental stage where peers are especially important (Coleman, 1980; Hartup, 1985), and the restrictions that traditional classroom structures place on their ability to interact with peers may be one factor that leads students to feel bored and restive. Second, as indicated previously, the competition that developed in the GPTutor classrooms seemed to have as much to do with meeting the challenges posed by the problems as beating others. One factor that enhanced this aspect of the competition was the fact that students' grades were not dependent on how fast they went. Thus, students could excel without being a direct threat to others' grades, an extremely important fact in reducing the potential for competition to create negative peer relations. In addition, as indicated earlier, since work on the tutor was quite private, students could generally opt out of the competition if they so desired or choose who they would share their progress reports with. This is quite unlike the competition inherent in practices like publicly announcing grades, where one cannot opt out and comparisons are made with the entire range of others, rather than with friends who are often relatively similar in skill level.

4

COMPUTERS IN THE CLOSET
Attitudinal and Organizational Barriers to Computer Use in Classrooms

T O LOOK ONLY AT THE IMPACT OF TECHNOLOGY ON CLASS-
room social processes is to miss half the picture. It has become
increasingly apparent that preexisting attitudes and social structures shape the extent to which technology is used as well as the
way it is used. The fact that a computer is in a classroom does not
mean that it will ever be used. It may be kept boxed in a closet or sit
gathering dust in a corner (Bowers, 1988; Piller, 1992). Decisions
made by the school system about what kind of hardware and software to buy and what kind of training and support to provide, by
teachers about how to integrate computer usage with their personal
style of teaching and the existing curriculum, and by students about
whether and how to use computers in their work all jointly create
the package of "technology in use," which in turn may alter existing
attitudes, interaction patterns, and social structures.

This chapter focuses on one striking finding that emerged from
the study of computer use at Whitmore. With a few notable exceptions, such as the geometry and computer science classes, computers were actually used very little in Whitmore's classrooms. The
purpose of this chapter is to explore the numerous intertwined
factors that led to this situation. However, before turning to a
discussion of why computers were used so little in most milieus in
which they were available it is necessary to lay out in some detail
the evidence on which this conclusion rests.

This chapter discusses three situations in which the low level of

94

utilization is particularly well illustrated – business classes, the library, and the computer room available to gifted students for their use. However, a similarly low level of use was quite apparent in many other places in the school as well. Of course, the claim that computers were not frequently used involves a comparison with some implicitly expected or desired level of use. For example, it would hardly be reasonable to claim that textbooks are used infrequently merely because they are not in constant use in every class in which they are available. One might take a similar view of computer use.

However, there are at least two important differences between these cases. First, computers are, relatively speaking, quite expensive so that a low level of use means that the time during which the computers are being employed must add something very significant to students' education to justify expenditures on them in an era in which many school districts are facing serious financial pressures. Second, at Whitmore, as is the case in many schools, computers, unlike textbooks, are used only during the school day. Although a few highly motivated students with computers at home sometimes took work back and forth from the machines at school to theirs at home, such behavior was very unusual. The rarity of this occurrence was undoubtedly not only a function of students' preferences about how to spend their time, but also a reflection of the practical difficulties inherent in using machines that may not be completely compatible.

Thus, although the conclusion that Whitmore's computers were used rather infrequently involves some judgments about what level of use one might expect, I believe the underutilization was a striking enough phenomenon that most individuals would agree that it is worthy of documentation and discussion. It is certainly true that most of the teachers at Whitmore who were familiar with computers felt that they were very definitely underutilized, as is apparent in the following excerpt from an interview with Mr. Edwards, a chemistry teacher who, on his own initiative, learned enough about computers that he ended up teaching computer science courses as well:

Interviewer: How much would you say in general that computers are used for instructional purposes here at Whitmore, ignoring computer science classes for the moment?

Mr. Edwards: Not anywhere near as much as they should be. Very little.

OFFICE AUTOMATION AND BUSINESS COMPUTER APPLICATIONS

As indicated in the Appendix, in each of the 2 years during which data were gathered for this study, one class called Office Automation and another called Business Computer Applications were systematically observed. Thus, a total of four different business classes taught by four different teachers participated in the study. The Office Automation classes covered basic material on secretarial and clerical work, including topics such as how to dress properly for office work, how to answer the telephone in a businesslike manner, and how to set up filing systems. Students were also familiarized with a wide array of office equipment including adding machines, dictaphones, typewriters, word processors of various sorts, and personal computers. During most of this study the Office Automation classroom was equipped with two Tandy personal computers and one printer. Four additional personal computers were installed in late October of the study's second year.

The Business Computer Applications classes were intended both to teach students about computers and to give them first-hand experience with using the machines to perform a variety of tasks, such as entering various kinds of data into tables, computing payrolls, preparing taxes, and doing accounts. Students worked from a text that had a disc designed to accompany each chapter. During most of this study the classroom in which this class was conducted was equipped with 4 Tandy personal computers and 2 printers. During the second semester of the second year, the class had available for its use 17 new computers and several new printers.

The typical class size for both Office Automation and Business Computer Applications classes was about 16. Roughly two-thirds of the students in the Business Computer Applications classes were girls, as were all the students in the two Office Automation classes we observed. The largest single group of students in all four classes were black females and the smallest group in three of the four classes were white males.

Computers were actually used quite rarely in Office Automation classes. For example, in one of the two classes observed the computers were not used at all in the first semester. In the second semester, the observer's best estimate was that the students used the computers roughly twice a month. This was consistent with the results of the student interviews in which 75% of the students said they used the computers infrequently. Although a few students reported using the machines two or three days a week, there were also a few students who claimed not to have used them more than once or twice the entire year and one who insisted she had never used a computer even once in that class.

The low level of computer use in the Office Automation class may not be too surprising given the rather elementary nature of the material covered in the course and the wide variety of office machines to which students were exposed. However, a similar pattern also emerged in the Business Computer Applications course. For example, Ms. Parelli, whose class was observed during the first year of the study, usually taught in a very traditional manner the first 3 days of the week, while the computers sat unused in the back of the room. Thus, these days were generally devoted to lectures, teacher-led question and answer periods, and written exercises in workbooks. Although Ms. Parelli planned to have students work on the computers at the end of these classes if there was time, very often there was not enough time left for students to do so.

The last 2 days of the week students worked individually or in small groups at their desks or on the computers. Desk work included vocabulary review, inventory exercises in which students physically cut out pieces of paper that were then arranged in alphabetical or numerical order, and the like. Computer work generally centered around the discs that came with the textbook. These covered a range of material including data entry and accounting

97

exercises. Since there were only four computers and most of the exercises were designed to be done individually, students could not get a great deal of computer time even had the machines been in constant use, which they were not. Specifically, even if the machines had been in constant use during the last 2 days of the week, students would have averaged less than 25 minutes each on the computers out of the roughly 4 hours they spent weekly in their Business Computer Applications classes. Since the computers often sat idle and usage was not equally distributed among all students, a substantial number of students used them much less than this. Computer use was so infrequent for some students that they were observed asking peers for extremely rudimentary information, such as how to turn the machines on, in November after more than 2 full months in the course.

Usage in the other Business Computer Applications class was also very limited. Rather surprisingly, observers encountered not a single example of student computer use in this class during the entire first semester of the course. Rather, the class was observed spending its time learning about computers and in some cases performing by hand tasks that could be easily automated, such as figuring payrolls based on information about wage rates and hours worked. The information about computers was conveyed through the textbook, which was not infrequently read aloud in class by students while the teacher inserted questions, clarifying comments, and additional explanations. Students spent their time learning basic material such as the name and function of the various parts of computer systems, how computers store and retrieve information, and the kinds of printers available and the functions for which they are most suited. They also had a library project for which they selected a topic from a list presented to them by the teacher and prepared a brief report. Computer use increased somewhat in the course's second semester after enough computers arrived so that all students could work on them simultaneously. Then, the majority of students used the computers at least two or three times a week after an initial period of lower usage. However, many students had trouble making much progress because they used the computers little enough that they had to be constantly checking on basic information the lack of which impeded their use of the software in the relatively short periods of time generally available for work on the computers.

THE LIBRARY

The school library was another milieu in which the computer resources available were used very little. The librarian received a terminal that was connected to the Bibliographical Retrieval Service database search system during the study's first year. Not only that, she was very strongly encouraged to use it by her supervisor. For reasons that will be discussed later, the librarian was very slow getting started using the system herself and in teaching students to use it. In fact, the lack of system usage became a real bone of contention between the librarian and her supervisor. As the librarian put it in an interview:

> I had been given a directive. "You *will* learn it. You *will* do the searching." It was almost like somebody had stock in BRS. [They insisted] you will *use* it. . . . My principal was receiving letters every month or so about my inability to push these searches here at this school.

The situation got so bad that the librarian at one point told researchers that she thought her job was in jeopardy because she was not able to get usage of the system's database searching capability up to a level acceptable to her supervisor. In addition, the strong pressures for use combined with the difficulty the librarian had getting students to use the system led to cases in which she allowed the search system to be used very inefficiently or unproductively because that at least used up some of the budget allocated for the searches:

Ms. Jackson: At each grade level there are on-line data bases that the librarian has to teach. Some teachers are library users and some are reluctant. . . . I have to sell it. It's like I'm selling it.

Interviewer: When you said you have to spend the money, do you mean you are allotted a certain amount of connection time and then you are supposed to use it?

Ms. Jackson: I think so. Yeah. That's what [they] want. . . . One student . . . was doing a research paper on Buddhism. He went into a database here – into the American Academic Encyclopedia [which the school library has on its shelves]. . . . He ran up a bill of two hundred something [dollars]. It was the full text. He sat there and he got his entire report off of that thing there [pointing to the terminal] . . . I let him. . . . Even the student himself [said,] "Mrs. Jackson this is costly. Why can't I just go and get it from the encyclopedia?"

This might seem like an example of overuse rather than underuse since the terminal was used for something that could have been done at least as rapidly and at a fraction of the cost with the library's copy machine. However, it was clear from conversations with Ms. Jackson that she allowed this overuse to occur because there were strong pressures for utilization of the terminal that she felt she could not meet more productively.

THE COMPUTER ROOM FOR GIFTED STUDENTS

The computer room for gifted students contained 13 Apple IIe computers, 7 printers, and an expensive color plotter that was never actually connected to the other machines so it could be used. The equipment in the room arrived at the school in two or three small shipments over the 2 years preceding the start of this study. It was paid for by special state funds designated for use in the education of gifted children. Initially the computers had been placed individually in the classrooms of teachers who taught students in the program for gifted students. However, there was wide agreement that they were used very little when distributed that way. As Mr. East, a chemistry teacher who was involved in the program for gifted students, explained in an interview:

100

> They [the computers] were being underutilized. . . . They were just sitting in the rooms and the teachers were not using them. . . . [Some] had never even been turned on.

Mr. East's assertions were supported by the comments of Mr. Walters, who initially served as the co-coordinator of the program for gifted students and as such was responsible for the computers purchased through this project. He characterized use of the machines during their first 2 years at the school as "very minimal." Interestingly, he reported that what little use there was of the machines went primarily for record keeping or basic word processing by teachers rather than for instruction.

The coordinators of the gifted student program decided to place the computers together in a single room in the hope that they would be used more. One of the coordinators explained the decision this way: "We [created] the computer lab because many people found the computer an inconvenient electronic device that they didn't have time for in the classroom." Only two teachers, Mr. East and Mr. Deppe, objected to this decision, expressing a strong desire to have a computer in their classrooms. Their wishes were honored. Mr. East kept his computer locked up most of the time, but occasionally used it for classroom demonstrations or individual student projects. Mr. Deppe kept his in the back of his room and used a rather extensive collection of discs he had for teaching various topics in biology. The other teachers relinquished their computers very readily. As a history teacher put it, "It was all right with me 'cause mine was just sitting there."

However, gathering the computers into one place did not do a great deal to increase their use. It did lead to their use during two lunch periods most days by roughly a dozen students who chose to come and spend that time playing educational games or word processing. However, with this one exception, which will be discussed in the next chapter, the use of this room remained extremely infrequent. In fact, this room was used on the average less than 1 of the remaining 30 class periods each week. The infrequency of use was made clear in an interview with Mr. East, who indicated that the two or three teachers who were the room's heaviest users brought

101

their classes there roughly two or three times a year. In addition, he asserted, consistent with our observations, that many teachers who were eligible to use the room never did so even once in the two years since the computers had been gathered there.

The one obvious exception to the general tendency not to use computers in instruction outside of the GPTutor and computer science classes was their rather frequent utilization in special education classes. Mr. Pike used his computer on a daily basis in his classes for socially and emotionally disturbed students. Ms. Green also used a computer consistently to instruct her educable mentally retarded students. Both of these teachers showed a degree of interest in using computers for instruction that contrasted very sharply with the general tendency to use them little or not at all. In fact, after trying to start out with a jerry-built system that included a TV screen and tape recorder he had scavenged from the school's audiovisual collection, Mr. Pike managed to put together a workable computer system through a serious personal effort that included persuading an acquaintance at the board of education to lend him a monitor and writing a small grant proposal to a community group to pay for a disc drive. Ms. Green also took the initiative to get her computer by going to Whitmore's principal and requesting that one of the computers paid for by funds for gifted students be transferred to her room, on the theory that both gifted students and the special education students she taught were in the category of "exceptional children." Since use of these machines in the room for gifted students was quite minimal, the principal approved her request. She also wrote a small grant proposal for the purchase of computer equipment, which she submitted to a local foundation. However, it was not funded.

BARRIERS TO COMPUTER USE
The Belief That Computer Use Will Add Little of Value to Current Practice

The factors that appeared to inhibit computer use at Whitmore were many and complex. The contrast between the intensive use of

102

computers in the field testing of the GPTutor as well as in computer science classes and their infrequent use in most of the other locales in which computers were available makes one of these barriers clear. Quite sensibly, teachers will not use computers to any noticeable extent if they do not feel there is some educational purpose to be furthered by doing so (Eurich-Fulcer & Schofield, in press). The developers of the GPTutor gave the teachers cooperating with them a clear rational for use of the machines. Specifically, they pointed out that the tutor could provide constant monitoring and structuring of students' problem-solving attempts, as well as immediate feedback, all of which seem likely to facilitate learning (Anderson et al., 1985). The usefulness of having computers to teach programming in computer science classes is readily apparent. Similarly, the special education teachers saw both motivational and social reasons to use computers; they used them at least weekly for drill and practice, as well as to help teach things like vocabulary and spelling in a gamelike context. Interestingly, one of these teachers pointed out that in addition to these instructional uses, there was another reason to have the special education students use the computer – using it gave them a badly needed ego boost, as the following excerpt from an interview with one of the special education teachers indicates:

Ms. Green: They [the special education students] are embarrassed to be in this room [the special education room] in the first place. The fact that other people see there's a computer in here and realize the kids are using it . . . has sort of lifted their egos a little bit.

However, in general, Whitmore's teachers saw little reason why computers should be used in their classrooms. It was not at all clear to them that their goals would be better or more easily met by doing so. As one teacher who did not use the computer he had been given for his gifted students put it, "It didn't do anything I couldn't do easier and cheaper on the blackboard." Another attributed his failure to use his computer with a world cultures class for gifted students to a difficulty in finding appropriate software, saying, "I can't see teachers using computers unless they can see how

103

it could be useful." A home economics teacher cited this issue as the crux of the matter, stating, "If I could see a really good use for a computer I would use one . . . but I have yet to think of anything I could do on a computer that I can't do by myself just as well." Similarly, Ms. Jackson, the librarian, attributed the low level of usage of the library's database search capabilities at least partly to their lack of usefulness. Specifically, she said that students had little need for the system because very few teachers assigned research papers that required the kind of intensive search of a variety of sources that database searches supply. Further, she pointed out that many of the students could not read well enough to make use of the kinds of sources they were likely to locate when using many of the databases available through the BRS search system.

It is worth noting that when teachers discussed whether or not they thought computer use would be valuable, they took what I will call an incrementalist view. From this perspective, the goal of computer use is not to facilitate fundamental changes in the goals or methods currently typifying the educational system. Instead, it is to help teachers and students do what they are currently doing more easily, efficiently, or effectively. So, for example, one might decide that rather than having students do worksheets using a pencil and paper, the same time could be devoted to having them use a computer-based drill and practice program that might hold their interest better and reduce the amount of time the teacher spends correcting papers.

Consistent with this incrementalist viewpoint, the teachers' emphasis on evaluating the potential usefulness of computer use was virtually always on how it would fit into ongoing classroom practice and the already established curriculum. Thus, the issues pertinent to teachers were the level of difficulty of the material, the precise subject material covered, and the way the software meshed with their textbooks, as is evident in the following remarks of one of Whitmore's longtime faculty members:

> Implementation of all this [the gifted student computer program] is not the way it should be. I never really understand how they [the district administrators] never think through the program

and its connection to the curriculum the way they ought to. It is just sort of pasted on top.

This emphasis on the fit between current practice and computer applications is also apparent in the following excerpt of an interview with another teacher, Mr. Walters:

Interviewer: If there were two or three things that somebody could do to make the computer a more useful tool for you what would they be?

Mr. Walters: I think [locating] software that would be applicable to the curriculum. Second, developing lesson plans specifying step by step how this can be worked into the curriculum. Third, providing paid summer seminars on how to utilize it.

This emphasis on how computer applications fit into the current curriculum is hardly surprising since teachers are, in fact, held responsible for covering certain material in their classes. Thus, innovations are likely to be judged on the basis of what they can contribute to the attainment of this goal. However, it is worth noting that this orientation differs dramatically from that of many proponents of computer use in schools, who see such usage as a vehicle for transforming education (Means et al., 1993). For example, the developer of the widely used LOGO software sees it as a way of increasing the emphasis on developing problem-solving skills and encouraging students to reflect on their own thinking processes in elementary schools (Papert, 1980). Others see the use of computers and related technology as a way of bringing the resources of the outside world into the classroom (Bossert, 1988; Hunter, 1992), of fostering the development of inquiry skills (Groen, 1985; Lawler, 1984), of letting students follow their own interests more than they currently can in most school settings (Feurzeig, 1988), or of changing the current emphasis on didactic approaches to teaching to more collaborative, learner-centered ones (Collins, in press). The point here is that many of the potential consequences of computer use that are most exciting to those outside of the schools are not given high priority by those working within that system who tend to ask whether these applications can

105

assist them with doing their work as they presently understand it better, quicker, or more easily.

The Disruption of the Classroom's Traditional Social Organization

The common belief on the part of teachers that there is little software that is likely to work better in teaching their subject matter than current methods is a factor contributing to the lack of use of computers in many fields. However, this does not account for the relatively infrequent utilization of computers in a class like Business Computer Applications, which was explicitly intended to give students a substantial amount of practical experience with computers. Teachers in these business classes spoke enthusiastically of the need for their students to learn to use computers:

Interviewer: What do you like best about teaching this course [Business Computer Applications]?

Ms. White: I think it is related to the world of work. . . . Jobs are going to be white collar . . . working with computers, and I feel I'm making a contribution. . . . Students [will] have the skills that they need to get jobs.

Yet, ironically, computers were used relatively little even in business classes. Two factors seemed to contribute to this situation. First, teachers were not easily able to solve the organizational problems posed by computer use when there were a great many more students than computers in their classrooms. Second, they were, generally speaking, not very knowledgeable about the computers or the software they were using. Although these two barriers stood out in clearest relief in Business Computer Applications classrooms, they were also very real inhibitors of computer use in other classrooms, as will become apparent.

The teachers in Business Computer Applications were much like their peers in the college preparatory courses in that they tended to use traditional whole class methods of instruction – that is, they lectured, conducted structured discussions, and had their students work individually at their desks on various kinds of written exer-

106

cises. Given this format, it was not immediately apparent how to integrate computer use into normal classroom procedures when there were so few computers that the entire class, or at least a large portion of it, could not work on the computers simultaneously. The problem was, of course, that students working on the computers would miss the material covered in class during that time. Since different students would miss different portions of the material covered by their peers as they rotated in and out of the larger group, there was no quick or easy way for the teacher to help them make up what they had missed.

There were other more prosaic kinds of problems as well. For example, the printers were noisy enough that it was distracting for students to use them while the teacher was trying to talk to their classmates. Thus, one of the teachers made it a rule that students could not use the printer when she was talking. Although this was reasonable given that one person's printing could disrupt the work of a dozen or more classmates, it led to inefficient use of the computers as students often sat at them for extended periods of time waiting for an appropriate moment to print out their work. Another problem with detaching a few students from a class's main activity was that it meant the teacher was not likely to be readily available to help them when they needed it. If a problem arose for one of these students, the teacher either had to ignore it or shift her attention from the large group of students with whom she was working to the single individual who needed help. Both of these ways of handling the situation had serious drawbacks, thus putting the teacher under some pressure as she decided between the lesser of the two evils. Other possible mechanisms for handling this problem, such as having a particularly knowledgeable student serve as a kind of informal resource person, were occasionally used on an ad hoc basis. However, this did not always go smoothly since to be successful it required that the knowledgeable students be both willing to divert attention from their own academic and social concerns and able to communicate their knowledge to others.

Such impediments to extensive computer use were found not only in Business Computer Applications classes. Teachers of a variety of subjects ranging from history to home economics who had just one or two computers in their classrooms also spoke frequently of the organizational issues this raised for them:

Mr. Specter: Personally, I never got into using the computer at all. My experience with the software is that not a whole lot of it is very valuable or useable. . . . And the other factor is how do you get kids, 30 or 25 or even 15 kids, to use one computer. The matter of scheduling . . . I was never willing to put the energy into answering those questions. Just too many other things to do.

Not too surprisingly, attempts to use one computer to teach an entire class simultaneously were both quite rare and generally rather unsuccessful. Mr. East occasionally used his computer for demonstrations in his chemistry class for gifted students, and Mrs. Jackson used hers in the library to demonstrate how to use the data base search system, but it was difficult to keep students' attention when one or two dozen of them were supposed to be attending to a standard-sized monitor that was hard for those not right up in front to see clearly. Although the development of LCD screens means that such problems are now less likely to occur because the larger screens allow more students to view what is occurring, unless a school has many such screens, teachers are likely to have to make advance arrangements to use them for classroom demonstrations. The importance of a screen of reasonable size is indicated by the comments of a math teacher who described his experience trying to use a computer with a regular-sized monitor for demonstrations:

Mr. Erie: I didn't find it very useful to have one terminal in the room. In the first place it was too small. It was about 10 inches. . . . Any demonstrations I could give, half the kids would have to gather round. [Then I would repeat it for the others.] I found I could put it on the board faster.

Mr. Powers, who taught a vocational course called Power and Energy, seemed to agree with his colleague, saying succinctly, "One machine in the classroom is not enough."

One French teacher, who did make the shift from a whole class format to one in which students rotated through a variety of work stations, including computers used for drill and practice and tape recorders for oral language practice, talked of the difficulty she had in making the adjustment. As her comments indicate, this shift is likely to mean not only that different students are working on different tasks, but that the classroom looks and sounds very different than it used to. Students are more likely to move around the classroom and talk with each other. The teacher's role as lecturer becomes much less important, and his or her ability to juggle the competing needs of students working on different tasks becomes crucial:

Ms. Wright: I'm for anything that will work. I had been on the committee that wrote the material for the gifted [student] French classes. I had picked the book . . . I had ordered the stuff, including the computer software. So I was anxious to see what it would do and how it could be incorporated. . . . It was a ninth-grade class, and most of the kids in ninth grade have already worked in a class where a number of things are going on at a time, so it didn't bother them at all. *It drove me crazy*, but I could see it was benefiting them. I felt torn. I wanted to be with this [person]. I wanted to be with that group. It was just a question of convincing my soul that when there is noise and everybody is doing something different learning is taking place. It's difficult for me. My natural reaction to that is not good. I think you can train yourself to do that if you find it is valuable. I was learning to do that with anguish.

Ms. Wright's anguish was not an idiosyncratic reaction. Prior studies have suggested that many teachers attempting to use computer technology in instruction have similar difficulty adjusting to what may appear to be a noisy, even disorderly, classroom (Sandholtz, Ringstaff, & Dwyer, 1990).

Many teachers, less motivated than Ms. Wright or less willing to experiment with classroom practices that were unfamiliar and initially uncomfortable, never made the transition from whole class instruction to formats more amenable to the incorporation of one or a small number of computers. Perhaps one factor that contributed to the frequent use of computers in the special education classrooms, which was so in contrast to the low level of use in other settings, is that instruction in these classes tended to be rather individualized whether or not the computer was being used. The small size of these classes, combined with the varying special needs of the students, meant that teachers did not generally use a whole class lecture format. Thus, their customary mode of classroom organization was compatible with computer use on the part of one of two students at a time.

Lack of Familiarity with Computer Hardware and Software

The large majority of Whitmore's teachers, like the majority of teachers nationally, completed their formal education before the advent of the widespread use of personal computers. Thus, many of them never encountered computers in their training, or if they did, their experience was with large and relatively inflexible mainframe machines. Thus, their preteaching experience did not present them with creative models of how computers might be used to enrich the curriculum or of how to adjust traditional classroom procedures to make effective use of computers possible. Neither did it provide them with knowledge of how to use personal computers and of the kinds of software available for use.

This lack of knowledge on the part of teachers was a real impediment to the use of computers in the classroom. Ms. Parelli freely admitted that she did not know enough about computers or the software she was using to teach effectively in Business Computer Applications, saying things like, "I just plain don't know enough to teach some of the things I need to." When asked what she liked least about teaching the course, her reply was that she disliked feeling unprepared to teach it. Her lack of knowledge was readily apparent to students, as evidenced by the following excerpt from field notes taken in her classroom when two of her students working on the computer encountered a problem they could not solve:

110

Lauretta says, "Maybe we should ask Ms. Parelli for help." Janette replies, "Ms. Parelli doesn't know anything about computers. She won't be any help."

The girls' decision not to consult their teacher may have been reasonable, as suggested by the poor advice she gave some of her students a week or two earlier:

Ms. Parelli leaves [after working with one of the students at a computer]. Lisa says to the boy sitting next to her, "She didn't help at all!" The boy replies, "Yeah, she spent one and a half weeks helping me to get started on the computer, but nothing worked . . . ." [Later] Ralph is having trouble with his disc drive. The red light is on and he remembers that the teacher told him never to put a disc in when the disc drive light was on. He calls Ms. Parelli over and says, "What should I do now? I can't put the disc in." She replies, "Oh, go ahead and put it in anyway." He responds, "No, I'd better not because the disc drive is moving in there." [He is right. Inserting the disc when the disc drive is moving will cause damage.]

Ms. Parelli was not the only business teacher plagued by a lack of thorough knowledge of the material she needed to teach. Another of the business teachers, Ms. Spring, explicitly told researchers that she avoided using the computers very much because she did not know how to teach students to use them very well.

I argued in Chapter 3 that it was motivating for high school students to see their teachers having to work to solve problems rather than seeing them as distant omniscient experts who just hand down facts. However, as also indicated in that chapter, to be effective teachers must know enough so that they can effectively help students solve problems that arise. Otherwise both the teacher and the student become annoyed and frustrated and learning is impeded.

This lack of real familiarity with computers was not restricted to the business teachers. In fact, because their jobs specifically included teaching students how to use computers, in general the business teachers appeared more familiar with computers than most other teachers. For example, Ms. Parelli spoke of several training sessions that were provided by the school system for business teachers, and Ms. Spring was one of the very few teachers who repeatedly checked books on computers out of the school library to increase her proficiency with them. With the exception of the computer science teachers and a few others, most teachers were even less familiar with computer technology than their peers in the business department. This posed a formidable barrier to utilization at Whitmore. However, this problem is by no means unique to Whitmore. National survey data suggest that fewer than 30% of the individuals in teacher training programs feel that they have been well prepared to use computers for instructional purposes (American Association of Colleges of Teacher Education Committee on Research and Information, 1987), thus suggesting that this barrier will remain a reality for some time to come.

Threat to Teachers' Sense of Competence and Authority

Frequently coupled with teachers' comments on their lack of knowledge about computers was a sense of concern that trying to use computers exposed them to potentially embarrassing situations, which undermined either their sense of competence, their classroom authority, or both. For example, Mr. Trowbridge, a geometry teacher who indicated that he found it hard to "get the hang of computers," argued that because of their youth students could learn to use computers more quickly than teachers. Thus, by attempting to use computers with his class he reversed the usual situation in which he was more in command of the knowledge needed to perform well than were his students. Ms. Wright, the French teacher quoted earlier, made a similar point:

> I took a little bit of a course [on computers], just so I wouldn't be a total fool. When they first came, even turning on the machine was a real trial. . . . Something like this is always an opportunity to make a fool of yourself. When the computer first came to my room even my dumbest student knew more about it than I did. If you are the kind of teacher who is frightened of making a fool of himself or herself, then that could be a real problem. . . . I'm a competent person but sometimes I do things wrong and that

112

doesn't bother me a lot. It doesn't bother me to say to the kids, "I can't turn this machine on. Will you turn it on for me?" They will say, "You're dumb." I say, "I know, but I know lots of other things."

Whitmore's teachers are not alone in feeling they know less about computers than their students. A national survey of 1,100 teachers from all regions of the United States demonstrated that more than half feel the same way (Staff, 1989).

In spite of the fact that a few teachers at Whitmore like Ms. Wright appeared to tolerate knowing less than their students without too much discomfort, many were quite leery of putting themselves in such a situation. Ms. Green, who used a computer for a variety of purposes with her special education students, felt that this fear of looking incompetent or foolish was a major deterrent to others:

Interviewer: Have any other teachers [aside from you and Mr. Pike] in the special education department decided to use them [computers]?

Ms. Green: No.

Interviewer: Do you think they would like to?

Ms. Green: They may when they feel more comfortable with it themselves so that they don't feel like a fool in front of these kids trying to tell them how to use it. That's the fear I see.

One of the Business Computer Applications teachers even contrasted her fear of the computer with the students' relaxed attitude, which she saw as conducive to their learning readily:

Ms. White: They [the students] are very good at figuring things out. A lot of things they taught me, 'cause they're not afraid of it [the computer]. This is their thing, even the ones you wouldn't expect.

The teachers' concern about being or appearing to be less knowledgeable than their students is understandable. In the United States, the social structure of the classroom has traditionally been built around two complementary roles – that of teacher and student. An important part of the teacher's role is the exercise of authority, that is, legitimated power over the student (Bierstedt, 1970). The teacher's authority has a number of bases, but one of these is unquestionably his or her expertise and, more specifically, the gap between that expertise and the student's own (Benne, 1970). Although teachers have authority by virtue of the role they occupy, they must work to express and maintain that authority in order that it not be eroded. In fact, Hughes (1959) has estimated on the basis of his research that 40% of teachers' actions are directed toward maintaining and displaying their authority.

Any change in the classroom that seriously undermines the teacher's image as a knowledgeable and competent individual has implications not only for the teachers' personal feelings of comfort and self-esteem, but also for important aspects of classroom functioning related to the teacher's authority. In a high school with a very diverse student body, concerns about maintaining authority are understandable and realistic. Many teachers felt that to display a lack of expertise would give students an opening to ridicule them that the students would be quick to take. This concern is clearly evident in the following excerpt from field notes of a conversation between a member of the research team and a physics teacher about why he failed to use the computer he had in his classroom:

> Mr. Barber said that students are waiting to jump on teachers. He went on to say that many of the gifted students don't see teachers as really human. Rather they expect teachers to know everything and when teachers don't they react to it very negatively. He said, "There are a lot of opportunities to make a fool of yourself and the kids are just waiting for them."

In fact, cases did arise in which teachers were literally unable to perform some of their authority-linked functions because of the students' greater knowledge of computers. For example, one math teacher was unable to grade a project turned in to him by a gifted student because it was a computer program designed to perform various mathematical operations. Not knowing anything about programming, the teacher had to go to a colleague, who graded it for him. In 2 years of close observation at Whitmore, we found no case of one teacher asking another teacher to grade his or her students' class assignments that did not involve computer-based projects.

Although teachers most often mentioned a fear of looking uninformed, stupid, or foolish in front of their students, it was not uncommon for them to experience the same feelings when trying to improve their computer skills in both formal and informal training contexts in which students were not present. For example, Mr. Miller described his unsuccessful attempts to learn from a colleague, Mr. East, a chemistry teacher who was Whitmore High School's foremost "hacker":

Mr. Miller: He's a computer whiz. He's way over my head. . . . A couple of times I've asked him to explain things to me, but it gets so complicated. He goes on and on and I just sit there and I say, "I gotcha . . . I got it. I understand." But I don't understand a thing!

This sense of threat to one's sense of self as a competent professional was felt by some even in formal training. For example, the school librarian spoke frankly of the strain of trying to learn about computers in a training session that obviously did not take adequate account of the level of knowledge that she brought to it:

Ms. Jackson: I went to an all-day training session. . . . I didn't even know the basics of computers. . . . At one point they were talking about a menu. I started wiping my glasses. . . . I kept cleaning my glasses looking for the word *menu*. Then I got upset, started running to the bathroom like a child because I don't know what is going on here. Finally I raised my hand timidly. [I said] "I don't see anything that looks like food . . . ." It was overwhelming for me. . . . I was not computer literate.

Computer Anxiety

Although much of the teachers' trepidation about using computers in their classrooms appeared to stem from concern about how their relative lack of expertise would influence their position in the classroom and their ability to effectively and efficiently teach students using them, another factor also seemed to contribute to their reluctance. Some teachers felt quite anxious about the mere idea of having to learn to use an unfamiliar and rather intimidating machine. Like some of the teachers interviewed by Honey and Moeller (1990), many teachers at Whitmore used words like *fear*, *anxiety*, and *phobia* in discussing their own or others' reactions to the idea of learning to use a computer. An excerpt from an interview with the coordinator of the program for gifted students supports the contention that fear was a common reaction:

Interviewer: How did you find the other teachers reacted that first year when you gave them one computer each?

Mr. Deppe: I'll be honest with you. Everybody was afraid of them.

This reaction was by no means limited to the teachers of the gifted students. Many of their colleagues throughout the school evidenced similar reactions. For example, Ms. Baker, a mathematics teacher, gave the following reply to an open-ended question about what one thing the school system could do to help her decide whether and how she might be able to use a computer effectively in her classes:

If I could have a few hours one-to-one with a really competent teacher that has used it – just let me ask questions – [about] what I'm afraid of about a computer, what I don't understand.

A computer science teacher, who arrived at Whitmore toward the end of the study, indicated that anxiety related to computers was not peculiar to Whitmore's faculty. She had encountered it in many teachers taking courses at a local university:

Interviewer: What do you think would be the biggest impediment to the utilization of computers [by teachers]? What sorts of barriers . . . ?

Ms. Patrick: I think it would be . . . how much they [teachers] know and their fears and prejudices toward the computer. . . . I was taking courses with a lot of teachers . . . and computers were a big topic. A lot of them seemed apprehensive.

116

Problems with Training

In general, there appeared to be four types of training experiences available to Whitmore's teachers. First, over a period of several years, a few in-service training sessions related to computing were offered by knowledgeable colleagues. These sessions were typically no more than an hour or two long and the material covered was very rudimentary. For example, roughly once a year one of the computer science teachers held a brief session on computers for interested teachers from all departments. Teachers asked him questions like, Do computers ever make mistakes? and Should I buy a computer to do things like balance my checkbook? In addition, Ms. Green once took her colleagues in the special education department to the room housing computers for the gifted students' use to familiarize them with the Apple IIe's there.

Another somewhat more extended kind of in-service training was offered at a Teachers' Center. All teachers in the school system were rotated through this center over a period of several years in a effort to provide a several-week period during which they, freed from their normal duties, could select among a variety of seminars and training experiences designed to enhance their professional development. Several workshops on computer usage were offered to interested teachers. As part of this experience it was also possible for teachers to visit a software library at a local university.

A third kind of training were the workshops organized by the vendors of computer equipment in conjunction with the sale of equipment to the school district. These workshops varied from about 1 day to 1 week in length and tended to focus on very basic issues connected with how to operate computers and associated equipment such as printers. Finally, a few teachers reported availing themselves of opportunities to learn about computers during evening or summer courses at local institutions of higher education. Some of these teachers reported paying the tuition for these courses themselves. Others indicated that the school district shared the cost.

The inability of all but a few of Whitmore's teachers who had access to computers to utilize them effectively, or to use them at all for that matter, makes it clear that the training provided was not particularly effective. It is worth noting that other staff members also appeared not to get the training they needed to use computers readily. For example, Mr. East complained in an interview that the secretaries in the school's main office received such rudimentary training that they were unable to operate their newly arrived personal computers and that they had to learn in a very inefficient manner on their own:

Interviewer: Did the school or the system provide you with any sort of training or incentive to help out in the gifted [student] computer lab?

Mr. East: No. This is a problem almost all the way across the board, not only in our program. . . . The secretaries have a Burroughs terminal downstairs that is supposed to help them in their record keeping. . . . They were given like a half hour [of training] quickly. [Like], "Here's the switch." They've learned it little by little on their own instead of [someone taking] a bit of time out and saying, "Let me show you what you can do with this." There's been nothing like that. It would make a good in-service program.

In addition, a new computerized system-wide procedure for recording grades and producing report cards operated so poorly that the start of summer school actually had to be delayed because students did not know in time to meet the deadline for registration whether they had failed courses and thus needed to retake them in the summer. Although part of this problem stemmed from glitches in the software, some of the delay appeared to be attributable to the unfamiliarity of district employees with the computer equipment and the procedures required to use it properly. Thus, issues connected to training must be considered in any analysis of the barriers to effective computer use at Whitmore.

Timing. Policymakers at the district level were aware of the dangers of letting the pace of computer hardware acquisition outstrip the development and implementation of appropriate training. In light of the problems described in this chapter, it is rather ironic

118

that Mr. Petrella, a high-level administrator at the Board of Education, had this to say about the district's policy:

> Unfortunately a large number of districts consistently go out and lead with their face, for lack of a better phrase. They buy equipment and say, "Here you go," and everybody says, "No," and it sits in closets or is misused. The intent here is that nothing is purchased until there is a relatively comprehensive plan that identified exactly what the outcomes are, what people will be doing with them, and how they will be trained before equipment is bought.

The process of computer acquisition and introduction at Whitmore did not appear to be as orderly and rational as one might expect from the preceding statement, as should be apparent from the earlier part of this chapter. Several factors may account for this. First, the school district decided to focus its major effort on encouraging computer use at the elementary level and was implementing a plan to introduce LOGO into all of its elementary schools. Thus, much of the effort of central staff with responsibility for computer use in the schools was devoted to this project. In addition, a number of fairly innovative attempts to explore how computers might be effectively introduced and utilized at the middle and high school levels were being made. So, for example, the district entered into an agreement with a local university and a foundation to field-test a program that gave relatively intensive computer training to middle school teachers with no prior computer experience in order to let them become expert enough to discover where and how such technology could enhance instruction in areas such as English, social studies, and language arts. Another program undertaken in cooperation with a different university gave a group of mathematics teachers considerable exposure to computer technology with the intention of having them serve as peer trainers in their home schools.

The problem was that while the district was concentrating on these many admittedly useful activities, computers were entering Whitmore and other high schools at a pace that exceeded the district's ability to ready teachers for the change. Various environmen-

119

tal forces contributed to this. For example, practices changed in the business world so rapidly in the 1980s that it became clear to district personnel that business students needed to learn to use computers rather than to focus on using typewriters, as they traditionally had in many classes. Thus, a moratorium was placed on the purchase of new electric typewriters, and a decision was made to purchase various kinds of word processors and computers for business classrooms instead. In addition, in the years just preceding this study, the district found itself in serious danger of losing state funding for its program for gifted students because of various deficiencies in it. The district knew as it drew up plans for revising the program that state funding for computers for gifted students was available. As a "free good" for which the state would pay, these computers were seen as desirable even though it is clear from the earlier part of this chapter that most teachers had relatively little idea what to do with them. Pressure to institute the use of computers also came from the existence of an evaluation of Whitmore issued a few years prior to this study by a visiting committee from the Middle States Association of Colleges and Secondary Schools, which, among its many other recommendations, called for additional computers at Whitmore.

In fact, Mr. East suggested that merely possessing the computers was seen as valuable, whether or not they were used, since it allowed the school to show them off on parents' nights as part of an effort to keep talented students, who might otherwise go to private schools, in the public school system. He was not alone in his view of the situation as evidenced by the words of one of his colleagues:

> It [having computers] is just another Band-Aid. Instead of suturing it into the system, we paste it on because we need it to look [good]. We need to bring people into the building or take them over there to the computer lab and say, "See this? Isn't this wonderful?" We need to bring in the press.

Thus, parents' belief that computers were the wave of the future and their desire to have their children prepared to live in a world in which computers are playing an increasingly important role also added pressure to acquire machines even when it was not clear exactly how they would be integrated with traditional policies and practices or what they would add to the students' education.

Lack of Coordination Between Training and Hardware Purchases. Coordination of the arrival of computer hardware and software with teacher training in its use was also a very real problem at Whitmore. From the teachers' perspective such coordination often appeared close to nonexistent. Teachers frequently reported either that a computer would just arrive in their classroom one day with virtually no advance warning or that one had been expected to arrive for months before the actual delivery was made. Some teachers reported receiving training in basic operational procedures and then waiting months for equipment to arrive in their classroom. Furthermore, teachers occasionally were trained using one system and then were expected to use a different one in their classes:

> Ms. McDonald: We had . . . training 'cause we were going to get a computer, but it really did nothing for me . . . because I didn't have anything to come back and use. . . . Plus it was on a different computer. Originally they ordered a TRS80 and they got one for us with no software. [Then] they realized . . . they don't have any software [for my subject]. Only Apple has Home Ec software. So they sold it to the business department and they reordered us new computers. So there was a lapse in there.

Frequently machines arrived in the middle of the semester, and teachers ended up using valuable class time to familiarize themselves with new hardware or software. This even happened in computer science:

> Carl [a student] told me [the observer] . . . that students have been mainly playing games during the last 2 weeks [in his computer science class]. I asked him why and he said because Mr. Davidson still appears to have a lot to learn about the new computers [so] he hasn't been teaching very actively. [Instead, he has] allowed students to play games.

121

All in all it was clear that issues of timing and coordination constituted a real barrier to the effective and efficient utilization of computers at Whitmore.

Matching Training to the Teacher's Level of Knowledge and Instructional Concerns. Although most teachers at Whitmore were novices when it came to computer use, the precise level of knowledge and previous exposure varied quite widely. Many, like the librarian who was quoted earlier, had so little previous experience that words like *menu* needed to be explained. A much smaller number, exemplified by Mr. East, were quite expert and enjoyed using the computer at home for recreational and other purposes. Some fell in between these extremes. Thus, problems arose in matching the kind of training offered with the teacher's existing level of knowledge. Training that was too rudimentary in nature was obviously wasteful and boring for those with some expertise. Yet training experiences that presumed any knowledge of computers at all left other teachers floundering. Many of the teachers who had access to one or more computers for instructional purposes could speak only vaguely of training sessions they remembered. For example, the comments of Ms. Prentiss, who volunteered to supervise the gifted students' use of computers after having seen her husband accomplish a lot on their personal computer at home, were quite typical:

Interviewer: How did you come to be in charge of the computer room [for gifted students] here?

Ms. Prentiss: I volunteered. . . . I didn't know much.

Interviewer: Did the school or the school system provide you with any training?

Ms. Prentiss [laughing]: That one 2-hour workshop at the Teachers' Center. That was it.

Interviewer: How long ago was that?

Ms. Prentiss: I have a hard time remembering. [Maybe 3 years ago]. . . . Right after that a friend of mine, a nontechnocrat, got an Apple [computer]. The two of us figured it out over the summer. And I figured if I can teach her I can teach anybody.

Those who could describe their training generally felt that it was inadequate. One of the characteristics of the training teachers were most likely to complain about was its restricted technical focus. Specifically, teachers tended to be critical of the fact that the training often focused primarily on such issues as how to operate the computer without giving them much advice or assistance with two fundamental issues discussed earlier – what software was available to assist in accomplishing their educational objectives and how to organize the class to make efficient and effective use of students' time when there were a small number of computers in the classroom. Mr. Powers's experience is related in the following excerpt from an interview:

Mr. Powers: I've had this thing [pointing to a computer] about $2\frac{1}{2}$ years. It came in the middle of the year. Nobody told us it was going to be part of the curriculum. Nobody told us what to do with them when they got here. They basically gave us the equipment and never said anything. . . . I actually had to teach myself how to work the computer.

Interviewer: Did you get any sort of in-service training?

Mr. Powers: Yeah. Included in the price of the computer they gave us 6 or 8 hours of instruction . . . telling you how to turn it on, load the printer, stuff like that. . . . It was very elementary.

Although most teachers needed training in basic operational procedures, they definitely needed much more than that to help them discover ways to use the computers effectively once they were turned on.

Lack of Concentrated Experiential Training. Training sessions tended to be relatively short and often covered a wide variety of issues. Thus, there was rarely time for teachers to become truly familiar with the machines and procedures they were learning. Rather, it was often a matter of hearing someone tell a class what command to use or seeing a demonstration in a training environment, which did not encourage or even allow the kind of repeated practice that builds and consolidates skills. To make matters even worse, a couple of individuals complained that the training sessions they had attended had more participants than computers. Therefore, they had not even been able to try out the procedures described to them because they did not have a computer on which to do so. Needless to say, they found this kind of experience extremely boring and felt that they had gained very little from it. A few of the teachers who were most interested in computers did arrange to borrow one from the school over the summer in order to develop their skills. This seemed to be very useful for those who were unusually motivated. The only problem was that occasionally teachers became so enamored of having a computer at home that they were quite dilatory in returning it for students' use after the school year had begun.

Inertia and Resistance

It was clear that the training offered to Whitmore's teachers did not generally prepare them to use the computers available to them effectively. However, two things seem necessary for training to be really effective. First, of course, one needs carefully timed and structured training experiences that speak to the questions and concerns individuals have and build the skills they will need. Second, the individuals involved must want to learn. Many of the teachers at Whitmore indicated that they were at least mildly interested in learning about computers. However, it is important not to ignore the existence of a great deal of inertia and even some outright resistance on the part of other faculty members. Mr. Powers, who used a computer in some of his Power and Energy classes, highlighted this problem in an interview:

Interviewer: Do you think most teachers would be anxious to have more access to computers or not?

Mr. Powers: I think a lot of them that aren't familiar with them are going to be afraid of them. . . . They are opposed to any change. They don't want to roll with the technology.

The following exchange with a geometry teacher suggests that Mr. Powers's assessment of the situation was quite accurate, at least with regard to some of his colleagues:

124

Interviewer: Have you had a chance to see the computer [tutor] that Mr. Adams and Mr. Brice . . . [are using]?

Mr. Carter: Yeah, but I'm not too fond [of] computers. . . . I'm the old-fashioned type. I don't want to learn anything new. Maybe that's my fault. I should go into learning computers . . . but I don't know. I just – after so many years, you build up a file on your subjects. . . . For me to go into teaching computers . . . I would have to start all over. I would have to actually sit down and work everything out, and it would require a lot more work on my part to run a class the way I want it run. . . . I suppose everybody gets lazy and . . . I just don't want to do it. . . . I'm doing what I'm doing. Don't want to change.

Thus, many teachers failed to take advantage of training that was available.

Infrastructure Problems

For those teachers who were interested in discovering if and how their students' learning could be enriched through the use of computers, the lack of readily available, timely, pertinent training was not the only barrier to be overcome. Another serious problem was the lack of structural arrangements within the school to facilitate the achievement of this goal. For example, although Whitmore had a teacher who received release time from teaching to take care of the school's audiovisual equipment, this individual's responsibilities did not include computer equipment. Nor were there others at Whitmore responsible for helping teachers with computer hardware or software problems. Teachers generally struggled individually with problems they encountered in using various software packages, sometimes utilizing informal networks including computer-using teachers in other schools or knowledgeable peers at Whitmore to help with problems they could not resolve. Repairs that a teacher or those the teacher consulted could not perform were referred to commercial companies with which the school district had arranged service contracts.

These procedures were very inefficient since teachers often had to wait a substantial amount of time to get assistance with problems that a knowledgeable person on the spot could have solved almost instantly. For example, we observed one situation in which a computer in a business class was not used for some time as the teacher waited for a repair person to return her call. After finally receiving this call, the teacher, as instructed, checked the machine and discovered that the cause of the problem was that the computer was not plugged in. Ms. Prentiss described the difficulties she encountered before she persuaded Mr. East to help her out during his free period, which luckily coincided with part of the time the computer room for gifted students was open:

Ms. Prentiss: At first . . . it was terrible. . . . I called my husband every day at work [for advice]. . . . I'd ask him all these question. I was awful. I could just see this was not going to work. . . . But having someone to talk over the problems with was invaluable.

Even with Ms. Prentiss and Mr. East doing their very best, the 6 to 12 students who usually came to the computer room at lunch time could not count on having machines and software operating smoothly, as the following excerpt from our field notes indicates:

The students . . . continue to have a lot of very nitty-gritty problems. Kathy can't get the printer going. . . . She's scowling and says in an annoyed tone of voice, "Please help me." Mr. East suggests several things, and after they try out four or five different approaches they finally get the paper to print out. Ms. Prentiss has been working with Sharon on word processing. . . . For the last 10 minutes cries like, "I don't believe it," and "Oh, no. Not again!" have been emanating from both of them. . . . Finally, Ms. Prentiss calls Mr. East over. . . . Sharon is clearly getting anxious, pacing around, picking her nails, and the like. She takes her disc and inserts it in another computer hooked up to a different printer. She can't get this printer to work. . . . Ms. Prentiss rushes over to try to fix it saying, "I just don't believe it!" Ms. Prentiss comes over to me [the observer] and says, "I feel like quitting this . . . ." At this point Mark calls to Ms. Prentiss, "I need help . . . ." Ms. Prentiss puts her head down on the desk briefly. She looks at me with what appears to be a mixture of mock and real despair and trudges over to Mark. [Later in the same period] Dan is trying to use a printer that Mr. East thought he had fixed. Dan's essay comes out quadruple spaced. In addition, every single word is underlined. Ms. Prentiss looks at it and breaks into almost hysterical laughter. Dan looks annoyed. Ms. Prentiss says, "I'm sorry, this is just too much – too, too much! . . . " Mr. Adams and Mr. East are still working on the second malfunctioning printer. Mr. Adams says, "You know I have a trick. What I do with my Radio Shack computer is just turn it on its side and hit it. Maybe that will work here . . . ." They turn it on its side and give it a whack as one of them holds the tension on the paper feed. The machine begins to work.

The knowledge needed to make minor hardware repairs, to be able to distinguish which problems one can fix and which require outside help, and to operate specific pieces of software is only part of what is needed to utilize computers effectively in teaching. Locating, trying out, and keeping abreast of new and better software also takes time and energy. Many of the teachers interested in using their computers felt that they did not get adequate assistance with this task:

Mr. Powers: I've been ordering software out of catalogs because these's no person around the school board that's familiar with Power and Energy, that knows what software is available. . . . [There is no one here who] says, "Hey, this is a good program. Let's buy it," or "We want you to try this program or preview this program." It's basically look in the catalog. If it looks like it has anything to do with the curriculum I'll order it. . . . All the [Power and Energy] teachers got a computer at the same time. However, all of them are not using them in the same way because there is no standard set for this part of the curriculum.

Other teachers had the same kind of problems. Without a knowledgeable person available for ready consultation, they failed to order software out of inertia or a sense of uncertainty about whether it would be useful. Those who did order it were frequently disappointed and reported that such disappointments discouraged them from further similar expenditures. All this is not to say that it was impossible for teachers to get useful information on software. Whitmore was only 4 or 5 miles from a university-based educational software library. Teachers reported that if and when they attended professional conferences, sessions about educational software were common. For some subject areas the school district did purchase software and provided teachers with some opportunities to learn about it. However, effective utilization of most of these avenues required some degree of extra energy, initiative, or time. Many teachers just preferred not to add any extra activities to what they perceived to be their already overburdened schedules. Others were skeptical enough about the value of computing for their students that they chose to invest their energies elsewhere. Peer norms among the teachers clearly did not require teachers to go out of their way to give students the opportunity to work with computers, as indicated by this excerpt from an interview with Ms. Prentiss:

Interviewer: How have other teachers responded to your efforts to make computers available [by opening the gifted student computer room at lunchtime]?

Ms. Prentiss: Generally surprise. . . . and . . . just "Why?" "Why?" It's one thing if you can do *your own* work on it, but why would you [do the extra work]? . . . I've never been so isolated from teachers as I have [been] this year. I don't even eat with them. . . . So they . . . think I'm weird because I want to socialize with kids.

Without someone on hand to encourage and facilitate their efforts, many teachers never really tried to explore what use they could make of computers in instruction, and those who did try often became discouraged.

Overload of Knowledgeable Teachers

Becker's (1984) work suggests that individual teachers very often play a major role in providing the impetus for a school's obtaining instructional computers. Although Becker reports a trend for administrators to become more involved in this process than was the case in earlier years, individual teachers still play a crucial role in the implementation stage with regard to issues such as deciding what software will be purchased and providing informal training for other teachers.

Such was certainly the case at Whitmore. For example, from all reports if Ms. Prentiss had not volunteered to supervise the computer room that was open for gifted students at lunchtime as her "duty" period instead of doing something like monitoring the halls, it would not have been used on a daily basis. Similarly, Mr. Adams often served as a resource for his colleagues at Whitmore. Since there was no individual or group at Whitmore with formal responsibility for helping teachers learn to use computers and assisting them with problems they encountered after they had learned enough to attempt to use the computers in their classroom, any increase in the use of computers within the school meant added burdens on teachers like Mr. Adams, Mr. East, and Ms. Prentiss. This put knowledgeable teachers in a position of conflict when colleagues or students requested help because that help had to be taken from either their own personal time or from time officially allocated to other more traditional purposes, namely, teaching or preparing to teach. Although in principle the teachers were glad to share their knowledge, in practice helping others sometimes felt like a burden:

Interviewer: What are the one or two major impediments to greater usage of the computers?

Ms. Prentiss: The time for some *one* person to coordinate the use of the room. . . . What I didn't realize when we started is that a teacher who doesn't have complete control of the class . . . and know everything about the machines . . . could cause so much damage. They walk out of the room and who's got to deal with it? You know who. . . . It's selfish, but I didn't bargain to . . . I often give two periods a day and lots of extra time. . . . One time that other teacher asked [to use the room]. I had to teach her class – make up the dittos [about using the computers]. Hey, I don't want word to get out I'm doing this. Then every . . . teacher . . .

The Lack of Incentives and the Presence of Disincentives

As has already been discussed, few teachers willingly devoted energy to learning about the potential of the instructional use of computers out of an a priori conviction that computers have a great deal to offer their students. Incentives for them to try to make effective use of computers in instruction at Whitmore were few and far between. Disincentives were easier to find. In addition to the lack of either really effective training or a supportive infrastructure, teachers often encountered difficulty in getting appropriate supplies when they did use computers in their classes, as indicated by the following excerpt from project field notes:

> Tammy tells me that Mr. Checkhov wants them to conserve the printer ribbons. There is only one left for the rest of the year [today is March 10]. Students were urged to use the computer less.

On occasion, teachers even reported bringing in computer-related supplies from home because they were unable to get them through the school:

Interviewer: Are you able to get the supplies you need [for the computer], like paper or anything of that sort?

Mr. Powers: I order one case of paper each semester, which really isn't enough. I have to go and try to bum it from other departments. I've already brought some in from home.

Interviewer: Is it just that it's hard [to get] or is it that you're not *able* to order as much as you need?

Mr. Powers: When we order as much as we want . . . they start cutting things off the requisition. So I find that if I keep the orders low, at least I get that rather than nothing.

The disincentives for computer use were not all material. Teachers faced the risk of looking bad not only in front of their students,

130

as discussed earlier, but also in front of administrators whose evaluations were important to them:

> Allen is working on a biology project [in the room where the computers for gifted students are]. Steve is helping Ms. Prentiss load paper in a printer. Ms. Prentiss formally introduces Steve to the two vice-principals [who are visiting the room today]. One of them says to Ms. Prentiss, "I thought this would be an organized lab. . . ." After they tire of watching Allen, they go over to Ms. Prentiss. One of them says very audibly [to the other], "Boy, I don't see anyone doing anything . . . except for Ms. Prentiss." He [then] says to Ms. Prentiss, "You told us that you've got everything down to a T!" Then the vice-principals watch Ms. Prentiss try to print out something on the printer, but the printer wasn't cooperating. Dave . . . asks, . . . "Will you take the computers away?" The vice-principal replies, "No, we'll take Ms. Prentiss away." Ms. Prentiss smiles somewhat nervously and says that she'll try to get the printer to work. . . . At this point another vice-principal comes in. One of the vice-principals who was there before him turns to him and says, "Ms. Prentiss is showing us how computers don't work today." Two of the vice-principals leave.

Given that the school system provided Ms. Prentiss with virtually no training and that she voluntarily gave up her lunch break to supervise the lab so that the computers would not sit idle, the rather unsupportive attitude of the vice-principals was quite striking.

The partial payment of tuition for courses designed to build teachers' computer skills was one incentive to which a few of Whitmore's teachers responded. However, this was clearly not enough to induce most teachers to spend their own time and money on taking computer courses. A more obvious incentive would be to pay teachers to build their skills. Even Mr. Carter, whose fairly strong resistance to computer use was apparent in an earlier excerpt from an interview, might have been willing to explore the possibilities if paid to do so:

Interviewer: Let me ask you a hypothetical question. Is there anything that the school or the school board could do if they wanted to entice teachers to see whether there was anything useful they could find in using computers? What would they have to do?

Mr. Carter: They'd have to pay me money.

When asked a similar question, many of Whitmore's other teachers mentioned similar ideas such as paid summer workshops that would give teachers a reasonably extended time in which to explore the computer's possibilities. The problem with these suggestions is, of course, that they would be quite expensive. Furthermore, there is at least the possibility that some teachers who have little serious interest in actually using computers in their classrooms might see such workshops as a reasonably painless way to supplement their income, thus wasting money from the perspective of the school system.

One other possible incentive is suggested by the fact that a number of teachers reported that they had initially started using computers to create tests and to compute grades, that is, in ways that made it easier or more efficient to perform administrative or clerical parts of their jobs. Some of these teachers then proceeded to experiment with ways in which they could use computers for instructional purposes. To the extent that the motivation to perform these parts of a teacher's job in an easier or more efficient way is salient, it might be used to overcome the inertia and anxiety that kept some teachers from ever venturing to touch a computer in classroom settings. It is possible that a familiarity with the technology gained through such use might then lead at least some teachers to venture further and see how and if they might use computers in their teaching.

SUMMARY AND CONCLUSIONS

Computers available for instructional purposes were not used very much outside of computer science classes and the geometry classrooms that served as the field test site for the GPTutor. A wide variety of factors appeared to contribute to this situation. One factor of fundamental importance was the teachers' perception that much existing educational software does not have enough educational potential to make it worth using. In addition, many teachers found it difficult to envision how they could integrate the use of one or two computers into their rather traditional whole class methods of instruction. Furthermore, they were not anxious to adopt new methods that might be more compatible with extensive computer use, which Honey and Moeller (1990) suggest importantly influences teachers' decisions about integrating technology into their curricula. Most teachers were also quite unfamiliar with computers and with educational software. Inertia, concern about the impact of low levels of computer competence on their authority in the classroom, and anxiety about dealing with a new and unfamiliar machine all conspired to keep things this way. In addition, real problems with the training available to teachers at Whitmore and the fact that the school had neither an infrastructure to support teachers' attempts to learn nor many incentives designed to induce them to take the first steps toward increasing their knowledge in this domain contributed to the fact that many of the computers available for students' use at Whitmore were used quite infrequently.

5

THE COMPUTER ROOM
FOR GIFTED STUDENTS
A (Bright, White Boys')
Lunch Club

THE PRECEDING CHAPTER ADDRESSED ONE FACET OF THE issue of how the social context of the school shapes computer use. This chapter and the next continue exploration of this issue with a focus on students rather than teachers, in particular on the role that gender played in influencing computer use at Whitmore.

My goal here is not just to add to the literature suggesting that gender is indeed related to student computer use, since the existing evidence related to this general point is substantial (Anderson, Welch, & Harris, 1984; Becker & Sterling, 1987; Chen, 1986; Hess & Miura, 1985; Linn, 1985; Lockheed, 1985; Miura, 1986). As Sutton (1991) points out: "The inequalities are known. The future task should be to understand the complexities of the problem better" (p. 494). Consistent with this point of view, this chapter and the next will attempt to analyze the forces that conspired to create the differences observed at Whitmore and to discuss some of the complexities of the situation that contributed to building and maintaining these differences.

There are many possible ways to approach discussing the impact of gender on students' opportunities for using, and reactions to, computers at Whitmore since the influence seemed so ubiquitous. I have chosen to explore these issues in the context of discussing two very different milieus at Whitmore – the room full of computers reserved for gifted students and the Computer Science 2 classes.

The computer room for gifted students, although admittedly not typical of Whitmore's classrooms either in terms of the kind of students observed or the activities in which the students engaged, is an especially revealing milieu in which to observe students' attitudes toward, and reactions to, computers for two reasons. First, students used the computers voluntarily during their lunch break. They were thus much freer than in their regular classes to decide what they wanted to do when using the computers and to talk with each other about their reactions. Second, the students' behavior on the computers in this setting was not shaped by the fact that working with the machines was a requirement or contributed directly to their grades, as it was elsewhere at Whitmore. Thus, again, students were free to act on their preferences rather than having to weigh the impact of their behavior on their grades. The computer science classes to be discussed in Chapter 6 function as a useful contrast since the students there were both from a different academic track in the school and worked under conditions more representative of most of the students' school day. In spite of the marked differences between the nature of these two milieus and the students who frequented them, the two cases have two important things in common – girls were much less likely to be found than their male counterparts in both settings. In addition, the experiences they had in those settings were quite different from the experiences their male peers had.

Before proceeding in this chapter to discuss how gender influenced gifted students' reactions to the availability of computers for their use at lunchtime, I will do two things. First, I will briefly discuss the nature of sex roles at Whitmore in order to lay the groundwork for that discussion. Second, I will describe how the room reserved for gifted students' computer use was set up and run to give the reader an idea of the way it functioned.

SEX ROLES AT WHITMORE

In spite of all the changes that have occurred in our society in the past several decades with regard to male and female roles in both the home and the workplace, students at Whitmore behaved in a way very consistent with traditional gender roles and stereotypes.

135

The school, in general, seemed to accept and sometimes even reinforce this tendency. Many aspects of the school situation reflected or modeled rather traditional gender roles and relations. For example, the principal and most of the high-level administrators were male in spite of the fact that almost precisely half of the faculty were women. Similarly, as mentioned in Chapter 1, the faculty tended to teach subjects traditional for their gender, with 70% to 80% of the English teachers being women, and 70% to 80% of the math and science teachers being men.

Several male faculty members used terms of endearment such as *honey* or *sweetheart* in addressing female students. Neither they nor female teachers were observed addressing male students in this way. In contrast, male teachers were more likely to engage in displays of strength or toughness when interacting in a friendly way with boys:

> Mr. Deppe, a biology teacher, joins Dick in kidding Steve, who yesterday climbed inside a computer security cover. They tease him about being small enough to fit in. . . . The question of Steve's size raises the whole issue of male prowess, and Mr. Deppe challenges Dick to punch him saying solidly, "You can't hurt me!" Dick says, "Really? Do you want me to?" The teacher says, "Sure, go ahead!" Dick . . . gives him a fairly hard punch in the abdomen and Mr. Deppe just smiles.

Many of Whitmore's teachers clearly expected that a substantial proportion of the female students would work during at least some period of their lives. However, there were clearly forces at work that encouraged any tendencies students might have to stay within career paths traditional for their gender, as Mr. Powers' remarks in an interview indicate:

Interviewer: Do you have any girls in your [Power and Energy] classes?

Mr. Powers: Yea, I had two. One decided she didn't want to get her hands dirty. I blame [the small number of female students] on the counselors. The guidance department in this school is very old. I would say that the youngest [counselor]

136

is in their middle fifties. They are under the impression that there are girls' industrial arts classes and boys' industrial arts classes. I've had girls go through this course extremely successfully, As and Bs, and they earned every last point. . . . Yet these people when they go to schedule these kids . . . they'll say, "Well, girls got to take the sewing and the cooking . . . " and that nonsense and not put them in an industrial arts course unless they insist on it. I've been here 20 years and I haven't been able to change . . . [what] goes on up there with those people. They do what they want to do. . . . Come September, whoever walks in the door walks in the door and 99% of them are boys.

Although many teachers encouraged the career aspirations of female students, there were also those who conveyed a very traditional message as evidenced by the following field notes:

Mr. Carter [a math teacher] begins to talk with Tessie. They . . . discuss things such as marriage, the function of a wife, love, and relationships. Mr. Carter says jokingly that the function of a wife is "to cook and make babies." Tessie is thinking about getting married soon to her boyfriend . . . who would be a senior now at Whitmore if he had not dropped out.

Traditional assumptions about sex roles were apparent not only in explicit discussions of students' futures, like the interaction just presented, but also in the casual jokes and comments that were a part of everyday classroom life, as the following field notes from a geometry class suggest:

The teacher says, "Now pi, that doesn't stand for your mom's pies, the kind she made for you. It stands for 3.14 or 22/7."

Student interactions in the classroom, lunchroom, and hallways made it clear that gender was an important organizing principle of student social life and that traditional gender roles had a strong hold on students' ways of thinking and acting. At the most basic level, gender clearly influenced who students chose to spend their time with in class settings. Typically, students did the majority of their classroom socializing with students of their own gender.

When they were free to choose their own seats, they showed a very strong tendency to sit near those of the same gender. For example, it was common for field notes from computer science classes to indicate that even in classes with a roughly equal number of boys and girls seating was segregated by gender, with the very large majority of students sitting next to others of the same sex in the lab.

This is not to say that boys and girls ignored each other. Quite the contrary, they did interact a substantial amount. Furthermore, it sometimes appeared that some interactions within the single-sex peer group occurred as much for the sake of opposite-sex others who might be observing them as for their value in the ongoing interaction. Nonetheless, except in the cases in which classmates were involved in ongoing dating relationships, most students entered and left classes with same-sex peers and chatted with same-sex peers during the majority of the time they devoted to socializing in the classroom. Similarly, when students had to select partners for academic tasks the clear tendency was to choose students of their own gender. For example, virtually all of the students in the GPTutor classes who worked in pairs chose partners of the same sex. The tendency to work in same-sex pairs was also apparent in computer science:

> Of the 16 students in Mr. Edwards's computer science class today, 14 are consistently working in pairs with their neighbors [i.e., the student at the computer next to theirs]. One girl begins to work as the third party in a group with two other white females. . . . The pairing is all girls with girls and boys with boys except for one pair that is composed of a black fellow and a white girl. Talking appears to be completely within these groups.

Gender influenced not only who students tended to spend their time with in school, but also the themes and activities that characterized peer interactions. For example, an emphasis on the actual or symbolic display of male strength was quite apparent at Whitmore. Sometimes this was embedded in conversations about sports, which were a popular form of recreation for boys as well as a way for them to attempt to win status with peers of both sexes. However, the theme of prowess was also readily apparent in many

138

other contexts, as is clear from the following three excerpts from field notes:

> Chuck spent the whole period [in Visual Communication] drawing a sketch of a strong man. The man is depicted as being very muscular, something like you might see in a body-building magazine.

> Sara and Serena are sitting in Mr. Chekhov's office asking male students whether or not they can make muscles. . . . These two students are collecting names of boys and girls who will pose for the New Year's calendar [they are doing as a class project]. Copies of last year's calendars are in the back room. . . . There are girls in somewhat provocative poses and boys flexing their muscles.

> Jim showed me his new tatoo. It's on his right shoulder and is of a lion. It is 3 to 4 inches in diameter and is done in much detail. Jim is very proud of it and he shows it to many students. I ask whether or not it hurt and he replies that it didn't hurt much at all.

Consistent with this emphasis on attaining and displaying strength and athletic prowess, or symbols of these qualities, was a marked tendency for boys to call favorable attention to themselves by making remarks that highlighted their accomplishments, be they social, athletic, or academic:

> Rick and Denise are working together today in computer science class. I hear Rick say, "I'm a brain, a scholar student. I should own one of these," referring to his computer. ["Scholar" is Whitmore's name for the track for strong students with IQs well above average. It is different from the program for gifted students, which is for students with very high IQs regardless of their academic performance].

Sometimes these claims highlighted positive personal attributes or accomplishments, without any specific comparison with others. However, often this attempt to call attention to one's positive qualities and achievements involved direct competition and comparison with others, sometimes including clear denigration of them:

139

Bill . . . says, "Oh man. This is weak. Look at this." Evidently he has come up to another point where the GPTutor will not let him do the proof his way. . . . Bill clearly has a very superior attitude. He says to Mr. Adams, "I found a flaw in your system." Mr. Adams makes a sort of grimacing smile and throws a mock punch at Bill saying, "Well, we found plenty of flaws in you pal," referring I assume to Bill's superior attitude [about which Sonia was just complaining].

This emphasis on highlighting one's accomplishments and the often accompanying unblushing demand for approbation when challenges were met was much less apparent in the girls' interactions. In fact, it was not unusual for girls to take a quite different approach, downplaying or otherwise negating their accomplishments:

Mike turns to Roy [who is also working on the GPTutor] and says, "What problem are you on?" Roy replies that he is on problem 232. Mike replies, "I'm on 236 . . . 234 is a tough one." Mike then turns around and asks Ruth what problem Sharon is on. Ruth says, "I can't see." Then she turns to Sharon and says, "What problem are you on?" Sharon looks up and sees all three of the other students looking at her. She says, "None of your business," smiles, and turns around. Mark says, "She's way ahead, on 285 or something like that. What are you on Ruth?" Ruth replies, "225," very quietly. Mark says, "What?" Ruth replies, "Oh, I'm way behind."

It is probable that the contrast between boys' and girls' behavior was so clear because the majority of the classes we observed could be considered traditionally male subjects, such as geometry and computer science. Outstanding accomplishments or boastful behavior on the part of girls in such classes might call their femininity into question, either in their own eyes or in those of traditionally oriented peers. In contrast, meeting challenges and then boasting about one's talents in these areas was to some extent a way for boys to help build a masculine image for themselves. Most students were well aware that academic proficiency was a route to obtaining desired rewards, including, at least in the future, the kind of professional status or earning power that would serve men well in attracting women. Thus, the boys at Whitmore often appeared to act as male college students report they act when trying to impress women, that is, to boast of their accomplishments and, by implication, of their earning potential (Buss, 1988). This idea that academic accomplishment can yield sexual rewards for men was embodied in a poster that the chairman of the math department duplicated and circulated, as the following field notes indicate:

> Mr. Adams comes over to me [a male observer] and shows me a poster that Mr. Erie has photocopied. . . . It shows a slim young woman in a bikini, and the caption implies that men who like calculus are able to attract women like the one pictured.

Although the differences just described in boys' and girls' behavior may well have been partially due to the nature of the subject matter covered in many of the classes we observed, this does not seem to explain the phenomenon completely since similar, though perhaps less pronounced, patterns were apparent in students' interactions in milieus that were less stereotypically traditional male domains. In general, girls seemed somewhat less concerned about establishing a dominance hierarchy based on claims about their personal characteristics or accomplishments, which is consistent with cross-cultural findings in developmental psychology (Omark, Omark, & Edelman, 1975) as well as with other studies of peer interaction conducted in the Waterford school system (Schofield, 1981, 1989a) and elsewhere (Best, 1983; Goodwin, 1990).

In contrast to the boys' emphasis on outshining their peers in bodily strength, athletic ability, or academic ability, girls paid a great deal of obvious attention to aspects of their physical appearance related to traditional ideals of female sexual attractiveness, often combing their hair or applying nail polish or makeup in classroom situations. In addition, an interest in clothes, jewelry, and cosmetics figured prominently in girls' classroom social talk. Thus, their behavior was very similar to that in which female college students engage in an effort to make themselves appealing to men (Buss, 1988).

In addition to displaying a concern about how to enhance their

141

attractiveness through the grooming or decoration of their faces and bodies, girls at Whitmore also showed awareness of and concern about meeting standards of feminine beauty relating to their weight and bust size. Their attention to these aspects of themselves was clearly reinforced by boys, for whom it was very salient and who were not shy about making their interest in such matters obvious:

> Toward the end of the Visual Communication class Derrick and Serena are working together testing out a new sort of light meter on a camera. Derrick is taking photographs of Serena. . . . He says to her, *"Okay baby! Show me some cleavage!"* . . . He moves up closer to her and says, "Don't just stand there. Do something. Give me a pose. . . . Stick it out."

> I [the observer] ask Dick if he has a sister named Arlene since I discover his last name is the same of that of a female student in another class I'm observing. He says that Arlene is his sister. . . . [Soon afterwards] I overhear Mike asking Dick whether his sister "has a nice build." Dick replies that she doesn't.

> Tammie, Margie, and Rebecca . . . are talking about a geometry problem, but then Ron, a classmate, starts to kid Margie about being fat. [I, the observer, would say that she's about average build for a high school student. She is definitely not fat according to what I would consider any reasonable standard.] Margie stops smiling and rolls her eyes. She looks hurt. Ron says, as if he didn't expect her to take it so seriously, "No offense intended. You're not really fat. Some people spread out all over. That's fat!"

Also consistent with traditional sex role stereotypes and the findings of previous studies of friendship in high school (Kinney, 1993; Youniss & Smollar, 1985), girls seemed more oriented toward relating to others, including sharing their experiences, thoughts, and feelings with one another. For example, it was common for girls to bring in photographs of friends or family and to use the photos as a basis for relating tales of good times they had shared with others. Such behavior was never observed in male peer groups, which seemed to define friendship more in terms of doing things together than in terms of discussing reactions to experiences

142

in any very personal or revealing way. This contrast in behavior, apparent at Whitmore, is also consistent with prior research that has found that girls tend to emphasize intimacy more than boys in thinking about friendship (Grant & Fine, 1992; Lever, 1976; Mitchell, 1981; Rubin, 1980; Schofield, 1989a).

In sum, students at Whitmore acted in ways very consistent with many aspects of traditional gender roles and stereotypes. This conclusion should not be construed to mean that such strong gender-linked roles are inevitable or desirable. Rather, it seems clear that a variety of factors, including many aspects of the school's structure and functioning, help to shape and reinforce rather traditional gender roles, as was discussed briefly earlier. Of primary interest here are the implications of these patterns for students' reactions to the availability of computers in the room set aside for gifted students, which will be discussed after the following brief description of the room itself.

THE GIFTED STUDENT COMPUTER ROOM: THE LUNCHROOM

As was discussed in the preceding chapter, the computers purchased for the gifted student program were grouped together in one room after it became apparent that the original decision to distribute one computer to each of the teachers who had gifted student classes was not conducive to their use. The hope was that once the 15 or so Apple IIe's were all grouped together in an environment in which there would be roughly one machine per student, teachers would use them more. In fact, the computers were not used very frequently in this way, as indicated in Chapter 4. However, they did get used almost daily during the lunch hour after an English teacher, Ms. Prentiss, volunteered to supervise the room. The room was open for two consecutive lunch periods of about 25 minutes each. Ms. Prentiss assisted students as best she could within the limits imposed by her initially rudimentary level of knowledge and the fact that she received no release time from her teaching to help her deal with equipment problems or explore

143

the software available for use in the room. She also took the initiative to persuade Mr. East, a chemistry teacher who was a computer hobbyist, to come down to the room for one of these lunch periods on a regular basis to help out with problems she was not able to handle by herself.

Students were allowed to use any of the software available in the room. The majority of the software consisted of games with at least some educational component. The detective game, Where in the World is Carmen SanDiego?, was clearly the most popular. Other software available included typing tutorials, a biology game called Microbe, word processing programs, and software packages designed to prepare students to perform well on the Scholastic Aptitude Tests. Some of the software was purchased through the gifted student program. Some was donated by teachers or obtained in various sorts of informal trades with individuals ranging from staff at other schools to equipment repair people. Students were allowed to bring in software from home as long as Ms. Prentiss felt that it had at least some minimal intellectual or educational value. Thus, chess games, Mastermind, and bridge were allowed, but arcade-type video games were not. This did not stop students from occasionally trying to smuggle in Pacman and other purely recreational games. However, it did keep usage of such games to a minimum.

Although Ms. Prentiss strongly encouraged students to make use of the resources in the room, she recognized that it was their lunch break. Thus, she permitted a substantial amount of socializing, and the norms for student behavior were very different from classroom norms. The atmosphere was informal and relaxed. Students chatted in an animated manner, moved around freely, drank sodas and snacked as they used the computers, tried to score points in imaginary basketball games by throwing crumpled wads of paper into the wastebasket, and called to each other across the room when excited about some accomplishment. This atmosphere was reflected by the fact that in referring to the room, the students often called it "the lunchroom" but never "the lab."

The room in which the gifted students used computers was observed during both lunch periods during the 2 years of the study. Thus, there were four different groups observed regularly. These groups typically ranged in size from 5 to 10 students. Each lunch period had a fairly stable nucleus of students who came regularly. The different groups varied in the extent to which there were also other occasional attenders. However, members of the nucleus virtually always outnumbered others, giving a noticeable stability to the composition of the group. Students in a particular group were generally from the same grade, with 9th and 10th graders predominating. Many of the regular attendees were in one of Ms. Prentiss's English classes. Another substantial group were students who used the GPTutor in Mr. Adams's classes. (Mr. Adams was one of the few teachers who brought his gifted student classes down to this room on some relatively regular basis.) The large majority of the students were members of the gifted student program, which meant they had IQs near to or above 130. However, Ms. Prentiss did not discourage the interest of several students from the advanced track who regularly showed up. In fact, a number of these students were unusually helpful to Ms. Prentiss, almost as if they wanted to repay her for letting them participate. To the best of my knowledge, students from the regular or vocational tracks never visited the lab.

PEER INTERACTION IN THE COMPUTER ROOM: THE LUNCHROOM AS A BRIGHT, WHITE BOYS' CLUB

Whitmore's student body was very heterogeneous, as discussed in Chapter 1. The gifted student program was somewhat more homogeneous, tending to enroll students whose parents were relatively more educated and affluent than those of the average Whitmore student. Thus, although the numbers of boys and girls in the gifted student program were virtually identical, whites outnumbered African Americans by three or four to one. Given the composition of the program, one of the most striking things about the students who chose to come to the computer room was that with the exception of the students in one of the four groups observed, which had almost as many girls as boys in it, they were virtually all white males, as the following excerpts from two sets of field notes suggest:

Today, as is frequent, the second lunch period attendees are all white males.

I remained with Ms. Prentiss and Steve after the bell signaling the end of the lunch period rang. . . . After Steve left, Ms. Prentiss remarked to me, "Boy, it's always the same thing in here every day." I replied, "What do you mean?" She responded, "Well, it's always me and a bunch of young boys."

The boys who came to the computer room were generally white, very bright, and young, being typically 9th or 10th graders. Quite a few of them fit the stereotypical image of the computer hacker or nerd in many respects. Others certainly perceived them this way:

Interviewer: Are there certain kinds of students who use computers more than most?

Rick: Yeah, it's like "The Revenge of the Nerds." . . . The kind of person . . . who wouldn't go out. . . . They would rather sit at home playing games on a computer, typing programs. . . . All during lunch they go up to the computer room [referring to the gifted student computer room] instead of sitting around. . . . Everybody basically just sits around, and then there's the ones who go up to the computer room.

On occasion they could be heard describing themselves or their friends with such terms, as occurred in this interchange between students in the computer room at lunch:

Mark, who is talking to Allen, says very seriously, "You'd like Fairmount Avenue [the city's best-known and best-regarded high school]. I know you would. Seriously, you'd like it better [than Whitmore]." One of the other boys in the group looks skeptical and says, "I don't know." Allen says with a half-embarrassed smile, "I know you would because there are more nerds there."

Even those boys who did not fit this image well were hardly striking embodiments of the male image as previously described. For example, few of the boys who regularly came to this room at lunch were members of athletic teams at Whitmore, and those who were participated in low-status sports, such as track, rather than the higher prestige sports such as basketball and football. In addition, few, if any, appeared to be involved in the almost ostentatiously high-risk activities, such as fist fights or car theft, which created a macho image for some of their peers at the same time it sometimes brought them into conflict with the law.

As discussed earlier in this chapter, masculinity at Whitmore appeared to be understood in a very traditional way, including an emphasis on engaging in activities that allow for the demonstration of physical strength and athletic ability. Yet these were not typically the dimensions on which the brightest boys compared favorably with their peers from the other tracks with whom they mingled in the cafeteria. Many of the boys were consciously aware that the computer room was a kind of retreat from the pressures of the high school social scene with which they were not equipped to cope easily. One of them described it this way in an interview:

> The cafeteria isn't too hot. . . . If you don't fit into a clique you are sitting by yourself. A kid who transferred from Fairmount didn't like eating in the cafeteria because he didn't know anyone and he felt . . . secluded. So he came up [here].

The computer room, however, was more than a refuge from the hurly-burly of the cafeteria, with its attendant threat to the self-esteem of boys who were at a social disadvantage in that context. It provided a context in which these boys were able to build friendships and enact behaviors that supported a positive traditionally masculine image of themselves.

With regard to the room's function in fostering friendships, it is important to note that the atmosphere in the computer room was not serious or task-oriented. Rather, the room functioned more as a setting for a social club, with the computers providing the activity

147

around which socializing often centered. Although the students clearly enjoyed using the computers, especially to play Carmen SanDiego, they often just sat and chatted with each other about classes, grades, or sports as they ate their lunches. Similarly, it was common for students to watch while others played computer games, introjecting questions or comments frequently. A number of students who were participants in the production of a Shakespearean play supervised by Ms. Prentiss spent a substantial amount of time in this room rehearsing favorite scenes, especially those involving swordplay. Thus, this room provided a milieu in which boys who were not part of the popular in-group could develop activity-based friendships. This is consistent with Kinney's (1993) work, which suggests that as boys who have been labeled "nerds" in middle school enter high school they often engage in school-based clubs and activities to reduce their isolation, develop rewarding relationships, and begin to feel better about themselves. Commenting on the relaxed friendly atmosphere, Ms. Prentiss called the room the students' "home away from home."

There were a number of ways in which activities in the computer room also contributed to bolstering students' sense of masculinity. First, it provided a setting in which the boys could fantasize about their physical prowess without the potentially threatening presence of others who were actually nearer the traditional male ideal in this regard. This tendency was evident in both students' work on the computer and their social interactions. For example, one boy used a graphics program to produce a poster covered with pictures of a skull and crossbones. The poster, which he put up on a bulletin board in the room, proclaimed in large letters, "MESS with the BEST, DIE with the REST." An emphasis on high-prestige sports and other masculine activities was also frequently evident in the boys' playful socializing:

> Steve and Dick . . . laugh and talk loudly. On several occasions Dick throws pieces of paper in the trash basket. . . . Sometimes he pretends he is a basketball player making a basket. Other times he pretends he is the center on a football team hiking the paper into the trash can.

148

In addition, many of the games that were available for use let students take on, in fantasy, valued, traditionally male roles such as that of a physician or a pilot. In Carmen SanDiego, the most popular game, students played the role of a detective following a glamorous thief around the world. Thus, they were able to assume in their fantasies a role that has commonly been presented in books, movies, and television as typically requiring a rather tough traditionally masculine kind of personality:

> Ernie is seated at the computer [playing Carmen SanDiego]. . . . He tells me [the observer], "We really get into games," meaning that the students become very involved in them. . . . He finally catches the fugitive who has been hiding from him in various parts of the world. . . . Ernie appears to be enjoying this very much. He says to the fugitive, who is being led off to the judge, *"Okay, you're busted! You're gone! Good-bye!"*

The boys were not shy about calling attention to their success at these games. In fact, they often trumpeted it in loud tones, asking implicitly or explicitly for approbation from their peers or Ms. Prentiss:

> Charles is back at his terminal. He exclaims triumphantly, "Am I excellent or what?" Ms. Prentiss responds from where she is working on a computer with Tom, "Yes, you are."

The one piece of gamelike software that could have been construed as dealing primarily with traditionally feminine themes or roles was the typing tutorial. However, even this piece of software was masculinized. For example, its name was Typo Attack, invoking a military image, and it used themes of destruction and violence to add excitement to the learning process:

> Everet is working on Typo Attack. . . . The object is to hit the key on the keyboard that appears on the screen. So, for example, if an A appears on the upper left corner of the screen, the student is to type in the letter A. If he or she does so [quickly enough] and then hits the return key an incoming object explodes. . . . If the student is not fast enough . . . the incoming object hits an object

representing the flying saucer in which the student is supposedly seated and it explodes.

The computer room not only provided an environment that supported fantasy behavior reinforcing certain aspects of traditional masculinity for the students who attended; it also fostered competitive behaviors, another very obvious aspect of male social behavior at Whitmore. The focus for much of this competition was the students' performance on the games they played on the computers. The fact that many of the games had built-in features that displayed and ranked the scores of the various players and awarded honorific titles to the high scorers played an important role in promoting keen competition:

> Mitchell has checked two or three of the Carmen SanDiego discs to see if they are working. He plays the game for about 5 minutes after checking the third disc. He says, "My year-long goal is to be the high scorer on all nine discs."

> Theodore has never played Carmen SanDiego before. . . . He sees . . . that Ernie is an ace detective and asks how he gained that status. Ernie tells him that you must solve 10 crimes in order to become an ace and adds that everybody should bow down before him for this accomplishment. [Ernie is the only student who has become an ace.] Theodore wonders aloud how he can enter his name. . . . Bill tells him to delete someone who hasn't been playing very much. . . . Ernie says in a serious tone, "If you delete me, I'll kill you." As Theodore plays he asks Ernie questions such as, "Where is Swahili spoken?" Ernie helps him out and then adds before leaving that he [Ernie] is an ace sleuth, whereas Theodore is only a novice.

Interestingly, there were a number of features of the competition that either minimized the chances of losing or mitigated the sting of defeat, while nonetheless not appearing to undermine the satisfaction students gained from doing well. First, the competition students engaged in was focused on activities that were, after all, just games. The thrill of winning did not seem to be dimmed by this. Yet the fact that the competition had no implications for students' grades or future educational options may have allowed students to engage in it playfully and for enjoyment rather than in a way that created tension and strain. Second, since the games varied widely in some respects, with knowledge in biology most pertinent for success in some, knowledge in geography and social studies most useful in others, and logical or strategic abilities crucial in yet others, it was possible for students to play games in areas that reflected their strengths and thus to enhance their chances of winning or at least ranking well. Third, the fact that a relatively small number of students came to each session and that those in one's own particular lunch period rather than the larger group were the most salient comparison group increased the chances that a given student could find some game at which to excel.

For a subset of the boys who regularly came to the computer room at lunchtime, the positive feelings generated by the opportunities to build friendships, indulge in fantasies, and enjoy the computer games were quite regularly supplemented by gratifying experiences of challenge and mastery provided by the fact that they often worked with Ms. Prentiss to solve problems arising in operating the computers there. The students' assistance was particularly helpful to Ms. Prentiss when Mr. East was not there because a number of these students clearly knew more about certain aspects of computing than she did. Thus, rather than being in a position of receiving knowledge from a more expert teacher, the students often helped her solve stubborn hardware and software problems. The extent of the shift in the usual relation between teacher and student, and the linkage between technical skill and maleness in the students' minds, was exemplified the day one of these boys complemented Ms. Prentiss on her successful removal and return of a disc drive to a computer by saying in an encouraging but also somewhat patronizing way, "See, women *can* do these kinds of things."

In sum, the computer room for gifted students served several functions for the boys who went there. It provided a retreat from the social pressures of the cafeteria. Perhaps more importantly, it provided a relaxed and congenial atmosphere in which they could build activity-centered friendships as well as enact fantasies, satisfy their competitive urges, and indulge their desire to be challenged in an environment in which succeeding was gratifying but losing did not have serious life consequences.

Bright girls have their own special set of problems to contend with as they enter high school, but they may be less likely than bright boys to handle them by retreating to a place like the computer room for a number of reasons. First, the girls' emphasis on talking with friends, as opposed to the boys somewhat greater emphasis on engaging in sportslike activities with them, means that girls could engage in one of their most preferred social activities quite readily without coming to the computer room. In fact, Kinney (1993) suggests that unlike boys who have been labeled nerds, girls of this type tend to try to build a positive self-identity in high school through developing close relationships that are not based on school-centered activities. Second, given traditional dating patterns, freshman and sophomore girls had open to them the possibility of dating older students, which did not realistically exist for their male counterparts. Thus, for many of the younger girls, time in the cafeteria was an opportunity – not a potential threat to their sense of self:

Ms. Prentiss: [The computer room] has become a social haven for some kids that obviously need it, and I didn't anticipate that when we started it. It's pretty clear that's what happened. . . . Unfortunately, in our sexist world, most of the computer nerds are male, and also probably – maybe not in the social swing of things – so they're more comfortable here than they would be down in the lunchroom, for instance. This is a safe and comfortable place for them. They're welcome. I certainly make a huge fuss over them because they're so wonderful to help me do this and that! They enjoy themselves here. They look forward to coming and they have status here. They might not have it somewhere else. . . . I asked them, "Don't you have any girls in your class? Why don't I ever see any [girls here]?" They said, "Well they're in a clique and they like to go down and eat together and talk to older boys."

Not only was the cafeteria more attractive to many of the gifted girls than to their male counterparts, but the computer room and

152

the potential activities it provided were less attractive for a number of reasons. First, and most generally, computers were clearly associated with males at Whitmore, just as other research has suggested they often are elsewhere (Wilder, Mackie, & Cooper, 1985). The reaction of Ms. Prentiss's colleagues to her involvement with computers demonstrates this association:

Ms. Prentiss: Generally [their reaction to my involvement with the computer lab is] surprise. I think I'm still a bit of an anomaly. . . . Not that many women do these things.

Students also saw gender as being linked to an interest in computers – with this interest being seen as more typical of boys, as evidenced by excerpts from two different interviews:

Interviewer: It seems like most of the students in the [computer room] during lunch are boys. Why do you think that is?

Richard: They're more computer-oriented, possibly. Most girls don't like computers.

Interviewer: It seems like most of the students in the [computer room] during lunch are boys. Why do you think that is?

Arlene: Well . . . the girls in my class . . . don't really like computers. . . . Most girls don't. It's usually boys who are into it. . . . My brother got me hooked on computers. At first I was the only girl in there [the computer room], but then Toni started coming up because she needed help from Ms. Prentiss and then she got her friend Margaret to come up too. At first the girls are really hesitant. They don't really want to come up.

Another fascinating indication of the link between maleness and computers was the fact that when students in the GPTutor classes referred to the computer-based tutors with personal pronouns indicating gender, as quite a number of them did from time to time, they virtually without exception referred to them as "he" rather than "she."

Thus, while going to the computer room for lunch fit rather comfortably with male sex roles, it was not so congruent with the female sex role as it was understood at Whitmore. Ms. Prentiss felt proud of herself for taking on responsibility for the room and

153

stated that she did it partly because she thought it was important for women to develop such competencies and thus break down traditional expectations. However, behaving in a way that does not fit well with traditional expectations for one's sex may be rather threatening for those who are less mature. Specifically, adolescence, especially early adolescence, is a time of intense self-consciousness and concern about fitting in with the peer group (Elkind, 1978). To do something unusual for a member of one's social category is to at least raise the possibility that one is in some way odd, an uncomfortable thought to many at any stage of life but particularly threatening to adolescents for whom issues relating to their identity and others' perceptions of this identity are so salient (Coleman, 1980; Hartup, 1985; Lerner, 1982).

Another factor reducing the likelihood that girls would become habitués of the computer room at lunchtime was that the games, which so attracted many of the boys, did not hold the same fascination for most of the girls. The comments of Willa, one of the girls who came to the computer room relatively frequently to do word processing, capture this lack of interest in the games:

Interviewer: How often do you play games [on the computers in the gifted student computer room]?

Willa: I've never played any games. I've heard of the games they are playing. . . . I've seen a couple of them, but I don't see the point.

This difference in appeal was no doubt enhanced by the fact that many of the games revolved around traditionally masculine themes of conflict, war, and exploration and required the players to assume fantasy occupational identities traditionally associated with males, as previously discussed. Perhaps even more important, though, was the fact that competition, which was such a major element in the boys enjoyment of the games, did not fit as well with girls' preferred social behaviors.

Consistent with existing sex roles at Whitmore, the gifted girls did not flaunt their talents and intellectual accomplishments in the obvious way that their male peers did. Thus, overt competition highlighting such characteristics did not generally play the prominent role in girls' interactions that it played in boys'. Not surprisingly then, the games available in the computer room that sparked so much animated competition among the boys did not seem to attract the girls very much. Also, as previously mentioned, compared with the boys, girls at Whitmore placed more emphasis on talking with their friends about their concerns or feelings as opposed to engaging in various activities with them. Thus, whereas the computer room promoted friendly interactions among the boys by giving them an activity that could serve as the focus of their interactions, it was not as useful in the formation of female friendships. Playing computer games and using the computer more generally were seen by some girls as a way boys filled up the void in their lives left by the difficulties they faced in forming meaningful friendships:

> Arlene [a girl in the gifted student program]: My brother [a regular in the computer room] doesn't do any sports or anything. [We] girls can always just talk [with our friends], but he doesn't have anything to do and so he uses his computer. He learned BASIC and all these other languages since he didn't have anybody to do anything with. It's true for some of the rest of the fellows [too].

This interpretation of the computer room's attraction to some of the boys was supported by the fact that boys were much more likely than girls to say in interviews that they came to the computer room because it was "something to do" to fill an otherwise aimless or boring lunch period. Mr. East, himself the school's foremost hacker, saw things in a similar way, although his view of the situation was somewhat less negative in tone:

> Mr. East said that typically in the Community College computer courses and at the user groups you get fathers and sons [when you have parent–child duos attending]. I asked if there were any girls in these activities and he said, "Well, there are one or two girls, but they're the powerful type." I asked him what he meant and he said, "Well, you know, boy-type girls." He then went on to say that he thinks computer hacking is in many ways a sport like hunting or fishing and that men and boys use it the same

way. That is, it gives them something to discuss, something to compare their skills at, and the like.

The tendency for girls not to come to the computer room for the reasons just discussed itself created yet another barrier inhibiting girls' attendance there. Given that interaction patterns at Whitmore were very much influenced by race and gender, it took considerably more initiative, perhaps even a kind of courage, for a student to decide to enter a domain in which he or she stood a good chance of being the only student of a particular social category. The isolation of the few girls (and of the African American boys) who did come to the computer room was very apparent. There were many days when no more than a word or two, if that, passed between these students and the white boys. The girls' isolation was reduced somewhat by the fact that they often requested and received assistance from Ms. Prentiss or Mr. East. Interestingly, they rarely requested assistance from their male peers, although the teachers would sometimes ask one or more of the boys to assist a particular girl with a problem she was having. The isolation of the African American boys was even more complete than that of the few white or African American girls who came, since the former generally did not use the computers themselves. Thus, their level of interaction with even Ms. Prentiss and Mr. East was low because they were not engaged with them in helping interchanges. Typically, the African American boys who came to the lab stood around and observed the activities of their white peers, as is illustrated in the following field notes:

> Then an African American student whom I've never seen before comes in [to the computer room] very quietly and unobtrusively. He stands around in the middle of the room rather aimlessly. After a minute or two Mr. East says politely to him, "Can I help you?" The student replies, "I'm waiting for Ned" [a white student who comes quite regularly]. After 2 or 3 minutes more . . . the student exits.

> An African American male student enters the room. He stands about 4 feet away from all the others watching a white boy named Ernie demonstrating how to use Microbe. . . . [Several

156

minutes pass with a great deal of conversation between Ernie and various students.] The black student hasn't touched a computer yet and he hasn't talked to or been spoken to by anyone, either students or teachers, although there is a lot of talk going on . . . about how to use Microbe. [Several more minutes elapse.] Another African American fellow comes in and starts to watch the students playing. There are three or four watchers now, including the only two black students in the room. However, the black students both leave soon [as the play continues].

Since attendance was completely voluntary, student friendship networks were an important recruiting mechanism, as implied by the first of the two field notes just excerpted. Students who enjoyed coming to the computer room tended to talk about it to their friends and to encourage their friends to join them there. Since friendship networks were clearly influenced by similarity in race and gender, girls and African American boys not only faced the prospect of being isolated if they went to the computer room on their own initiative; they were also less likely than the white boys to have others actively urge them to come and to sponsor them to ease the transition as a new member of the group. The female student quoted earlier, Arlene, was the first girl to come to the computer room during the one lunch period that ended up having three or four regular girls in attendance. She specifically stated in an interview that she first came to the lab because her brother urged her to come. Once Arlene started coming regularly, another girl started coming and then the second girl persuaded a friend to come as well. It is probably no accident that girls were more likely to mention in interviews having initially come to the computer room with a class than were boys, who often came with no prior exposure to it, since prior experience there could help to ease the concerns of individuals who know they are likely to be isolated about whether they will enjoy the experience and can figure out how to use the computers in the ways they want to.

Sponsorship was especially likely to be important to girls and African American boys since they were less likely to have experience with home computers than were their white male counterparts. Thus, they were often unable to participate unless someone was willing to help them get started. The size of the gender disparity in this realm is illustrated by the fact that every single boy who was interviewed because of his frequent appearance in the computer room at lunch time reported having a computer at home, whereas not a single girl did so. Although not enough African American students regularly attended the computer room to make a corresponding comparison between white and black students meaningful, conversations with both teachers and students suggested a similar pattern in the student body more generally – with white students more often having access to home computers than their black classmates.

Not only were boys more likely to come to the computer room than the girls, but the behavior of the two groups while there differed greatly. As indicated earlier, the boys intently played games or chatted with their friends. In contrast, the girls who came regularly, whether white or African American, generally behaved in an extremely task-oriented manner. Typically, they entered the room and went straight to a computer, where they used the word processing programs or, much less commonly, the SAT preparation discs. The difference in the approach of the boys and girls was succinctly captured in the following excerpt from an interview with a student who attended the computer room quite regularly:

Interviewer: Do boys and girls do the same things on the computers?

Charlie: Girls mostly word process. Guys will do games and such.

The girls typically used the word processing programs to complete class assignments or to prepare articles for the school newspaper or a literary magazine produced by Ms. Prentiss and her students. On occasion, one student who had some personal problems would write diarylike entries, in which she reflected on these problems and how she might deal with them. These kinds of behaviors stood in sharp contrast to the boys' behaviors on the relatively infrequent occasions in which they did use word processing software. Here again, the boys tended to be less task-oriented and serious than the girls. For example, one day a group of boys

158

laughed and fooled around as they helped one of their peers use the word processor to compose a bogus letter to the well-known sexologist, Dr. Ruth. They raucously competed to come up with suggestions about the problem that should be posed and the person whose name should be signed to the letter.

The difference in the general orientation of the boys and girls who came to the computer room is well illustrated by the fact that with the exception of Arlene, who first came there at her brother's behest, all of the girls interviewed about why they first came to the computer room mentioned task-related motivations, compared with fewer than 15% of the boys. The following two responses to questions about why students initially came to the computer room capture very well the difference between the boys and the girls more generally:

Melanie: [I came] because I had to word process a poem. Ms. Johnson gave us an assignment and we had to word process it.

Chuck: I went there with my friends because we were into computers. We went there and played some video games and pirated some stuff. It was basically just a social thing.

The girls' task orientation in this setting is further demonstrated by the fact that when asked what they disliked about the computer room, half of the girls, but not a single boy, mentioned that it was noisy or crowded, characteristics of a milieu that interfere with work. It is possible to attribute the marked difference in girls' and boys' behavior in the computer room to the fact that the girls generally had few same-sex peers with whom to interact. Thus, their situation was not conducive to informal social behavior. Although this most likely contributed to the girls' task orientation in the computer room, this explanation does not seem sufficient in light of the fact that the girls in the one group that regularly had three or more girls in attendance focused on word processing in a task-oriented way, just as their more isolated peers in the other groups did.

There was one other striking difference between the boys' and girls' reactions to computers, foreshadowed by comparing the

159

comments of Melanie and Chuck excerpted earlier, that also seemed to contribute to this difference in their behavior in the computer room: The girls who came to the computer room, almost without exception, related to the computer as a tool to accomplish specific tasks. Their positive reactions on it were based on its utility, as suggested in the following excerpt from an interview:

Interviewer: What's the best thing about being able to come up to the computer room during lunch?

Charlene: It's a lot easier than using a typewriter to type up all the poems. It can be corrected so easily. It doesn't take much to type it in.

Although the boys also recognized that computers were useful, especially in the context of possible future careers, their positive reactions to using them did not seem to rest completely on their assessment of the computer's utility for specific tasks they wanted to complete. Rather, consistent with Turkle and Papert's (1990) observations, many of them appeared to be attracted to computers by the enjoyment and sense of mastery and accomplishment they got from exploring them as well as from using them in a way that let the boys test themselves against others or against the computer (e.g., by being high scorer on a game, by figuring out how to illegally copy software that was designed to prevent ready copying, by bending the machine to their will through programming it, and by figuring out why the machine would not perform as it was supposed to and changing things so it would react as desired). This sense of active enjoyment in interacting with the computer is reflected in Chuck's response to the same question that Charlene answered:

Interviewer: What is the best thing about being able to come to the computer room during lunch?

Chuck: It's basically, the computers are there, the programs are there . . . . It's a good feeling to be able to sit down and throw something in the disc drive, play around with it for a half hour.

This difference in boys' and girls' reactions to computers was evident not only in the computer room for gifted students. The same underlying pattern emerged again and again, manifesting itself in a variety of ways in different settings, for both adults and students. For example, a number of male teachers spoke of what they sometimes termed the almost addictive pleasure they or other males found in computing, often, as the teacher interviewed next does, linking the fascination to the power of the machine:

Interviewer: Did you find it difficult at all to learn to use the Apple once it came [into your classroom]?

Mr. Powers: No, not too difficult, I caught on to mine pretty easy and it's sort of addictive, you know, once you get into it. It's a powerful machine.

A number of male teachers also reported doing things such as building computers for fun or deciding to teach computer science out of a deep-enough fascination with the subject to lead them to switch fields, although it required a major investment of time and effort. Not a single female teacher we interviewed spoke of the kind of fascination with the computer that a number of their male peers evidenced. Rather, those who responded positively to them tended to speak about their actual or potential usefulness:

Ms. Wright [speaking about why she had decided to use computers in her French class]: You could use it for a lot of things. You could use it for quizzing them [students]. The computer would keep score for you. . . . But just to use the computer for the sake of using the computer is not my idea of fun.

A parallel difference appeared between boys and girls outside the gifted student program. The schools' preeminent student hacker was a boy, as was a legendary former student who was reputed to have frequently carried $20,000 worth of pirated software around in a suitcase. When naming computer nerds or wizards, who were popularly seen as being engrossed by, as well as extremely competent with, computers, students never, with one exception, nominated girls, whereas half a dozen or more different boys were singled out for this title. Over 40% of the boys that we interviewed from Computer Science 1 classes reported talking more about that class than other classes with their friends (implying an unusually high level of interest in it), with a number of them making comments like Rob's:

> Some of my friends and I do a lot of hardwiring. One of my friends hooked up this television to the monitor. . . . He does all kinds of neat stuff. He runs the VCR off of it. One of my friends is a systems engineer. I guess I do talk about it [computer science class] a lot.

The comparable figure for girls was very much lower, 14%. In fact, the majority of girls (57%) said they talked less about computer science than other classes. However, it is important to note that a number of these girls spontaneously indicated that the fact that their friends did not know anything about computers, and hence would not understand such conversations, contributed to this situation.

SUMMARY AND CONCLUSIONS

Before closing this chapter, it is necessary to make one very important point. The conclusions drawn here – that girls were less likely than boys to choose to come to the computer room at lunchtime and that they were more likely to respond to the computer primarily as a tool to be judged in terms of its utility rather than with a deep fascination with the process of interacting with it – should not be taken as evidence that there is some inevitable link between gender and reactions to computers. My conclusion is not that there is some inherent biologically based incompatibility between femininity and computing. Neither is it the less draconian position that due to certain aspects of our current culture girls actively dislike or are afraid of computing – a position that quite a number of other researchers have taken (Kramer & Lehman, 1990; Sutton, 1991). Both of these conclusions would be strikingly inconsistent with the analyses presented in Chapters 2 and 3 which suggest that both girls and boys reacted positively to the GPTutor and, generally speaking, enjoyed working with computers in Computer Science 1 classes.

Rather, this chapter suggests that social arrangements and educational practices that isolate girls who want to use computers, that emphasize the link in our society between computing and masculinity, and that do not effectively compensate for the likely initial disparity in prior experience between male and female students tend to reinforce preexisting differences in interest and expertise by discouraging many girls from seeking out opportunities to use computers. Furthermore, although these factors do not actually create a *negative* attitude toward computing on the part of most girls, they are conducive to girls developing somewhat *less positive* attitudes toward computing than boys. Consistent with this general theme, the next chapter examines in detail a number of social and organizational factors that contributed to girls being quite unlikely to enroll in the advanced computer science courses offered at Whitmore. In addition, it explores the rather unhappy situation of the few girls who went ahead and enrolled nonetheless.

6

GIRLS AND COMPUTER SCIENCE
Fitting In, Fighting Back, and Fleeing

THE PRECEDING CHAPTER EXAMINED BOYS' AND GIRLS' reactions to the opportunity to use a computer lab at lunchtime. However, gender differences in students' reactions to computing were not restricted to that milieu. Enrollment patterns at Whitmore for courses involving computing reflected gender-linked patterns that have been documented elsewhere in large-scale surveys. For example, as mentioned earlier, Whitmore girls were much more likely than boys to enroll in the business courses in which computers were used for word processing, consistent with Becker and Sterling's (1987) finding that the only computer-intensive courses in which girls were overrepresented relative to their proportion in the student population are word processing classes.

Also consistent with national trends was the finding that girls at Whitmore were somewhat less likely than boys to enroll in programming courses (Anderson, Welch, & Harris, 1984; Chen, 1986; Linn, 1985; Lockheed, 1985; Sutton, 1991). The difference between the male and female enrollment in Computer Science 1 was relatively small. However, in both years of the study male enrollment outpaced female enrollment, resulting in a total of 95 male Computer Science 1 students over the 2-year period compared with 80 female students. (African American students enrolled in Computer Science 1 in numbers just slightly under their representation in the track from which most computer science students came, constituting 56% of the computer science students and about 60% of the

164

students in the regular track.) The disparity between male and female enrollment in computer science increased substantially as students progressed from the introductory to the more advanced courses, a trend also found in previous studies (Linn, 1985; Oakes, 1990). Specifically, in each of the 2 years of the study, only 2 female students, 1 white and 1 black, enrolled in Computer Science 2 classes at Whitmore, constituting 17% (2 out of 12 students) and 25% (2 out of 8 students) of these more advanced classes, respectively. (Overall the numbers of white and black students in Computer Science 2 classes were quite similar, there being a total of 9 white students and 11 African American students.)[1]

The goal of this chapter is twofold. First, it will discuss the factors that seemed to contribute to the girls' tendency not to enroll in computer science classes, especially the advanced classes, in numbers proportional to their enrollment at Whitmore. If this pattern at Whitmore did not mirror national trends so closely, it might not be worth such close attention, since it is possible that the enrollment differences could arise by chance. However, observation of these classes and interviews with students suggested that these patterns were more than flukes and that a complex set of interwoven factors contributed to the fact that girls were not likely to enroll in the advanced courses. These factors will be addressed in some detail here since they illustrate the many subtle ways in which girls can be discouraged from pursuing an interest in computing and computers.[2] In addition to exploring factors that con-

1 The numbers and percentages presented are based on the teachers' class lists. Since the student population routinely changed somewhat over the course of the year due to transfers, dropouts, and the like, the exact number of students actually enrolled in computer science classes varied slightly depending on the particular point in time this information was gathered.
2 One question that might be raised is why factors discussed in the next section, such as a lack of role models and stereotyping in course materials, did not lead to low enrollment by African American students in Computer Science 2, if they contributed to this phenomenon in female students. One possibility is that the argument to be presented about their impact on girls is just plain incorrect. Another, which I believe is more likely, is that these factors in and of themselves were not decisive; however, in combination with the other factors that were not

tributed to the very low female enrollment in advanced computer science classes, this chapter will examine a related question – what the classroom experience was like for those girls who did go ahead and enroll, especially in the advanced courses, in which they were a very clear minority.

THE LACK OF FEMALE ROLE MODELS

Five of the 6 computer science teachers at Whitmore during the 2 years of the study were men, as were almost all the substitutes used to replace these teachers when they were ill or attending professional development experiences. The only woman hired to teach computer science was a temporary one-term replacement teacher. An even more striking way to capture the gender-linked disparity is to point out that $12\frac{1}{2}$ of the 13 computer science classes conducted during the 2-year study were taught by men. This was in sharp contrast to the all-female faculty of the business education department, which was responsible for teaching word processing. It even contrasted, to a lesser extent, with the composition of the 10-person math department, which was responsible for teaching computer science. Not a single 1 of the 4 permanent women math teachers taught computer science. In fact, whereas the male faculty taught the majority of computer science and "fast track" math classes, the female faculty taught three-quarters of the classes offered in the more basic general math sequence.

so inconsistent for African Americans (e.g., the classroom examples and games that were neither obviously "white" or "black" in any real sense), they exerted some effect. Another possibility, which could well combine with the one just raised to explain the difference in enrollment patterns for girls and blacks, is that the situation for blacks and girls is somewhat different. Specifically, girls in the college-bound track could decide not to take computer science and instead fill up their elective credits with courses typically associated with feminity and taught by women (art, typing, fashion, food, and nutrition). For college-bound African Americans there was not any set of courses taught primarily by black teachers that seemed particularly congruent with a traditional group-based sense of self. As one black student put it when asked if computer science was much different from other classes, "Every class I go to, a different white teacher runs it, and this class [computer science] just happens to be about computers."

166

Women faculty were not actively barred from teaching computer science. Rather, they tended to be distinctly unenthusiastic about it:

Ms. Baker: Everybody thinks because I'm a math teacher I'm supposed to be able to do it [to use computers]. It's not my field. I do not plan on ever teaching computers. . . . I don't care if it's the wave of the future. It's just not mentally in my . . . I will try to learn how to use it in my classroom because that is what they [students] will need. But, I would never volunteer to take 30 computer courses so I could teach it. That's just not in my nature. I just don't want to do it. . . . I have computer anxiety.

There were male mathematics teachers who had no interest in computers, like Mr. Carter, quoted in Chapter 3, or Mr. Erie, who taught computer science because he was needed, even though he greatly preferred teaching math courses. However, the majority of the male computer science teachers had taken the initiative to learn about computers on their own out of an interest in the field and a desire to teach it. For example, Mr. Brice indicated that he decided he would like to teach computer science when teaching algebra. So he took evening courses and got the School Board to give him a temporary certificate to teach it while he finished up getting the credentials he needed to meet district and state certification requirements. Mr. Edwards's responses in an interview showed similar initiative and enthusiasm about the field:

Interviewer: Did you plan to teach computer science when you were preparing to become a teacher?

Mr. Edwards: No.

Interviewer: How did it happen that you ended up teaching it then?

Mr. Edwards: . . . I had expressed an interest in teaching it and I had had experience with computers. . . . I have three at home. . . . The day my wife went into the hospital to have the baby I went out and bought a computer. That was 4 years ago. I really enjoy them. I think they are wonderful . . . I had taken a correspondence course. I built a computer through that course.

167

Ms. Prentiss was very much aware of the paucity of female role models at Whitmore with expertise in the use of computers for applications other than word processing. In fact, one of the reasons she assumed responsibility for the computer room for gifted students was that she felt such role models were important, as suggested in the following excerpt from project field notes:

> I [the researcher] started to interview Ms. Prentiss about her experiences in the room for gifted students. By way of introduction I reminded her . . . that we will be using pseudonyms for all teachers. . . . She replied, "Well, it's okay as long as you don't make me a man." I told her that we wouldn't . . . transform her gender, saying [based on earlier conversations with her] that I believe it is important that she as a woman is taking responsibility for the computer room. She replied, "I'm glad you understand. That's what I meant."

However, even in cases like the business classes or the computer room for gifted students in which women did play a major role in teaching students how to use computers, they were generally dependent on men for expertise related to programming and computer hardware. For example, only men were observed repairing or installing the machines at Whitmore under the service contracts the district had with computer vendors. Not surprisingly, then, male and female teachers and students alike referred to the "repairmen" when talking about these personnel. Furthermore, even Ms. Prentiss, who, as the preceding field notes suggest, was quite sensitive about gender stereotypes, divided up responsibility with Mr. East in the gifted student computer room in a way that reflected the association of women with word processing and men with programming and hardware issues, as the following excerpt from an interview suggests:

Ms. Prentiss: Mr. East . . . can answer the questions [having] to do with programming and hardware that the kids want [answered]. My thing is the word processing and a lot of interpersonal exchange with the kids, so I think we make a real good team.

DECISIONS ABOUT THE DEPARTMENTAL LOCATION AND NAME OF THE COURSE

The fact that computer science was located in the math department and was generally taught by math teachers may have discouraged some girls from enrolling in computer science courses, because it is clear that by high school girls feel less at home with mathematics than boys (Chipman & Thomas, 1987). Whether this is evidenced in higher levels of anxiety about mathematics, in course selection that tends to avoid mathematics, or in students' beliefs about their own competence, the general pattern is similar.

In light of this potential negative effect, it is interesting that teachers were unable to present a convincing rationale for placing responsibility for computer science instruction in the math department. The placement seemed more a matter of custom, convenience, and historical accident than a carefully thought through decision, as indicated in the following interview with the chairman of the mathematics department at Whitmore, who had offered Whitmore's first computer science classes and was quite familiar with the history of the subject within the Waterford School System:

Interviewer: Can you tell me why instruction in computer science is handled through the math department at Whitmore?

Mr. Erie: Well, that's just the way it is in the Waterford Public Schools. . . . It just started off that way. . . . Computer science is not mathematics.

In fact, in spite of its name, computer *science*, and its location in the math department, computer science was not considered as either math or science in counting students' courses in various areas for purposes of graduation, suggesting that the material covered had neither a strong mathematical nor a strong scientific component. Although this disjunction between the material covered and the course's name and placement did not seem to trouble faculty or administrators, it was not without some impact on students:

Rhonda: I went down [to the counselor's office] to make up my schedule [for this year]. They said, "What about computer science?" and I was like, "I didn't know it was a computer *science* class." I mean I know computers, but . . . I work on the newspaper. What I really like . . . is that I can keep all my articles and everything on the computer.

COURSE CONTENT: AN EXCLUSIVE FOCUS ON PROGRAMMING

The computer science teachers at Whitmore had somewhat varied goals, as illustrated by the following excerpts from interviews in which they were asked what their major goal was for their students:

Mr. Fox: My goal for computer science is not to produce programmers. It's sort of, if they can become familiar [with computers] and get something positive, okay.

Mr. Edwards: [The goal] is the same major goal as it is in any subject – to [teach students to] think in a logical pattern about anything.

Mr. Brice: First of all, I want the kids to be comfortable with the machine. . . . You heard Linda talking here. She feels nervous with it. A lot of kids are like that at the beginning. I want to make sure that they are comfortable with the machine so that they can take software, purchase it, put it in, and figure out how to use it by themselves, which is literacy. I also like to teach programming. I like to teach the kids how to do graphics, . . . animation, . . . and sound. They get a genuine interest in that. I want to make sure they enjoy it.

Given this emphasis on getting familiar with computers in an atmosphere that will build students' confidence, comfort, and competence with a variety of computer applications, it is striking that the material covered in the course was virtually exclusively programming, an activity that appears to appeal more to boys than girls (Becker & Sterling, 1987). Thus, the focus was on only one of the three components of computer competence specified in the National Assessment of Educational Progress (1985) as important for students to learn. Other important components, such as a broad introduction to varied computer applications, which might well have been more attractive to female students, were not included. Since the course was called computer science (which in common use implies a substantial focus on programming) and definitions of computer literacy current in the early 1980s stressed programming, the situation at Whitmore was hardly surprising. However, as indicated earlier in the excerpt from the interview with the student named Rhonda, the decision not to structure the course more broadly to cover a variety of computer applications including word processing decreased its attractiveness to at least some female students. This is especially significant in light of the fact that, with a few notable exceptions, the use of computers for instructional purposes was not widespread at Whitmore, as discussed at length in Chapter 4. The implication of this fact was that whatever material was covered in computer science was in fact the core, and more often the sum total, of what even those students most interested in computers learned about them as part of their high school education.

This relatively narrow focus did not seem to be a direct result of district policies forcing teachers to emphasize programming against their better judgement or preferences, although it is undoubtedly true that at the district level the course was seen as a programming course. According to Mr. Brice, who taught the majority of the computer science courses at Whitmore, "Computer Science 1 in every school is different." His assertion was supported by the fact that one of the other computer science teachers who was familiar with these classes in one of the district's other high schools remarked on the variation in content across schools. Teachers' freedom to shape the course was enhanced by the fact that students did not have textbooks that they could take home, which might have structured the material covered more. Rather, since the texts were expensive and the district was in the process of deciding what direction it wanted to take in the instruction of computer science, there was a set of 30 or so textbooks that students in the

171

various classes could use in school when they were in the computer science room. Of course, had any of the teachers tried to cover broader material, they would have run up against practical and organizational barriers. For example, the computer science lab was not equipped with word processing or spreadsheet software. Had teachers tried to obtain it, questions about cost and redundancy with material covered in the various business classes would undoubtedly have been raised. However, since the teachers generally enjoyed programming themselves and saw teaching it as a reasonable way to achieve their rather general goals they acquiesced readily with the district's emphasis on programming. Unfortunately, it appeared that the issue of whether this differentially influenced the boys' and girls' enrollment in or reactions to the class was never raised.

STEREOTYPED COURSE MATERIALS

Although students could not take the computer science textbooks home, one common practice was for the teacher to give students in-class reading assignments. A content analysis of the pictures in the text suggested that they contained a considerable amount of gender stereotyping, which may have contributed to creating an atmosphere that discouraged girls from enrolling in Computer Science 2 (Britt, Eurich-Fulcer, & Schofield, 1991). To begin with, women were pictured in the text markedly less than men. This is quite consistent with earlier studies of science and mathematics textbooks (Arnold, 1975; Bazler, 1988; Gallagher, 1980; Heikkinen, 1978; Scardina, 1972; Taylor, 1979; Walford, 1981; Weitzman & Rizzo, 1974), as well as with studies of advertisements for computer hardware and software (Birmaimah, 1989; Demetrulias & Rosenthal, 1985; Ware & Stuck, 1985). In addition, when women were pictured, it tended to be in ways that reinforced traditional stereotypes about male and female occupations and status relations. For example, men were more often depicted as professionals, scientists, technicians, and computer scientists than were women who were shown more often than men as secretaries, clerical work-

172

ers, and data entry personnel. In addition, men were much more likely than women to be pictured as supervisors rather than subordinates. The most common combination of supervisor and subordinate was a male supervisor and a female subordinate. Given this, and its consistency with traditional sex roles, it is perhaps not too surprising that scenes like the following were observed in the computer science classrooms:

> Carl and Linda, who are working together, have worked out a division of labor. Linda is typing in the information. Carl, her friend, who appears to be helping her write the program, is looking in a manual. After Linda makes a typing mistake, I hear Carl tell her she's fired.

The same kind of gender stereotyping found in the computer science textbook used at Whitmore was also apparent in the books relating to computers found in the library, although no formal content analysis of these materials was conducted. Illustrative of such stereotyping was the fact that word processing books seemed aimed at women. For example, *A Definitive Study of Your Future in Word Processing*, found in the careers section of Whitmore's library, pictured four women on its front cover. In contrast, books that dealt with hardware or programming and displayed individuals prominently on their covers typically featured men. For example, the library's copy of a book entitled *How a Computer System Works* depicts three men in a very elaborate computer room full of big machines. Gender stereotyping was also apparent in other materials presented to the students, as suggested by the following excerpt from field notes made just a few weeks into our observation of computer science classrooms, when gender issues had not yet become a specific focus of analysis.[3]

---

3 A detailed 65-page proposal (Schofield, 1985) that laid out the issues taken as the initial focus of the research on which this book is based did not even discuss the topic of gender stereotyping. As a social psychologist, the principal investigator was familiar with research on gender stereotyping, which no doubt increased the chances that this issue would emerge as one of concern in examining computer science classes. However, this focus developed as a consequence of classroom observations and reflections on them.

[After setting up the projector] Mr. Davidson reminded the students, "Have your notebooks out. You may want to take notes. This is not one of those ancestral films. It was made just last year." . . . The general point being made by the film is that the computer is a tool. As I watch the film I [a female observer] suddenly notice how gender roles are presented in an extremely traditional manner. For example, a woman talks about the computer as a tool for office work. Another woman talks about the computer as a tool that nurses use. Then a man in a white coat who is clearly portrayed as a physician by the props and the context talks about using the computer as a diagnostic tool.

TEACHERS' CLASSROOM EXAMPLES

As indicated in Chapter 3, the computer science teachers generally gave students a substantial amount a freedom to create the kinds of programs they wanted, and the strong impact of traditional sex roles was reflected in the kinds of programs students choose to write. This impact was also evident even in some cases in which students merely modified programs:

Chuck and his friend Harold are playing Concentration, but they are also . . . trying to modify it. They're adding new prizes . . . including a prostitute whose services normally cost $200. They laugh and chuckle while they're entering the new prizes and tell me [a male observer] that I shouldn't tell Mr. Davidson about it.

Male and female students were often free to follow their own interests. However, observation of the computer science classrooms suggested that when illustrating programming procedures and when developing specific assignments in which students did not have a choice teachers were often inclined to select topics that were closely connected to domains traditionally associated with men. Although examples and assignments that might reasonably be considered gender-neutral were also often made, the frequent male-linked examples and assignments were not balanced with some female-oriented ones as well.

In particular, teachers were prone to use examples relating to sports statistics. The pattern was so clear that female students occasionally took issue with it. However, this did not seem to change the situation. In fact, the very idea of creating programs in traditionally female domains was so foreign to many students that it stimulated laughter:

> Arlene asks, "Mr. Brice, how come you are always doing stuff on football?" Mr. Brice replies, "You can do it [the program] on anything you want, Arlene." Tim turns and says, "Do it on sewing," which draws a few laughs.

The atmosphere created by these practices was reinforced by the fact that the available games tended to relate to traditionally male rather than female themes and interests. Thus, the games called Exterminator, Destroyer, Crossfire, Battle Zone, and Robotron and those whose content involved oil drilling and traditionally male sports events were not counterbalanced by ones whose focus was on activities more typically associated with women.

DIFFERENCES IN PRIOR EXPOSURE
TO COMPUTERS

One striking difference among computer science students was the extent to which the boys were more likely than girls to have had prior exposure to computers. For example, well over 75% of the male Computer Science 1 students interviewed reported having home computers compared with just 20% of the female students. (A parallel phenomenon was found for white and African American students, with white students being over three times as likely to report having home computer as black students.) Not surprisingly, given the magnitude of this difference, boys were more likely than girls to report that their introduction to a computer occurred at home rather than in school (73% vs. 0%). These findings are consistent with those suggesting that the parents of boys are more likely to buy home computers than are those of girls (Brady & Slesnick, 1985; Chen, 1986; Sanders, 1984). It is also consistent with Ms. Prentiss' observation that boys in the gifted student program were much more likely to have had experience with computers, including home computers, than were girls.

There is no way one can know for certain from these facts whether boys were initially more interested in computers and hence more strongly encouraged their families to buy them or whether parents were more likely to try to encourage the development of computer skills in their sons than their daughters. However, there is some fragmentary evidence suggesting that the latter may be the case. Specifically, girls were somewhat more likely than boys to mention spontaneously in interviews that they wished they had a home computer, whereas boys were more likely to report having a home computer that they rarely used. It is also of interest to note that the only student who reported taking a job in order to earn the money to buy a home computer was a girl.

Not only was there a clear difference in girls' and boys' exposure to computers at home, there was also a difference in the age at which they were introduced to computers. Although almost two-thirds of the boys interviewed from Computer Science 1 classes first used a computer before reaching high school age, the comparable figure for the girls was less than 15%. In fact, although none of the boys reported that their computer science class was their first experience with computers, almost 30% of the girls did so. Thus, boys were much more likely to have had the kind of experiences that prepared them to feel at ease with the idea of working with computers. Such experiences seem likely to have contributed to the boys' tendency to enroll in computer science somewhat more often than girls. It is also not unreasonable to suggest that this head start was likely to create, at least initially, a more relaxed and comfortable classroom situation for the boys than the girls, since they entered computer science classes with a clear advantage.

THE ROLE OF FEMALE STUDENTS IN COMPUTER SCIENCE 2 CLASSES

In spite of the preceding factors, both boys and girls generally liked Computer Science 1, and a few girls did enroll in Computer Science

2. As mentioned earlier, in each year of the study only two girls enrolled in this course, clearly a very small number. Weekly observations gave us a close look at how these classes functioned. I will now present a brief description of the girls in each of the two classes. Then, I will turn to an analysis of the similarities and differences of the four students' experiences and reactions. The goal of this analysis is to shed some light on the pressures that girls who wish to pursue a traditionally male subject like computer science face. This analysis may help to explain why none of the students who enrolled in the third class in Whitmore's computer science sequence were girls.

Phyllis and Mary

Phyllis and Mary, who were in the first Computer Science 2 class observed, appeared to have little in common, aside from the fact, which turned out to be quite important, that they were both girls and markedly overweight. (The observer estimated Phyllis's weight at around 210 pounds and Mary's as around 180.) Phyllis was Jewish, a junior, outgoing, and an active, even somewhat boisterous, member of the class. Although she almost always worked by herself or with Mr. Brice rather than as part of a pair, Phyllis went out of her way to try to become part of the social give and take in the classroom and to gain acceptance as "just one of the boys." Thus, she frequently took the initiative to chat with a pair of boys who routinely worked and socialized together, often attempting to join in their games. She was unusually generous with compliments about others' work and with candy she brought to class, almost as if she were bribing her classmates to interact with her. The following excerpt from field notes captures the way she often approached her peers.

> Phyllis walks over to put her disc away. She stops and watches Harry, who is playing a football game [on one of the computers]. She says to him, "Never use a long pass. It doesn't work. I swear to God the end run works best." Harry asks her [in a challenging manner] what she knows about football. She replies, "You should do real well in this game. . . ." She continues to comment on the

game Harry is playing saying things like, "Touchdown!" when he scores.

As is apparent from this exchange, becoming a part of the social give and take in the classroom often meant getting involved in software and interactions that were traditionally male in their content. Mary appeared to accept this, remarking on sporting events with gusto, swearing when annoyed, attempting to enter into the informal competition that sprang up to see who could score highest on computer games, and generally acting like "one of the boys."

The behavior of the classes' other female student, Mary, was strikingly different. An African American and a senior, Mary was very isolated, often sitting by herself in the classroom doing nothing in particular. There were two African American boys with whom she sometimes spoke, gossiping about parties and mutual friends or occasionally consulting about schoolwork. However, it was not uncommon for these interactions to turn hostile or critical in tone. It is difficult to characterize Mary's interactions with her peers in computer science more generally since she was so often late, absent, or completely solitary.

Although the two girls were very different in many ways, they had one thing in common. They were both the object of a considerable amount of teasing, taunting, and even outright sexual harassment. In Phyllis's case the main source of the teasing was Bill, a white computer wizard, who was one of the two boys with whom she frequently initiated interaction. Although he occasionally focused his attention on other attributes, such as Phyllis's distinctive last name, most of Bill's negative comments concerned Phyllis's physical appearance, especially her weight:

> Phyllis gets a piece of matzo from her purse and hands it to Bill. [She often hands out food in what appears to be a bid for attention.] Bill says to Tim, who is black, "Try it, you'll like it." Tim takes a taste and says, "It's a cracker." Phyllis replies, "Yeah, but it's missing something." Then she starts to list the things she can't eat [during Passover]. Bill says to Phyllis, "I won't say how Mark was looking at you. You'd beat him up. . . . He was looking at you as if to say, 'Maybe she'll lose some weight.'" Phyllis

178

replies good-naturedly, "This is the most fattening holiday there is. There's lots of junk food to eat." Bill . . . smiles and says to Mike, "I can afford to gain a few . . . Phyllis is the kind who stands in line and starts eating before she has even paid." When Phyllis says indignantly that she doesn't do this, Bill replies, "I just said you were the *kind* of person who does."

Although it was far from unheard of for students to taunt their classmates about alleged or actual undesirable personal attributes, the frequency with which Phyllis was the object of such behavior was striking, especially given that she rarely provoked other students by criticizing or teasing them and that she was so generous with her praise of others. Bill was clearly not the only student who went out of his way to make fun of Phyllis's physical attributes:

Phyllis comes over to Don who has a cigarette made out of chewing gum sticking out of his mouth. She says to him, "Joe Cool. How long do you smoke that cigarette?" Phyllis's hand [apparently accidently] touches Don's on the keyboard. Don says dramatically as if in great pain, "Oh no, your hands are sweaty." He then ostentatiously wipes his hands on Bill's shirt adding emphatically, "It's slimy."

The only other student in the class in addition to Phyllis who was frequently the target of others' denigrating remarks was Mary, the only other girl in class. Comments directed toward her were much like those directed toward Phyllis, except that they more often explicitly indicated her unattractiveness as a romantic or sexual partner:

Tim is writing on the board. He writes . . . , "Mary smells like a fish," and calls over to Mary, "Close your legs."

Mary and Tim get to talking about a Saturday night party and Mike says [to Mary], "Did you have to pay someone to take you?" Mary looks very angry but makes no reply. . . . About 15 seconds later she gets up rapidly, leaves her terminal, and goes into the classroom where she puts her head on the desk, pillowed in her folded arms. She remains in that position for the last 30 minutes of class, barely appearing to move a muscle.

> Tim says to Mary, after she made an inaudible comment to him, "What the hell would I try to impress *you* for?" putting great scorn in his voice and emphasis on the word *you*. He then continues, "No way!"

Mary did not appear to be able to shrug off these nasty remarks. Her most common reaction was to fight back by criticizing her attacker. Alternatively, she withdrew from classroom interaction, a very common reaction among girls, especially African American girls, to sexual harassment (Wellesley College Center for Research on Women, 1992). Her classmates and teacher generally ignored her when she did this, although her hurt seemed poignant and palpable to the observer. For example, one day after one of the boys called across the lab, "Mary was denied a nice face," she almost immediately turned to working on her makeup, applying eyeliner, and repeatedly applying and blotting lipstick, apparently studying intently the three or four pairs of perfect lip prints resulting from that process.

Although the boys' taunts generally suggested that Mary was unattractive, they also sometimes behaved toward her in ways that suggested that they saw her as someone with whom they might become sexually involved. As is apparent from the following example, this kind of behavior sometimes disrupted her work:

> Don leans over and starts to type on Mary's keyboard. She shouts angrily, "*Stop!* . . . " Mr. Bruce comes over and looks at her screen. Mary says, "I'm trying to do this, but Don keeps breathing down my neck." She is clearly very irritated as you can tell from the tone of her voice and the scowl on her face. Mr Brice smiles and says in a very unusual and overtly sexy voice, "Does that distract you?" Mary scowls and says indignantly, "No!" Don smiles in a very pleased way and . . . leans over and literally breathes on her neck. . . . [A few minutes later] Don starts to massage Mary's neck and back. She says, "*Stop!*" indignantly. He continues for 15 or 20 seconds and then stops.

I indicated in Chapter 5 that many of the male students at Whitmore were very conscious of the physical attributes of their female classmates and that some of them felt free to comment publicly on these attributes, either positively or negatively. National surveys suggest that this kind of harassment of female students is commonplace in many schools (Wellesley College Center for Research on Women, 1992). However, there is no doubt that the Computer Science 2 classrooms stood out markedly in this regard from the very large number of other classes observed in this study. It is certainly possible that this was due to the unusual opportunity for negative comment provided by the fact that both Phyllis's and Mary's appearance fell far short of the traditional ideal. It is also possible that the pattern of taunting about the girls' physical deficiencies in their peers' eyes may have been a function of the particular boys who were in this class, since some of their classmates were much more likely to engage in this sort of behavior than others. However, I would suggest that the fact that this was an advanced computer programming class with a heavily male enrollment also played its part.

There is a substantial body of work suggesting that stereotyping related to category membership is more likely to affect others' reactions to individuals when those individuals are functioning in a situation that is not traditional for members of their group (Fiske, Bersoff, Borgida, Deaux, & Heilman, 1991). Being female in a heavily male, advanced programming course seems to fit this criterion. In addition, there is evidence from experimental work in social psychology that being distinctive by virtue of being a "solo," that is, being the only or one of a very few individuals of a particular gender or race in a social situation, has certain predictable effects on others' reactions. Solo individuals, like Phyllis and Mary, tend to be evaluated more extremely than individuals embedded in a larger group of people with the same category membership (Fiske & Taylor, 1978; Taylor, Fiske, Etcoff, & Ruderman, 1978). Although this can lead to unduly positive evaluations if the individuals are judged favorably, it also leads to unduly negative evaluations if they are not, as was the case with Phyllis and Mary.

In addition to influencing others' reactions to an individual, solo status can also influence an individual's subjective sense of comfort and belonging. This fact is clearly illustrated by the words of a Computer Science 1 student who was one of only two white girls in her class. When asked in an interview to imagine what she would tell a friend who was transferring to Whitmore about her computer science class, Elaine said:

> At first when I saw my class I was not very happy. I had a feeling I wasn't going to have any friends or [that] I'd just be sitting alone, cowering in a corner.

Elaine went on to say that she had adjusted to the situation and found that, contrary to her expectations, the situation was "not stiff or tense." However, she clearly had to deal with a barrier to enjoying the class that other students who had many classmates like them in race and gender did not. The fact that Elaine mentioned this initial reaction to the class in response to a very general question in an interview conducted months after her first exposure to it suggests that the composition of the class made a substantial impression on her.

Finally, it is worth noting that Mr. Brice criticized both Phyllis and Mary for not exhibiting sufficient interest to do nearly as well as they were able to in the course, a reaction consistent with the results of a national survey that explored students' responses to sexual harassment (Wellesley College Center for Research on Women, 1992). An example of this can be found in the following interchange between Mr. Brice and Phyllis:

> Mr. Brice then tells Phyllis that she could have done a much better job [on her program]. He says, "It would have been better if you worked at it instead of playing games for a couple of weeks." Phyllis replies that she couldn't think of anything else to add. Mr. Brice says, "Well, you could have had music or a smiley face when they get it right, or something like that. But you'd rather play games than get an A, so that's what you did." Phyllis replies without any particular inflection in her voice, "I guess I'm lazy," and stretches her arms over her head casually.

Although Mr. Brice occasionally made similar comments to boys, this was not a stock observation that he used routinely to chide students or to attempt to motivate them. Rather, he reserved such comments for situations in which he felt students were indeed achieving markedly less than they could given their potential. Although there are many possible explanations for why the girls were prone to appear to be working at less than their full capacity, one very consistent with the picture of the Computer Science 2 classrooms drawn here is that excelling in computer science had a real cost for the girls that it did not entail for the boys. Specifically, excelling raised questions about their femininity, and in a situation in which they were already isolated, teased, harassed, or marginal in other ways only an unusually motivated student would take that risk.

Denise and Terry

The experiences of the two girls in the second Computer Science 2 class observed also appeared to be significantly shaped by their gender. Denise, an African American senior, was extremely isolated from her classmates, as Mary was a year earlier. In fact, an observer noted that she and Stan, a male classmate who ended up hospitalized with psychiatric problems, stood out as the only two students in the class who virtually never interacted with their peers. However, Denise's reaction to this isolation was somewhat different than Mary's. Specifically, she seemed markedly less alienated. When asked whether or not her male classmates "give girls a hard time because they are taking computer science," she replied succinctly, "No," reflecting the fact that neither she nor Terry received the kind of repeated teasing, taunting, and sexual harassment described earlier. (Both girls had body builds much closer to those typical of their peers than Mary or Phyllis.) Rather, Denise was almost totally ignored by her classmates, whom she routinely ignored in return. However, even Denise occasionally came in for teasing connected with the fact that she exhibited what male classmates considered laughable ignorance about certain sports-related information that she needed in order to do programs like those her peers did:

> Denise . . . starts to work on her computer program which is similar to everyone else's since it deals with football [statistics].

> Doug laughs at Denise's program because he notices that some of the . . . teams . . . [she listed] were not football teams, but baseball teams like the Red Sox. . . . He laughs because she does not know which of the teams are football teams and which are not.

Terry, an attractive white cheerleader, was the only girl in Computer Science 2 who appeared able to create a comfortable niche for herself. Although she did her programs individually like the other three girls, she was able to build and maintain fairly positive ongoing social relationships with her peers, especially two African American classmates, John and Doug. The following excerpt from project field notes catches the tone of these interactions quite well:

> Terry and John are working together. . . . Terry is talking constantly. . . . While I observe them, the conversation concerns their computer program. Terry looks at John's screen and he looks at hers. They often point to each other's screens and laugh, giggle, and then start typing.

A good though not extraordinary student, Terry often provided her peers with help, ranging from letting them copy her chemistry homework to working with them on their programs:

> Doug is working on a graphic display of housing sales. He is receiving a considerable amount of help from Terry. He types in information as Terry makes suggestions or instructs him on what to do. [Terry tells me she has finished her program.] . . . Doug finishes up his work and . . . says, "Thank you," to Terry. He then says to the other students who can hear, "I did two programs in the same week." Dick, however, corrects Doug, saying, "You did one and a half. Terry should get half of your grade."

Although Terry gave help more often than she received it, she appeared to feel free to ask her male peers for help when she needed it, and her requests for assistance usually elicited help. Thus, her situation was quite different from that of the other girls, who never knew whether they could obtain help from their peers or whether they would be rudely rejected.

PARALLELS AND DIVERGENCES
IN THE TWO CLASSES

As should be clear from the preceding discussion, the four female students enrolled in Computer Science 2 during the 2 years of this study were quite different individuals. There were also some marked differences in their male classmates' reactions to them. However, there are some clear patterns that seem worthy of discussion. The most notable pattern was one of social isolation. Not one of the four girls entered into the kind of continuing working partnership with peers that a large number of their male classmates did. With the exception of Terry, who managed at least some task-oriented give-and-take with her male peers, they worked alone, almost exclusively, being isolated to a very marked degree.

It is one thing to work independently in a class where all students do so. It is another to be isolated from human resources that one's peers can readily call on in their work. Recall the very important roll of peers in assisting each other with work on individual programming projects that was emphasized in Chapter 3. Students found these kinds of helping interactions to be efficient ways of solving problems they encountered. In addition, as discussed earlier, they greatly enjoyed these interactions and the social give-and-take in which they were embedded. Since three of the four girls who took advanced computer science were markedly isolated, they were not able to give and receive help, as did most of their peers. Thus, their choice was between working alone, as Denise virtually always did, or trying to elicit help when it was needed from others with whom they did not have some sort of special bond or ongoing positive social relationship. Such efforts were often unsuccessful and sometimes exposed the students, who were already socially marginal in the class, to potentially embarrassing refusals of their requests for assistance:

> Phyllis walks over to Bill . . . and asks for help. Bill says, "I've got no time for you." Phyllis replies, "Come on, I helped you yesterday." Bill refuses to help. . . . Phyllis goes back to her computer and sits and waits for Mr. Brice.

Mary asks Micky, "Micky can I ask you something?" Micky, who is across the room working on a different program, replies, "No."

In neither of the classes did the two girls come together to form a dyad for either task-oriented or social interactions. In fact, in both classes the girls were rarely, if ever, observed speaking to each other. This should not be surprising. First, these students had relatively little but their gender in common. In both cases, one was white and the other was African American, which was a significant barrier given the marked role that racial background played in structuring interaction patterns at Whitmore. There were also clear differences between the girls in other factors influencing social interaction patterns at Whitmore, such as social class background and grades in school, not to mention personality. Second, Phyllis and Terry may have realized that forming an alliance with the other girls in their respective classes, who clearly were not part of the general flow of classroom activity, would have further marginalized them. Instead, the two girls who chose to initiate interaction with their classmates oriented themselves towards boys who were quite central figures in their classes.

Terry's efforts to gain acceptance by her male peers were strikingly more successful than were Phyllis's, as should be apparent from the preceding. Many factors undoubtedly contributed to this. However, I would like to focus on two that I believe are both important and easily overlooked. First, the two girls were very different to the extent in which their physical appearance and behavior were consistent with traditional female roles and stereotypes. Phyllis's physical appearance and her attempts to be "one of the boys" were quite at odds with traditional notions of femininity. In contrast, Terry was widely known to be a cheerleader, a role that in many ways epitomizes traditional notions of femininity. Although these differences between the two students would undoubtedly have resulted in greater acceptance for Terry than Phyllis in most situations at Whitmore, the students' solo status in a class traditionally associated with males seemed to amplify the magnitude of these reactions.

Second, it is important to note that Phyllis selected Bill, a wizard, as the individual who received the largest number of overtures from her, whereas the two boys Terry chose to interact with frequently were not unusually advanced in their computer skills. (In fact, there was no wizard comparable to Bill in Terry's class.) Although Phyllis sometimes offered assistance to Bill, he was generally more skilled than she. Thus, her help was, generally speaking, not particularly valuable to him. Furthermore, her tendency to complement others on their work may have done less to win favor with him than it might have with other students, who were less likely to be able to win approbation from peers quite easily. Thus, Bill had relatively little to gain from developing a reciprocal relation with Phyllis. She was not a likely candidate for the role of girlfriend, and she was not particularly valuable as a collaborator.

In contrast, Terry was at least as good at programming, if not slightly better, than the two boys with whom she interacted most. Thus, she gave help more often than she received it, but in return she found friends to chat with as they worked. It is important to note that Terry gave this help in a way unlikely to threaten the egos of her male classmates. First, she focused on offering constructive suggestions, virtually never making disparaging comments or unfavorable comparisons. In addition, Terry minimized the extent to which she could be perceived as involved in or successful at "masculine" subjects by saying things like, "Let's go fail chemistry," when, at least according to teachers and peers who purported to know, she was quite competent in such subjects. Thus, Terry's help, while valuable, did not come at a high price to its recipients, and she was able to maintain an image consistent with traditional views of femininity while giving it.

Just as Phyllis and Terry exemplified rather different styles of interacting with their male peers, so too Mary and Denise exemplified different styles in their isolation. Mary's isolation was somewhat less constant and extreme, yet it had a much more negative tone to it. Mary seemed quite visibly alienated, skipping class, sitting alone doing nothing while others worked on their programs and chatted, and often arguing with peers when she did interact with them. In contrast, Denise, who virtually never interacted with her peers, devoted much of the time freed up by her isolation to learning how to program. She had definite plans to enroll in a 9-month training course once she graduated, and this goal was quite salient to her.

> Denise . . . just finished a program . . . designed to collect information on employees of a company. She entered her own name as an employee to test the program. She entered herself in the database as a computer programmer earning $45,000 a year.

SUMMARY AND CONCLUSIONS

Male and female students at Whitmore evidenced some initial differences in their interest in and experience with computing, as shown by the slight differences in enrollment in Computer Science 1 classes and preexisting differences in home computer ownership. This is certainly consistent with the discussion in Chapter 5 of the gifted students' view that computers were more likely to be of interest to boys than to girls. However, in spite of the fact that both boys and girls enjoyed working with computers in Computer Science 1 classes, as discussed in Chapter 3, girls constituted a very small percentage of those enrolling in the advanced computer science classes. A number of factors appeared to reinforce students' existing association of computers with males, including the lack of female computer science teachers; decisions about the name, content, and departmental location of the computer science courses; and gender-stereotyped course materials.

A close look at the situation of the girls who enrolled in Computer Science 2 during the 2 years of this study, in spite of all the foregoing factors, revealed a rather bleak picture. None of these students entered into an ongoing working partnership when doing their programs, although many of their male peers did so. Three were so isolated that they were virtually never able to get assistance or advice from their male peers in spite of the fact that, generally speaking, Computer Science 2 classes were characterized by the kind of helpful camaraderie that was described in the Computer Science 1 classes in Chapter 3. Neither did the two female students in each of the advanced computer science classes studied band together to assist each other. Only one student was able to achieve relatively relaxed acceptance from her male classmates. This acceptance seemed due, at least in part, to the traditionally feminine image projected by her status as a cheerleader and her public denigration of her own scientific ability. In addition to being very isolated, two of the girls were subject to a considerable amount of teasing, taunting, and even some outright sexual harassment. The fact that this behavior occurred in only one of the two classes observed suggests that it is not inevitable in such situations. However, research on the solo effect (Fiske et al., 1991), as well as the fact that the level of such behavior in this class was dramatically above that in any of the more than two dozen other classes observed at Whitmore, suggests that such behavior may be particularly likely in a situation such as the advanced programming classes in which female students are few and the topic under study is one perceived as associated with traditional masculine rather than feminine sex roles.

7

COMPUTERS, CLASSROOMS, AND CHANGE

T HE PRECEDING CHAPTERS HAVE ADDRESSED TWO VERY important questions about the relationship between technology and education. Expressed in its most general form, the first of these is, What is the effect of the instructional use of computer technology on students and on classroom social process? The second is, How does the social context in which computers are used for instruction shape their use? These two questions are inextricably related since factors that shape the use of instructional technology are thereby likely to influence its impact. This point is made in its starkest form by noting that educational technology that remains completely unused, because teachers see little to be gained from it or because they do not have the institutional support they need to learn how to use it readily, will be unlikely to affect students, teachers, or their classrooms in any substantial manner.

Anyone who has read the preceding chapters, or who is for other reasons familiar with the plethora of computer applications that are available today, will realize that the quest to delineate a set of inevitable consequences of instructional computing is, most likely, futile. Applications are as varied as artificially intelligent tutors, word processing packages, drill and practice programs, and widearea networking. As discussed in Chapter 1, computer use varies in its nature, frequency, intensity, and centrality to the curriculum. Students work singly or with others. Expecting unvarying effects from such disparate uses of computer technology is unrealistic. In fact, the two questions that guided this study might be profitably merged into one more complex question to focus subsequent theory and research: What factors influence the likely impact of the instructional use of computing on students, teachers, and classrooms? This phrasing has the advantage of explicitly drawing attention to the fact that students are not the only ones likely to be influenced by the instructional use of computing – that such use puts new and different demands on their teachers and can change classroom process and structure. This phrasing also has the clear advantage of suggesting it is unlikely that the many varied instructional uses of computing will have a predictable and uniform impact, such as dependably increasing learning of a given type. Finally, it also makes salient the fact that the influence of any particular technology on teachers, students, or others may depend on a wide variety of contextual factors that shape the way it is used.

Policymakers faced with the difficult task of deciding how much money to spend on instructional technology might prefer an unambiguous answer about the consequences of such purchases. However, it is vital to recognize the extent to which any impact is likely to depend on factors all the way from economic realities that determine the number of computers available, to assumptions that determine the nature and amount of training teachers receive; to organizational norms, values, and practices that influence when, how, and by whom the computers are used; to very specific design decisions made on the part of software developers. One can then attempt to understand the influence of these factors rather than assuming that the important decisions have been made once the equipment has been purchased.

One generalization that does seem safe, based on this study, is that using computers for instructional purposes will most likely change potentially important aspects of the classroom's social functioning. Acknowledging the great variety of uses of computer technology in the classroom and the consequent variety in the ways the presence of these machines may affect classrooms and the students in them does not prevent one from asking if there are any effects of computer use that are relatively common and then seeking to explore why this might be the case. It is to this task that I turn now. In addressing this question, I will draw on material presented in earlier chapters, on new material from other classes at Whitmore that is relevant to exploring the extent to which the phenomena discussed in depth in earlier chapters were replicated

191

in other settings at the school, and from the small but expanding body of literature on the impact of computer use on students, teachers, and classroom social processes. After exploring this issue, I will turn to a question raised in Chapter 1 – whether computers are likely to transform education – and examine it in light of the findings presented in this book and other recent research.

COMMONLY FOUND CONSEQUENCES OF COMPUTER USE IN THE CLASSROOM

Students' Enhanced Motivation and Enjoyment

The one striking effect of computer use across the wide variety of applications studied at Whitmore was enhanced student enjoyment of, interest in, and attention to classroom activities. This effect was by no means limited to cases in which students played educational games that "sugar-coated" the hard work often involved in learning by surrounding it with attention-getting graphics, sound, or fantasy situations. Recall that Chapter 2 discusses students' very positive reactions to work on the rather straightforward and demanding GPTutor and Chapter 3 discusses students' positive reactions to programming in Computer Science 1 classes. In both kinds of classes students not only liked working on the computers, they worked harder and evidenced much more involvement with learning when using computers than they did otherwise. Such reactions were not limited to these two kinds of classes. Again and again, in a wide variety of situations, students seemed to be drawn to work on computers in a way they were not generally drawn to their other work. For example, a special education teacher who used a variety of drill and practice programs when teaching socially and emotionally disturbed students asserted that they were so enthusiastic about using computers that they were much less likely to cut his class than others in which the teacher did not use computers. In addition, a number of teachers used access to computers as a reward, which would not make sense unless students' attitudes toward computer use were very positive.

Further support for the assertion that students really enjoyed computer use and found it motivating comes from the business classes. Parallel to the findings presented in Chapter 3 that contrasted students' reactions in the Computer Science 1 classroom with those in the lab where they actually used the computers, business students also appeared to enjoy the actual use of the machines much more than learning about office work, and they showed more energy and focus when doing so. When asked whether working on the computers was one of the things they "liked best, least, or somewhere in the middle," over 80% of the business students interviewed said they liked computer usage best, in spite of the difficulties posed by the fact that their teachers often did not know enough about computing to help them reliably solve problems that arose. Not a single student said it was his or her least preferred activity. Furthermore, and significantly, students' comments often implied or explicitly linked their positive reactions to the computer to an increase in effort, interest in learning, or satisfaction with their accomplishments. As one business student put it:

> The class is so boring. I would rather get on the computer than sit there and talk about what we have to do in the workbook. Working on the computer . . . you have to know how to handle it. You have to know what you're doing. . . . It's fun.

Another spoke of working on the computer this way:

> It's different. It's exciting. . . . I was like, "*Oh. I did this!*" I try to go ahead – and it's fun.

The pattern of increased student motivation and enjoyment that was very frequently apparent in Whitmore's classrooms when students worked on computers is not an anomaly. Both advocates of the increased use of computers in schools and the relatively few researchers who have attempted to study the noncognitive impact of the use of various computer applications on students often assert that computer use enhances student motivation (Brown, 1985; Campbell, 1984; Ferrell, 1986; Johnston, 1987; Kleiman, 1984; Lepper & Gurtner, 1989; Papert, 1980; Podmore, 1991; Ritter, 1988; Sandholtz, Ringstaff, & Dwyer, 1990; Schank, 1984). This same belief is one of the factors that contributes to the intensive use of computers and related technology in numerous after-school and club activities designed specifically for students who are considered to be at risk of academic failure or dropping out of school (Blanton & Zimmerman, 1994; King et al., 1994).

Although the idea that computer use often enhances students' motivation has gained currency in recent years, and the study reported in this book strongly supports this conclusion, we are far from understanding precisely why this might be. Thus, I would like to turn to a discussion of the factors that seemed to be important at Whitmore. It must be acknowledged that a qualitative study like the one reported here cannot make definitive statements about cause and effect or completely untangle the relative contributions of different factors. However, such a study can suggest, better than more narrowly focused ones, the full range of factors that may play a role in creating or maintaining the link between computer use and motivation.

One factor that a number of teachers suggested might help to account for students' high motivation while working on computers was their novelty value. There were two related, but not identical, lines of argument here. The first was that students respond well to computers because they are relatively new in their school experience. The second is that students seem drawn to working on computers because computers introduce variety into the school routine. Our observations and student interviews suggest that the latter factor plays a bigger role than the former. Students' comments in interviews rarely focused on the first of these factors, the computers' newness per se, as enhancing their motivation. Furthermore, our observations suggested, at least within the time frame of a year or two, that students did not generally lose their enthusiasm for working with computers as the first sense of newness wore off. So, for example, there was no obvious diminution in the students' interest in working on the GPTutor as the school year progressed. Nor did students in computer science or business classes appear to lose their enthusiasm for using computers as time passed. As one teacher put it, referring to the possible "halo effect" from newness per se, "If it's a halo effect, it's been glowing for over a year now."

194

In contrast, students' comments in interviews did indicate that variety might play a significant role in their positive reactions to working with computers. However, as Chapters 2 and 3 suggest, the attraction of working with computers was not only that they were a change from other activities, but that they provided relief from certain aspects of the school situation that students found aversive – most notably, listening to their teachers lecture.

Another clear source of students' enthusiasm about working with computers was their conviction that knowing how to use a computer would be useful to them in later life. In striking contrast, a large number of students felt that many of the other things they were learning in school had little real use, aside sometimes from the admittedly important instrumental one of helping them gain admission to college. For example, when asked why they had enrolled in geometry class, almost 85% of the students interviewed replied that it was necessary to meet high school graduation or college entrance requirements or that it was the expected course after algebra. Fewer than 20% of the students interviewed on this topic mentioned either liking math or seeing it as valuable, aside from meeting the requirements just mentioned. Occasionally the things individual students dismissed as irrelevant to their lives, which included learning about "boring" things like Hitler, the Vietnam War, and Shakespeare, were startling or even shocking to researchers who were a generation older and academically inclined. Yet, even if students were wrong in their assessment of the potential value of understanding some of the topics covered in their classes, this assessment appeared to influence their day-to-day behavior, including the enthusiasm with which they approached their work.

There is no doubt that a very broad array of students at Whitmore felt that it was important for them to learn how to use computers. As discussed in Chapter 3, this was certainly the case for computer science students, who were close to unanimous in seeing computers as likely to be useful in their careers. Business students, too, almost uniformly recognized the important role of certain kinds of computer skills in the job market. But such views were not restricted to students whose course selection evidenced a desire to learn potentially marketable computer skills. It was also prevalent in the geometry students we interviewed as well.

Students not only believed that a familiarity with computers would be of use to them in the job market. They also saw computers as becoming so pervasive that familiarity with them would be increasingly important in many areas of their personal lives as well. Thus, in describing the role computers will play in the coming decades, students frequently used phrases like "The wave of the future." Their vision, which is most likely accurate, is of a society increasingly permeated by computers in which those who cannot use them or do not understand them will be severely disadvantaged in their personal as well as professional lives. Thus, to Whitmore students, learning how to use computers seemed to be an important investment in their future. This vision was shared by students in both vocational and college preparatory classes.

Although this sense that computers will play an important part in the future did seem to heighten students' desire to work with computers in a variety of settings, it was clearly not the only, and probably not even the primary, reason for the enhanced motivation that they so often showed when using computers. Just as believing that exercise will improve one's health does not guarantee that one will embark upon an exercise regime or enjoy whatever exercise one gets, so believing that computer skills will be useful does not guarantee that students will choose to work with them or enjoy the process.

As mentioned in Chapter 2, during the past decade Lepper and his colleagues have looked more closely than anyone else at the link between computer use and motivation. After reviewing the huge body of research on motivation, they suggest that computers are motivating to the extent that they increase challenge, control, curiosity, and fantasy that allows for personalization of one's work (Lepper & Chabay, 1985; Lepper & Malone, 1987). Consistent with this point of view, both challenge and control did seem to play very significant roles in shaping students' interest and persistence when working on computers, as discussed in Chapters 2, 3, and 5. One theme that emerged again and again from interviews, as well as classroom observations, was that students found working on computers challenging in a way that much of their other schoolwork was not.

Numerous factors appear to have contributed to this link between computer use and a sense of challenge. Clearly important among these was the ability of students to work at their own pace. This let them push ahead as fast and as far as they could, rather than at a pace dictated by the teacher's concern for other students in the class, which often left some feeling bored and others lost.

The rapid feedback provided in many of the situations in which students used computers most likely also contributed to this sense of challenge. Such feedback quickly and regularly let them know when they had done something correctly, thus reinforcing a sense of competence that researchers have suggested is strongly motivating (Deci & Ryan, 1992). Of course, the feedback also included signals of problems when things were not going well (help from the GPTutor, error messages in computer science classes, and various kinds of immediate negative feedback in computer games).

Negative feedback can reduce motivation when it is seen as a sign of failure (Garber & Seligman, 1980). However, in most of the situations we studied, this feedback seemed to serve more as a signal to try new approaches within a context that provided help than as a mark of failure. So, for example, the GPTutor was structured to supply help soon after a student began having problems. Furthermore, students could not proceed to the next problem until they had successfully solved the problem on which they were working. So even if they experienced difficulty, they ultimately had to find a way to succeed rather than leaving problems unsolved and proceeding on to the next in the hope they could do it. Similarly, help from both peers and the teacher was generally available when computer science students ran into a problem, and such situations were so common for even the best programmers that needing help was not generally seen as a sign of failure. Furthermore, even if the students were unable to figure out how to make their programs do everything desired, it was extremely rare for them not to be able to complete a rudimentary program that contained the required elements. Thus, much of students' work was focused on the challenge of improving an already "successful" program.

The work of Lepper and his colleagues focuses primarily on the extent to which the design of the computer software itself promotes things like a sense of challenge, increased control, and the opportunity for fantasy. Thus, their approach tends to focus attention on issues such as the ways in which the developers of the GPTutor changed the initial versions of the software to provide more control to the students after they objected to the speed with which the tutor took things out of their hands once they had made a mistake.

However, the preceding chapters draw attention to quite different sources of challenge and control that are connected to computer use – changes in the larger classroom environment. So, for example, the fact that students using computers frequently gained more control than they had otherwise over the source (teacher, peer, feedback from the computer) and content of the help they received appeared to play a significant role in their positive reactions to working on the computers. Control was also enhanced in arenas varying from the students' ability to express negative sentiments when frustrated to their freedom to leave their seats and talk with other students. As yet another example, it is clear that students made a strong differentiation between classroom situations in which their primary task was to record and assimilate information presented to them by the teacher and situations in which they actively used what they knew to accomplish valued ends. The latter situations, which were commonly although by no means inevitably associated with computer use, were also conducive to a sense of challenge and control. These observations highlight a point made by Kling (1987) that was exemplified in Chapters 2 and 3 – the introduction of computer technology is often accompanied by alterations in social organization that may be as or even more important than the technological change itself. Ignoring this possibility can lead to a serious misunderstanding of why and how technology use leads to change.

A natural and important question that readers may ask at this point is whether the increased motivation that this and other studies suggest is frequently associated with computer use actually results in increased learning. Although the research reported in this book did not set out to address this question, I would like to suggest two thoughts on the issues. First, even if one cannot demonstrate immediate increased learning flowing from the use of computers in instruction, the same level of learning accompanied by increased motivation is an outcome not to be scorned. Second, it seems a reasonable supposition that increased motivation is likely to translate into increased learning with some frequency. I will discuss each of these points briefly.

With regard to the first point, I would argue, as Ames and Ames (1989) and others have, that enhanced motivation may be valuable in a number of ways even if it does not result in immediately measurable increases in students' content knowledge. For example, to the extent that students' motivation to study a given area, like mathematics, is linked to subsequent course choices or even career choices, it has a potentially powerful effect on their adult lives. More immediately, in a country where the high school dropout rate is often deplored, an educational innovation that stimulates interest in schoolwork on the part of minority and majority group students alike is valuable.

With regard to the link between motivation and learning, it seems eminently reasonable to postulate that increased engagement in the form of greater interest, attention, or persistence in the face of difficulty is likely to increase learning, and there are studies that support such a contention (Anderson, Shirey, Wilson, & Fielding, 1987; Asher, 1980). There is a also a substantial body of research that supports the very plausible assertion that the more time students spend actually working on a particular topic, the more they are likely to learn (Caldwell, Huitt, & Graeber, 1982; Carroll, 1963; Egbert & Kluender, 1984; Fredrick & Walberg, 1980; Sjogren, 1967), which again suggests that increased motivation should often translate into increased learning when it results, as it appeared to in the GPTutor classrooms, in students actually working more.

A relatively large number of studies of traditional kinds of computer assisted instruction (CAI) suggest that it often has some positive effect on learning (Becker, 1987; Bialo & Sivin, 1990; Mevarech & Rich, 1985; Office of Technology Assessment, 1988). Consistent with these results, a study of the GPTutor classrooms suggested some gains in the students' ability to do geometry proofs compared with control students (Wertheimer, 1990), although unavoidable methodological problems weaken the certainty of this conclusion. However, neither the study of the GPTutor just mentioned nor the studies of more traditional CAI typically measure individual's motivation and relate it to learning, so that gains documented cannot be confidently attributed to changes in motivation rather than to other possible mechanisms. Although such a link seems likely, it is not inevitable, as suggested by the fact that a large-scale survey of teachers who used computers in their classrooms found that teachers were five times as likely to report that using computers increased students' general enthusiasm as to indicate that it helped the average students learn more (Becker, 1983).

One very important factor likely to moderate the connection between the increased motivation that often accompanies computer use and learning is the structure of the software that students use. For example, Lepper and Malone (1987) make the point that software in which the results of making a mistake or failing to solve a problem are more exciting or interesting than the results of succeeding at the task is not likely to be conducive to learning, although students may be very motivated to work with it if it provides them with enjoyable experiences.

Similarly, software that rewards students for completing certain sequences of problems without ensuring that they have learned the material in them may be fun but not conducive to learning. An example of this kind of software is a program designed to teach filing that was used in one of the business classes observed in the study on which this book is based. This software presented students with a series of rules on alphabetization, each followed by one or more multiple-choice questions that tested students on that rule. If the student answered a question incorrectly, the rule was reiterated with further explanation or examples. Then, the same question was repeated. There were no penalties for wrong answers.

When using this program students sometimes just raced through the rule and example screens selecting answers to the questions that followed close to randomly. Some did not even leave the rule and explanation screens on long enough to read them, let alone think about the rules and try to assimilate them. Rather, they proceeded through the questions as quickly as possible, knowing that if there were four answer options, they could always get the answer right in four or fewer tries just by selecting all possible answers in turn. This strategy often appeared to lead to completion of the lesson more quickly but less productively than the designers of the software presumably intended. Students were able to enjoy many attractive features of working with this software (e.g., the rapid feedback, the congratulations for completing the answers correctly, independence from the teacher's demands for attention to her lectures) without necessarily learning much from it. Although it is possible to dismiss this example as just one unfortunate case, Malone and Lepper's (1987) analysis suggests that the structure of a distressing number of programs fails to reflect careful analysis of such issues.

Shifts in the Teacher's Role

A second change in many of the classrooms observed at Whitmore in which computers were used were the kinds of shifts in the teacher's role discussed at length in Chapters 2 and 3. Specifically, in the apt words of one observer of this kind of phenomenon, the teacher's role tends to change "from the sage on the stage to the guide at the side."[1] Thus, as discussed at the end of Chapter 3, in both the lab part of computer science classes and the GPTutor classes the teacher's role tended to change from that of the expert who presented information to be assimilated by students to that of a coach or tutor who assisted students when they encountered

---

1 The phrase was used by an audience member at a symposium held during the 1992 meetings of the American Educational Research Association. The context in which it was used suggested that it had been borrowed from someone else, although no specific attribution was made. I use it because it captures the phenomenon we are discussing so aptly. I regret not being able to identify its originator.

difficulties in their relatively independent work. This shift meant not only that the students received more individualized help, but also that they, generally speaking, worked more actively on their own rather than having the pace and content of their work controlled quite minutely by the teacher.

The findings presented in Chapters 2 and 3 are very consistent with the small body of other work that exists on the impact of instructional computing on classroom social processes. The most commonly shared theme among studies of the impact of classroom computer use on teacher's roles is that in one way or another the classroom becomes less teacher-centered (Schofield, Eurich-Fulcer, & Britt, 1994). For example, Bracey (1988) concluded that teachers using computers in their classrooms increasingly see themselves as facilitators of learning rather than authority figures whose job it is to impart knowledge didactically. Sandholtz, Ringstaff, & Dwyer (1990) concluded that when computers are used for instructional purposes teachers become more comfortable with evidence of student expertise. In addition, studies by Bracey (1988) and Bialo and Sivin (1990) conclude that students in classes that use computers have more input into structuring classroom activities and feel more in control than those in which computers are not in use.

Although this kind of change seems quite common, it is not inevitable just because one or more computers are located in a classroom. First, of course, is the issue of whether the computers are used, which Chapter 4 suggests is a very real one. Second, the occurrence of such a shift may depend on a number of factors, including the preexisting structure of the class and the number of computers available. Recall, for example, that the special education teachers, who were unusually enthusiastic about using computers in their classrooms, employed quite student-centered individualized approaches whether or not their students were using computers. Thus, computer use did not create a marked shift in their behavior from a predominance of the whole class lecture approach to a greater use of individualized coaching behaviors because they were already doing a substantial amount of coaching. Furthermore, Mr. East, who often acted like a coach with students in the computer room for gifted students, where the ratio of computers to students was high, behaved in a much more didactic way in his science classes when he used the one computer available there for demonstrations.

Changes in the teacher's role resulting from computer use are potentially quite important, but they are not as dramatic as the possible change suggested by the section heading of the Computer Science 1 textbook used at Whitmore, which asked, "Will the Computer Replace the Teacher?" the same question Mr. Adams found himself repeatedly asked by reporters interested in his experiences with the GPTutor. Observation of classes at Whitmore suggest that the computer science text (Shelly & Cashman, 1980, p. 233) was most likely correct in concluding that the answer to this question is probably not. However, since interest in this question appeared so widespread among those inquiring about the GPTutor, I will briefly address it here.

The first and simplest factor contributing to the conclusion that computers are unlikely to replace teachers in the foreseeable future is that most software applications are not made with this goal in mind and have virtually no chance of achieving it inadvertently. Drill and practice programs that assume prior instruction by a human teacher are common. Students learning programming languages like BASIC or PASCAL in high school are assumed to have someone to help them use these languages to create programs. The tutorial software that comes with word processing programs is almost without exception quite rudimentary, and manuals for a wide variety of applications are generally acknowledged to be very difficult for novice users to wade through.

The question of whether a computer can replace the teacher becomes more complex and difficult to answer when one considers artificially intelligent applications like the GPTutor. It was clear in the classrooms using the GPTutor that the current state of the art does not come near to creating a situation in which the computer can truly replace the teacher. Mr. Adams and Mr. Brice were extremely busy in these classes, circulating around the room, helping students who were stymied, and answering questions. Given that most of their classes were very small in size, even a very substantial improvement in the tutor's capabilities would leave a major role for the teacher to play in providing individualized help to the more numerous students in classrooms of normal size. Furthermore, the tutor was not designed to cover all phases of the teachers' work. Specifically, it provided students with assistance while they practiced constructing proofs. It was not intended to give them the initial introduction to the conceptual knowledge they needed to draw upon in doing the proofs. How effectively it could do this remains an open question.

Some of the team who worked on developing the GPTutor thought it was at least theoretically possible to create a tutor that could essentially replace the teacher, given enough time and money to invest in creating the appropriate software. However, teachers and students seemed quite dubious that computers could do so. As discussed in Chapter 4, some teachers felt that computers were just one more in a series of highly touted innovations that in the end would make little difference in the traditional structure and functioning of the classroom and thus could definitely not replace teachers. Mr. Erie's remarks to an interviewer reflect this point of view:

> I've been teaching 36 years, so I've seen almost everything. This [computers] has made an impact on the schools, but it's like anything else. In the end what counts is the teacher in the front of the room and the kids sitting in a chair.

Others pointed out important characteristics of teachers that computers do not have and cannot obtain in any meaningful sense, even should it become possible to improve artificially intelligent tutors to the point where the kinds of major intellectual demands that remained unmet by the GPTutor are well met by the tutors themselves. First among these was a set of rather ineffable qualities that is perhaps best captured with the word *humanness*. Included here are the kind of flexible intelligence that allows for the use of judgement rather than a rather formulaic adherence to rules and procedures, as well as the capacity to feel things and to use one's own feelings and knowledge of other's feelings to regulate one's behavior and inform one's decision making. Students often referred, in a negative way, to what they called the computer's strictness – its failure in interacting with them and evaluating their work to make allowances for minor errors or factors such as personal or family crises with which the student might be contending. It is unlikely that computers will be capable of interpreting physical or behavioral cues about the students' state of mind or health or to factor such information into their interactions with students. Both students and teachers saw this kind of behavior as important in the learning process and in making school the kind of place in which students feel comfortable spending a large portion of their waking hours. Furthermore, students pointed out that even if a computer were programmed to express feelings, such as pleasure when a student learned something particularly difficult, that they would know that these were not "real" feelings, but rather programmed words designed to influence them. The difference was felt to be very important.

Although they rarely, if ever, used the formal term *role model*, students also sometimes spoke of the importance of teachers as figures who embody important values or behavioral patterns that they can emulate. Exemplifying this point of view is the following excerpt from one of Mr. Adams's student's responses to a question about whether teachers can be replaced by computers:

Brian: Humans are better than computers or robots. . . . Let's say Mr. Ryan [the principal] ordered a robot to replace Mrs. Knowles. The robot may have certain things that we will be taught and then it will just shut itself off. Mrs. Knowles would teach us, go over it with us, go over it again and again to make sure we know it.

Interviewer: Just to be difficult, let's say Mr. Ryan programmed the robot to go over things several times. Would there still be a difference?

Brian: Yes, because she's her! She can do things a robot can't. . . . She can go out and get a drink of water. A robot will rust.

Interviewer: She won't rust. Okay, but does that make her better as a teacher?

Brian: [She's better] because she's honest. She's her. She's got

205

her degree. She worked for it instead of being programmed. . . . If two different people had a chance to become
stars, if one worked for it and the other just got put up there,
I'd rather be the one who worked for it.

Teachers occasionally expressed their awareness of themselves
as role models and spoke of doing things, such as responding to
mistakes they had made, in a way that modeled the way they
hoped students would respond to such situations. However, it is
also true that they were aware of sometimes behaving in ways they
would not like students to emulate, in the heat of anger, frustration, or disappointment.

Of course, classroom management is another function served by
teachers that is not likely to be taken over by a machine such as a
computer:

Ruby: The computer can't control the kids. There has to be a
teacher there [to] show them what to do. . . . At Whitmore,
. . . students . . . run, . . . they're loud and they scream and
everything. You have to have somebody there to calm them
down and the computer's not going to do that.

In sum, in spite of their impressive capabilities, even artificially
intelligent tutors seem unlikely to be capable of replacing teachers
in the foreseeable future. First, and most important, to the extent
the GPTutor is a reasonable example of this class of software, such
tutors' capacity to perform tasks that are central to the act of teaching, like effectively explaining why something is the case or answering questions, are much too limited. In addition, teachers obviously perform not only such task-related functions; they fulfill a
variety of important social and emotional functions in the classroom and modulate the way they fulfill their task functions in
response to their perceptions of the students' social and emotional
state. It is difficult to imagine how computers could effectively
fulfill some of these functions. Even if they could, the question of
whether they should – that is, whether this would be the kind of
environment most conducive to preparing students to function in
the broader world – remains.

206

Changes in Peer Interaction Patterns

One issue that often comes up in studies of computing in the schools is how the instructional use of computers affects peer interaction patterns. Initially, many who drew attention to this issue raised the specter that it might lead to students being cut off from much of the human interaction that they now experience in the classroom. In sharp contrast to this fear, there is now an emerging consensus that the use of computers for instruction typically increases interaction among students (Carney, 1986; Dickinson, 1986; Hawkins et al., 1982; MacGregor, 1985; Schofield, Eurich-Fulcer, & Britt, 1994). A number of studies report more task-related talk among students when computers were present than otherwise (Bialo & Sivin, 1990; Podmore, 1991; Ringstaff, Sandholtz, & Dwyer, 1991), suggesting that this interaction is potentially an important vehicle for learning rather than a distraction from it.

Consistent with such findings and that of an apparent shift away from teacher-centered classrooms are studies suggesting that "peer experts" often emerge in classrooms that use computer technology and that many students turn to these experts for help (Bialo & Sivin, 1990; Clements, 1987; Hawkins et al., 1982; MacGregor, 1985; Paris & Morris, 1985; Podmore, 1991; Ringstaff, Sandholtz, & Dwyer, 1991; Shade, Nida, Lipinski, & Watson, 1986; Shrock & Stepp, 1991; Webb, 1987). One other change in peer interaction patterns that is frequently said to accompany the instructional use of computers is an increase in cooperation, which is implied in the findings about increased task-related talk among peers (Collins, in press).

The findings reported in this book are only partially consistent with the emerging consensus just described. In Whitmore's computer science classes, peer interaction increased when students used computers, and most of the interaction that occurred was cooperative, with widespread and substantial helping among peers even though students did not, generally speaking, share machines. Also consistent with other studies was the emergence in many of the computer science classes, and in the gifted student computer room, of peer experts who served as a major resource for others. However, the picture was very different in the GPTutor classrooms. There, student interaction typically decreased some-what, mainly due to a decrease in socializing at the beginning and end of class. More important, a very significant proportion of the interaction that did occur when students were using the GPTutor was competitive, with cooperative behavior being quite rare except in the two classes in which students were required to work in pairs. Although some students learned how to use the GPTutor's inter-face faster than others, no clear wizards emerged to play the help-ing role evident in other settings.

In contrast to both of these cases, and with the one exception of computer use in an adjacent room to be discussed later, computer use in the business classes did not clearly or consistently increase or decrease peer interaction. Students in these classes generally worked on the computers by themselves and interacted only occa-sionally with their classmates. However, this behavior was quite similar to that of their peers who were practicing using adding machines, typewriters, and transcribing equipment.

Finally, Chapters 5 and 6 suggest that the amount of interaction students engage in while using computers can vary dramatically within one setting by demonstrating that when girls who have an interest in computers find themselves in an environment with few female peers, they are likely to become very isolated. The isolation of the few African American boys who came to the gifted student computer room at lunchtime, as well as the substantial amount of interaction that girls engaged in while in Computer Science 1 classes (in which boys and girls enrolled in roughly equal num-bers), suggests that the isolation of female students in advanced computer science classes and the room for gifted students was more a function of the fact that there were few girls in those situa-tions than of girls' invariant reactions to using computers. This is consistent with research suggesting that when individuals are one of a very small number of people in their particular social category that category membership increases in salience (McQuire, McGuire, Child, & Fujioka, 1978).

The dramatic variation in the apparent impact of computer use on peer interaction patterns in these various classroom settings at Whitmore underscores the point made earlier in this chapter – that expecting any absolutely consistent impact of instructional computing on students or classroom social processes is unrealistic. Rather, the impact is shaped by a wide array of factors. For example, the physical setup of the computers is one rather mundane factor that can play an important role in shaping the way computer use influences peer interaction patterns. The physical placement of the computers on which students in the geometry classes worked was not conducive to interaction. In these classes the computers were spaced around the room far enough away from each other that students had to leave their seats to see each other's monitors very well. In addition, the distance between the computers was great enough that any conversation between students sitting in their assigned seats was likely to be audible to the teacher. In contrast, computers in the computer science lab were noticeably closer to each other, close enough to allow students to see their neighbors' screens and even use their keyboards without doing more than leaning over or sliding their chairs a few inches.

The contrasting physical placement of the computers in different classes at Whitmore reflected both the sheer number of computers located in classrooms of a given size and the teachers' preferences with regard to student interaction. For example, Mr. Adams admonished his geometry students numerous times to work by themselves. He was able to leave considerable space between his students' computers to encourage them to heed his admonitions because there were fewer than a dozen machines in his room. In contrast, Mr. Brice often encouraged at least a degree of cooperation in the computer science lab by asking students to help each other when he was tied up. Furthermore, it was rare for him to discourage the substantial amount of cooperation that occurred spontaneously among students unless he felt that one student was leaning so heavily on the other that learning would be inhibited. The fact that he had almost twice as many computers as Mr. Adams did in a room of roughly equal size meant that even if Mr. Brice had wanted to leave a lot of distance between his students to encourage individual work, this would have been relatively difficult to do. Furthermore, the fact that a number of the computers in his lab were wired together to form a local-area network also was conducive to placing them close to each other to minimize the necessary wiring and create an environment without electric cords running hither and yon.

One big factor affecting the way in which computer use influences the amount and nature of student interaction suggested by the preceding paragraph is the ratio of students to computers and how teachers choose to handle the situation when there are more students than computers. The clearest example of this kind of phenomenon comes from the GPTutor classes. As was briefly mentioned previously, two of the GPTutor classes were purposely made large enough so that students had to work in pairs sharing a computer rather than individually, as was the case in the large majority of the GPTutor classrooms. (The reasons for the pairing and the results of it are discussed briefly in the Appendix.) In these two classes, the amount of student interaction was strikingly larger than in the other GPTutor classes, although most of it was within the pairs of students working at the same computer. Since the students in these classes were required to construct their proofs jointly, it should not be surprising that there was a lot of cooperative interaction within the student pairs. Some of the pairs worked together more harmoniously and effectively than others, but the structure of their task virtually guaranteed a certain amount of cooperative effort. Overt competition was also a feature of these classrooms, when compared with the classes not using the GPTutor. However, it was most evident between pairs of students rather than within individual pairs.

A second example of how the ratio of students to computers and the teacher's response to this influences interaction patterns comes from the business classes. During the majority of the 2 years these classes were observed, there were only two computers in the Office Automation classroom. Since there were four computers in the back of an adjoining classroom whose teacher often did not use them at the time the Office Automation classes were offered, the Office Automation teacher frequently sent two to four students to that room to work even if another class was in session there. The teacher repeatedly cautioned her students not to talk with each other when working in the other classroom since that was likely to be distracting to the class in which they were guests. Because the students were quite motivated to use the computers and understood that their opportunity to do so would be cut back dramatically if they made themselves unwelcome, they generally curtailed even their usual rather modest level of peer interaction when working outside of their home classroom. As an aside, it is worth noting that students using this adjoining room also virtually never interacted with their own teacher since that would have required leaving the room in which they were working and seeking help from their teacher, who was most likely in the midst of working with other students.

Also important in shaping the impact of computer use on peer interaction patterns are features of the software in use. For example, to the extent that an artificially intelligent tutor is designed well enough to supply the help students need, task-related reasons for them to turn to peers for assistance are reduced. Also, recall that one feature that appeared to contribute to the competition between students in the GPTutor classes was the numbering of the problems, which provided a ready shorthand for referencing precisely where students stood relative to each other. In a similar manner, the fact that many of the games in the computer room used by gifted students at lunchtime had a "Hall of Fame" screen, or its equivalent, that preserved a ranked list of high scorers encouraged the development of competition in that milieu.

In sum, the emerging consensus that computer use tends to increase peer interaction and to foster cooperative behavior may be premature. This study suggests that a number of factors, ranging from the physical placement of computers in the classroom to the task structure imposed by the teacher, the financial and organizational factors that influence the number of computers purchased and their placement within the school, and the nature of the software work both singly and in combination to shape the way computer use influences peer interaction patterns. The existing consensus is most likely a function of the particular kinds of applications that have been studied and of the financial exigencies that have led school districts typically to equip their classrooms with few computers relative to the number of students in them.

211

CAN COMPUTER USE TRANSFORM EDUCATION?

Computer technology has some important features that distinguish it in fundamental ways from many of the earlier innovations that have profoundly disappointed their proponents by having much less of an impact on schools than anticipated. Perhaps the most important of these is that computers are interactive tools that can be used to accomplish extremely varied purposes, from editing text, to providing simulations of dangerous or prohibitively expensive laboratory experiments, to putting students in direct contact with others from around the world, to facilitating "virtual field trips" to far off locales. In contrast, film strips and television shows are very static, in the sense of being set presentations that are there for students to absorb. Thus, even though they are likely to provide much richer visual and auditory information than a teacher's lecture, they are not interactive as computers are. Nor can they teach in a way that is responsive to a student's current knowledge the way artificially intelligent tutors can. The power and flexibility of computer technology also means that individual students can use it quite differently, depending on their capabilities and goals. In contrast, films and television provide a set of common stimuli for all students regardless of their ability or prior knowledge. Finally, teachers can use computers to get prompt and clear feedback about student progress, another potentially important function that most other technologies do not serve. Thus, I would argue that the computer's potential for transforming the classroom is clearly of a different order of magnitude than that of earlier technologies like film or television, which have failed to deliver their once anticipated benefits.

In many schools this revolutionary potential is beginning to be realized as computers are more and more frequently used as tools for accomplishing varied ends rather than as didactic instructional delivery devices or objects of study (Means et al., 1993). Chapter 2 discussed the field test of an artificially intelligent tutor, the use of which led to a number of very important changes in classroom structure and functioning. Computers, combined with videodisc technology, have been used to let students explore a rain forest and an ancient Mayan ruin, using simulations that include slides, films, graphics, text, sound effects, and narration (Soloway, 1991; Wilson & Tally, 1991). The experiences made possible through the use of such technology hold the potential for notably enriching students' education through exposing them to environments they could never otherwise explore as part of their schooling because of logistical, financial, and safety considerations. Other projects have used computer networking technology to enable students from different states or nations to work jointly on significant projects and to put students in contact with practicing scientists so they can participate in ongoing data-gathering and analysis efforts (Levin, Riel, Miyake, & Cohen, 1987; Riel & Levin, 1990; Schofield et al., 1994a; Waugh & Levin, 1989). Such uses break down the walls of the classroom and put students in touch with those outside their school, enabling them to profit from and contribute to the broader community in a way that is quite unprecedented in modern day schools in the United States.

Many of these innovative uses of computers in development and demonstration projects have had a profound impact not only on the materials to which students are exposed, but on many other important aspects of their educational experience as well. For example, as indicated previously, the GPTutor changed the nature of the help that the teacher gave students, the distribution of the teacher's time and attention between different kinds of students, teachers' grading practices, and students' motivation levels among other things. In a very different study, Newman (1992) reported that a local-area network designed to facilitate collaborative work in elementary school earth science classes ended up weakening some of the rather arbitrary boundaries between class periods devoted to different subjects. Similarly, Futoran, Schofield, and Eurich-Fulcer (1994a) report that the use of wide-area networking in an honors science and math program for minority group students led to an increasing emphasis on the research component of the program and the initiation of cross-age peer tutoring. Thus, there is reason to believe that computer technology has the potential to alter substantially, and often improve, current educational practice.

IS COMPUTER USE TRANSFORMING EDUCATION?

Although computer use can contribute to changing current educational practice in fundamental, often very positive ways, it does not always do so. In fact, it can exacerbate long-standing problems. Also, more often than not, the transformative potential of computer technology has not been fulfilled. I will now address these two issues in turn.

The Exacerbation of Existing Problems

There were at least two kinds of problems exacerbated at Whitmore by computer use. First, the disparity between the "haves" and the "have nots" was increased somewhat. Just as the gifted students had special field trips and other desirable and sometimes expensive educational opportunities designed only for them, the academically more advanced students had more access to computers than did their peers. Recall that there was no equivalent of the gifted student computer room for their peers in the less advanced tracks. Although many students used this lab for playing games and hence may not have profited too greatly from it academically, software programs designed to enhance performance on the Scholastic Aptitude Tests were available and used. In addition, the girls who used the computer room for word processing their assignments had the advantage of the ready editing capability it provides. Finally, the students who helped Ms. Prentiss and Mr. East with hardware and software problems undoubtedly learned a substantial amount as they did so. Since use of the GPTutor was, quite naturally, restricted to those studying geometry, who were typically college-bound, the group of students who were likely to terminate their education after high school did not gain experience with artificially intelligent tutors. Furthermore, although a conscious effort was made to include geometry students from all three applicable tracks (regular, advanced, and the one for gifted students) in the tutor's field test, a much higher proportion of the students in the two upper tracks than from the regular track were invited to participate (roughly 80%, 70%, and 25%, respectively).

College-bound students, no matter what track they were in, had the option of enrolling in computer science. This opportunity was open to very few of the non-college-bound students since Algebra 1 served as an informal screen through which students who wished to enroll in computer science had to pass. For the non-college-bound students, who typically took general math classes rather than algebra, no courses with a comparable emphasis on computing were available. Instead, there were only business courses, which used computers very much less than their names implied, and classes like Power and Energy, Visual Communication, and Home Economics in which computer use was limited and sporadic. In fairness, it should be noted that toward the end of the study a substantial number of computers were acquired for the business classes and more arrived the following year. Yet that does not obviate the fact that the students in the upper tracks had substantially more computer access earlier. It should also be noted that contrary to the argument developed earlier, many special education students had more access to computers than their mainstream peers, since, as previously mentioned, two of their teachers had computers in their classrooms and used them regularly. However, this exception to the generalization that more privileged students had greater access to computers seemed due more to the dedication and initiative of a few individual teachers than to general school or district policies.

National surveys suggest that the tendency for more privileged students to have greater computer access is not unique to Whitmore. They have demonstrated the not surprising fact that richer schools have more computers than do poorer ones (Becker, 1986; Becker & Sterling, 1987; Sutton, 1991). Furthermore, there is evidence that children from relatively affluent backgrounds are more likely than their poorer peers to be exposed to software designed

215

to foster higher-order skills, whereas the latter group uses computers more for drill and practice (Cole & Griffin, 1987; Laboratory of Comparative Human Cognition, 1989). To the extent that computer usage enhances what students learn or how they learn it, such disparities are likely to widen the already marked gap in achievement between students from more and less affluent backgrounds.

In addition to potentially exacerbating differences between the skills of students in the different tracks, computer use patterns at Whitmore reflected and reinforced preexisting differences between boys and girls in this domain that have been well documented in prior research (Becker & Sterling, 1987; Hess & Miura, 1985; Linn, 1985; Sutton, 1991). It is true that a substantial number of girls who had little or no prior experience with computing gained this experience at Whitmore, most notably in the introductory computer science classes and business classes. However, the business classes tended to route students toward relatively unremunerative secretarial and clerical jobs traditional for women. Furthermore, although almost equal numbers of boys and girls enrolled in the introductory computer science classes, the factors discussed in Chapter 6 conspired to lead very few girls to enroll in the advanced computer science classes; those that did tended to be isolated from their peers or, even worse, to be the recipients of behavior ranging from teasing to occasional outright sexual harassment.

Although Ms. Prentiss took responsibility for the gifted student computer room at least partly because she wanted to demonstrate to students that women could be competently and productively involved with computing, that room became an environment much more inviting and comfortable for boys than girls. In a kind of vicious circle, one reason girls did not go there was that other girls did not go there either. Nor did the girls who went find the ready companionship in same-sex groups that their male peers could count on. The small number of girls attending meant that others were not actively recruited the way boys were. Furthermore, since the boys normally had a considerably larger amount of prior computing experience than the girls, and hence were markedly more

216

knowledgeable about them, the image of computing as a male domain was reinforced.

The Failure to Realize Transformative Potential

In addition to the fact that computer use can sometimes exacerbate preexisting problems, it is also true that more often than not the transformative potential of computers is not realized in schools. Indeed, transformative cases are the exception rather than the rule. Reports of computers sitting in schools virtually unused for substantial periods of time are common (Bowers, 1988; Piller, 1992). Thus, the failure to utilize fully many of the computers at Whitmore that was discussed in Chapter 4 is not an idiosyncratic finding. Furthermore, computer use in and of itself does not guarantee major changes in either the goals, processes, or outcomes of education. For example, one of the most popular current uses of computers is as part of what are called integrated learning systems (ILSs), which are typically fairly sophisticated computerized drill and practice programs generally compatible with traditional learning goals and procedures, except perhaps for the fact that students can work more at their own pace than is typically the case. More than 10,000 such ILSs are in place in U.S. schools in spite of their very substantial cost (Means et al., 1993).

There are a large number of factors that work together to mute the impact of computers on the educational system and to prevent the realization of the potential for far-reaching positive change inherent in their use. One of the most fundamental is that although many scholars and others involved in the development of educational technology believe intensely in the importance of transforming both the content emphasized in the current curriculum and current pedagogical methods, many educators and parents do not. As discussed briefly in Chapter 4, some scholars and developers of educational software hope to see computer technology enable students to follow their own interests significantly more than they are now able to in most classrooms (Feurzeig, 1988) or to foster more collaborative, learner-center methods of teaching (Collins, in

217

press). Others emphasize the important role computers can play in encouraging students to reflect on their own thinking processes (Papert, 1980), in fostering inquiry skills (Groen, 1985; Lawler, 1984), or in breaking down barriers between the classroom and the outside world (Bossert, 1988; Hunter, 1992).

The vision shared by many of the scholars who advocate the widespread use of computers to transform education or who develop innovative educational software with the goal of transforming students' educational experiences is to some extent a shared one revolving around several elements that are central to or consistent with a constructivist approach to education (Simon, 1993; Steffe, von Glasersfeld, Richards, & Cobb, 1983; von Glasersfeld, 1989). Heavily influenced by recent work in cognitive science, this approach emphasizes the importance of fostering the kind of higher-order skills, such as planning and problem solving, its proponents argue are likely to be necessary for individuals to participate effectively as citizens and workers in an increasingly complex environment characterized by a rapid pace of change. Calls for reform emanating from those taking a viewpoint influenced by constructivism often include several core themes including shifts (a) from teacher-directed work to student exploration that builds on students' existing knowledge, (b) from didactic teaching to interactive modes of instruction that actively involve students in learning, (c) from brief class periods devoted to single subjects to longer blocks of time devoted to multidisciplinary work on tasks that have some obvious connection to the world outside of school, and (d) from individual work to collaborative work (Means et al., 1993).

However, this study suggests that the likelihood that computer use will lead to such potentially valuable changes is greatly decreased by the fact that many practicing educators appear to take what I called in Chapter 4 an incrementalist view of the computer's potential for improving education. Recall that, in this view, which was the predominant one at Whitmore, the purpose of computer use is not to bring about fundamental transformative changes in the goals or methods currently typifying the educational system, such as those embedded in the reformer's visions. Rather, it is to

218

help teachers and students perform the work they already do more easily, efficiently, or effectively. In this view, the justification for using computers is that they allow some already existing goal to be accomplished better than previously without creating offsetting, undesired changes. While there are many very worthwhile and productive incremental uses of computing, the possible benefits of which should not be underrated, this vision of what computers can contribute will almost inevitably undercut the possibility that computer use can achieve its full potential for improving students' educational experiences.

Recognizing the differences between their goals and those widely instantiated in current educational practice, some software developers and scholars who advocate the widespread use of technology in education hope that computer use will serve as a kind of Trojan Horse to exert pressure for change in the classrooms of teachers who have adopted the software with more incremental goals in mind. To some degree this may occur, since it is clear from the earlier chapters that using computers can exert many unanticipated pressures for change. Further evidence of this possibility comes from Salomon (1991), who uses the Trojan Horse metaphor in describing the way in which an eighth-grade classroom changed after its teacher adopted the suggestion put forward by researchers that the students should construct a computerized database on the U.S. Constitution. Salomon reports that this innovation led to a great many marked changes in the classroom initially unanticipated by the teacher, including having the students begin to work more collaboratively and engage in spirited debates, both of which were very uncharacteristic of that classroom's normal procedures and consistent with the reform vision discussed earlier.

However, one cannot count on such Trojan Horse effects. Nor can one be sure that the unanticipated effects of technology use in classrooms in which the teachers do not understand and value the intended consequences of its use will be uniformly positive. Seymour Papert, the developer of LOGO, has suggested that LOGO may profoundly alter current educational practice by functioning as a kind of Trojan Horse in the classrooms of teachers who may not originally desire or anticipate much change (S. Papert, personal communication, July 7, 1994). However, Zorfass, Morocco, Russell, and Zuman (1989) report that teachers in the school they studied barely let the horse in the gate. To be more specific, they resented the fact that LOGO use was mandated in their school and saw little real use for it in accomplishing the goal of teaching the plethora of material already in their curriculum. Accordingly, many of them taught LOGO only to the extent absolutely required and made little effort to find ways to make it appealing to students or to integrate it into the existing curriculum. Under such conditions, major positive change is rather improbable. In another discouraging but not surprising report, Zorfass (1991) recounts how software designed to foster problem solving and the effective use of reference materials did no such thing until the teacher stepped in, assigned students to work in small cooperative groups, and taught them the skills they needed to use the program in a constructive way.

As just suggested, in order to have computer use result in potentially transformational positive change, one has to find ways to team the technology up with teachers who understand and share the transformational goals. Otherwise, the technology will be little used or used in ways that do not help it reach its potential educational value. Further support for this contention comes from many studies including Sheingold, Hawkins, and Char's (1984) study of the use of a multimedia program called Rescue Mission, a simulation game the manifest context of which concerns rescuing a whale trapped in a fishing net. This software was designed to help students learn general mathematical concepts such as degrees, angles, vectors, and speed / time / distance relationships in the context of solving a practical problem. Some teachers interpreted the software much as its designers had and utilized it to supplement their mathematics curriculum. Others saw the software as a game about boats and navigation and consequently limited its use to free periods or after-school hours, thus demonstrating that teachers' perceptions of the nature and purpose of software dramatically influences the way in which it is used.

Even when educators do want to use computer technology as a lever to achieve transformational rather than incremental change in existing goals or practices, the obstacles are formidable (Cohen,

1988; Cole and Laboratory of Comparative Human Cognition, 1990; and Cuban, 1986). Many of the barriers are a function of traditional classroom practices and culture. For example, as discussed in Chapter 4, many teachers are used to a classroom format that emphasizes lecturing to the class as a whole. Finding a way to let students use the computer for learning when just one or two machines are available for an entire class can pose a real problem, although using overhead transparencies combined with an LCD screen to project displays to be used as the basis for discussion is a highly promising format. In addition, as discussed earlier, computer use often brings with it strong pressure for the teacher's role to change (Cole & Griffin, 1987; Sheingold & Tucker, 1990) that presents a challenge to many teachers, since they can no longer depend on a prepared lesson plan that gives them a high degree of control over the material to be covered. Rather, they are called on to respond to the wide range of queries that arise when students work individually or in small groups. Even teachers who wish to transform their classroom may find the demands of their new role unsettling. Some teachers may persist with computer use if they find the software sufficiently valuable, but others may stop, deciding it just does not fit in with the way they work.

Factors at the level of the school and the school district pose a second set of barriers. For example, incentives for innovation are rare and generally small in magnitude when they do exist. Given the strong pressures to purchase computer technology to keep up with the times, coupled with equally strong pressures to keep expenses down from taxpayers weary of increasing expenditures on education, it is all too typical for districts to buy new technology but to skimp on providing the training and support that teachers need to use it effectively. Furthermore, it is clear that the training that is typically provided tends to focus heavily on learning the mechanics of using computers. Thus, although teachers may come to understand the rudiments of how to make the technology function, they often still must struggle individually with the more difficult issue of how to use it efficiently and effectively for goals that they value.

One other major barrier at the school and school district level to computer use having a transformative impact on education is the almost overwhelming importance attached to performance on traditional standardized tests and the accompanying practice of measuring the value of educational innovations by their impact on such tests. Thus, educational administrators, teachers, and even parents often expect that utilizing computers should improve standardized test scores, which are often not good measures of the kinds of skills students develop using computers, especially if the computers are used in innovative ways. This did not appear to be a major issue at Whitmore, perhaps because the two main concentrations of computers were in the computer science classes, where programming skills were the focus of attention, and the gifted student computer room, which was used for essentially recreational activities. However, the importance of these tests was made evident by the fact that students in the GPTutor classroom were given practice in doing proofs in the traditional two-column format in addition to the unique graph format that the developers of the GPTutor were convinced was preferable specifically because the two-column format was used on standardized tests.

The tremendous potential of standardized tests to inhibit the innovative use of computer technology is illustrated by events at the Belridge School in McKirrick, California, which, after receiving a financial windfall, purchased computers for all students and teachers, as well as laser disc players and television production equipment for the school. All this technology was used in projects, like producing a television news show, designed to give students experience working together on involving tasks that required substantial amounts of planning and thinking. When scores on the Iowa Test of Basic Skills for the first year of this project failed to show any increases, disillusionment set in. The computers were removed from students' desks or even sold, and a new school board, stressing a "back to basics" approach, was elected (Schulz, 1992). All this happened in spite of the fact that the new approach had hardly been in place long enough to reasonably be expected to show a strong impact and that the Iowa tests are not an appropriate measure of the ability to work cooperatively or to plan complex projects, two of the goals that the new curriculum was explicitly designed to foster.

Many of these problems sound like part of the familiar litany evoked to explain the resistance to many kinds of educational innovations, not just those related to computer technology. This is so, but makes them no less important. There are, however, a few impediments to achieving computers' transformative potential that are more closely linked to this particular innovation. First, the pool of available educational software emphasizes rote drill or skills practice, rather than taking advantage of the full range of possible applications (Cole and Laboratory of Comparative Human Cognition, 1990; Komoski, 1984; Melmed, 1993). Such software may well be very effective from an incrementalist perspective. However, it is not likely to change the education students receive in major ways, since it is not designed to do so. Rather, it fits well with traditional classroom practice in most respects. For example, as Means et al. (1993) point out, typically such software (a) presents information students are expected to assimilate rather than giving them significant input in selecting their goals, (b) deals with information in a single discipline rather than being interdisciplinary in nature, (c) requires relatively simple responses from students that can be judged right or wrong rather than more multifaceted and complex responses, and (d) assumes that students will work individually rather than in groups.

A second impediment to achieving transformative use of computers that is specific to this particular kind of innovation is that consistent with the findings reported in Chapter 4, there is substantial evidence that many people react to the thought of using computers with various negative feelings that have been dubbed computer anxiety or technophobia (Igbaria & Chakrabarti, 1990). Since many teachers were educated before personal computers became an everyday object, they are particularly likely to be leery of computer use. The impact of such attitudes is compounded by school districts' tendency to skimp on training and support funds. It may well also be intensified by the recognition on the part of many teachers, again as discussed in Chapter 4, that their students may be more competent computer users than they are, a possibility that leads some teachers to feel classroom computer use might undermine their expertise-based authority. Finally, a teacher who makes the computer a tool integral to his or her curriculum must be able to assume that if hardware or software problems arise, someone will be available to help in a timely manner. This is likely to mean that the teacher becomes more dependent on others, often those functioning in an educational bureaucracy, a form of organization never noted for its flexibility or efficiency. Thus, the general inertia and resistance to change that the educational system has evidenced over the years is reinforced by factors specifically linked to the nature of computers and people's reactions to them.

In spite of such problems, it is clear that computers are gaining a place for themselves in schools that most other highly touted technological changes in the past 50 years have not. The sheer number of computers in schools has increased drastically to a current figure of roughly 2.5 million (Melmed, 1993). The variety of uses to which they are being put has also expanded markedly (Becker, 1990; Mageau, 1991). Those who have studied implementation efforts suggest that transformative change is possible, though by no means inevitable.

A review of this literature by Means et al. (1993) suggests several lessons about what is necessary if computers are to have a transformative effect. First, as I have already argued, schools and teachers must have transformative goals for technology use. Otherwise, computers are not likely to be employed in transformative ways. Second, these authors suggest it is important to find ways to encourage software development that facilitates such goals. This will not be a simple task, since the market for educational software is currently minuscule in comparison with other software markets such as entertainment or productivity tools for business and industry.

Melmed (1993) has suggested that the federal government should "prime the pump," perhaps by redirecting funds already allocated to support certain school operating expenses to create loan banks or other arrangements that might stimulate the commercial production of high-quality educational software. More consistent with the historical preeminence of local and state government action in the area of education would be state-sponsored initiatives in this same area. One example of this is the California Department of Education's effort to provide seed money to encourage private companies to invest in the development of software consistent with the state's curricular goals. Such efforts can be successful without being an undue financial burden to the state if arrangements are made so that the state receives benefits, such as a share of the royalties, on materials stemming from such efforts. For example, Means et al. (1993) report that one of the first products developed under California's program both won an award for its quality and earned substantial sums of money quite rapidly.

Third, software, by itself, is not enough. As indicated earlier, efforts must be made to develop and bring into common use student assessment systems that test for the kinds of skills one expects the transformed education to develop. Otherwise, even successful efforts will appear unsuccessful to many, since an inappropriate measuring stick will have been used.

Finally, technology's potential to contribute to transforming elementary and secondary education does not appear to be primarily through providing students "teacher-proof" software or artificially intelligent tutors designed to function without any teacher to assist the students. Rather, its potential will be realized only when teachers who desire change have the knowledge they need to incorporate the technology into the curriculum, as well as the interpersonal and pedagogical skills they need to function effectively in their new roles. Thus, professional development experiences that not only provide teachers with the technical knowledge they need, but also assist them with preparing to use the software as an integrated part of their curriculum are vital. As carefully planned as software may be, its impact is only likely to be maximized when teachers understand and value what it is trying to achieve, know how best to incorporate it into their everyday practice, and have the ongoing support they need to deal with problems that may arise.

CONCLUSIONS

The rapidly increasing use of computer technology is changing the lives of millions of people and the social organizations in which they are embedded. It is changing the way we work and play, as well as making fundamental alterations in the meaning of concepts such as physical distance, since people can now interact readily with others half a world apart in ways that were virtually unimaginable less than a century ago. This book has attempted to explore the meaning of computer technology for one vital institution in our society – its schools. I chose to do this in one of many possible ways – by the very close study of a particular school as its students and teachers encountered a wide variety of computer applications ranging from the commonplace to the advanced. In spite of the inevitable limitations imposed by any one approach to such a far-reaching and important issue, I hope readers will conclude that this book sheds some light on important issues related to this topic.

I also hope readers will take with them several main ideas. First, the task of introducing computer technology into the schools is more than the relatively straightforward insertion of a physical object with remarkable properties into an ongoing social milieu with no important coincident adjustments in that milieu. On the contrary, the decision to use computers often brings with it quite unexamined decisions that are not recognized as important choices with possible educational consequences. Yet things as varied as the name given to a computer course, the physical location of the computers within a room, or the extent to which students are allowed or encouraged to assist each other while working on the computers can have their own impact. Thus, the use of technology is likely to bring with it a surrounding envelope of change that is often an ad hoc response to the practical and logistical imperatives of the situation, rather than a carefully thought out integrated plan for change.

Recognition of this point leads to the second point – that using computers is likely to have unanticipated effects on students, teachers, and classrooms because in adopting the technology one is

226

likely to be accepting, or more probably evolving, an entire set of unplanned changes as well as the planned technological ones. These changes also have implications for the kinds of outcomes that the use of technology fosters. Thus, even if one could somehow know how the technology "in and of itself" would affect students, one does not know how it will do so in actual use. Furthermore, in interpreting any effect on students that seems to result from the introduction of computers into a school or classroom, one needs to be extremely cautious. There is always the possibility, even the probability, that the effects are connected to changes in the social functioning of the classroom either by themselves or in combination with changes more intimately tied to the technology itself.

A third finding, discussed at length earlier, is that in spite of the potential for very disparate changes in the social functioning of classrooms related to computer use, two such changes were fairly common. The first of these was a shift in the teacher's role from an emphasis on lecturing to a whole class, with the expectation that students will assimilate the information contained in the lecture, to a more individualized approach in which the teacher functions as a coach or guide when students encounter problems in their work. The second was heightened interest and involvement when students worked on computers. Although these two shifts are by no means inevitable consequences of computer use, they seem to be widespread, both at Whitmore and elsewhere.

Finally, the study reported in this book makes it clear that although computers have the potential to create important changes in the classroom, the ways in which they are received and used in the schools also reflect current social reality. Thus, many teachers avoid them – out of inertia, anxiety about technology, or the belief that computers have little or nothing to offer to the curriculum as it now stands. Those who do attempt to use them often struggle within a social system that does not give them the kind of training they need or the support they want.

Although students' attitudes toward computers and their reactions to using them are generally positive, traditional gender roles shape their experiences in very marked ways. Girls are more likely than boys to be socially isolated from their peers if they pursue an interest in developing their computer skills, and factors ranging from the gender composition of the pool of computer science teachers to the kinds of examples used in class reinforce this linkage between masculinity and computers to the point that students, as we found at Whitmore, laugh at the idea that one could create a program relating to sewing, a traditionally feminine domain.

This suggests that the view that computers will suddenly revolutionize education is most likely mistaken. Computers by themselves cannot and will not have such an impact. They are social as well as technological objects, and their use is subject to the vagaries of the social milieu in which they are available for use, although over time they may profoundly influence that milieu. If they are too out of step with existing practice, they are likely not to be used extensively, or they will be used in ways that do not take full advantage of their potential.

Yet in the long run, the use of computers and associated technology in schools and in society more generally may create pressure for and facilitate transformational change in our educational system. The full impact of inventions to which they have been compared, such as the invention of writing or the printing press, was not felt for centuries. Had studies of the impact of the printing press or writing been feasible only decades after these innovations appeared, it seems inevitable, in retrospect, that their eventual impact would have been vastly underrated. Furthermore, the rapidity with which computer technology itself is now evolving means that one must consider not the probable impact of the kinds of technology that are now available, but the likely impact of successive generations of computerized devices whose capabilities may only be foreshadowed currently in schools. With this longer view in mind, it is reasonable to expect that computer use will play a major role in reshaping education and that the potential for positive change is enormous.

APPENDIX

METHODOLOGY

The Research Team

In the past decade or so there has been increasingly wide acceptance of the idea that both the data generated in a research project and the conclusions drawn are to some extent influenced by the personal characteristics of the researchers involved, even in projects designed to minimize the impact of such characteristics (Phillips, 1990; Ratcliffe, 1983; Reinharz, 1992). For example, a researcher's disciplinary background clearly shapes the formulation of a problem, and researchers' gender and race often affect their access to certain kinds of information (Martin, 1978; Reinharz, 1992). Reactions to this realization have varied dramatically, especially among those engaged in the many forms of qualitative research. Some scholars, while acknowledging this situation, have sought to find ways to minimize its impact (Miles & Huberman, 1984). Others almost glory in it, arguing that this realization frees us from pernicious myths about objectivity (Roman & Apple, 1990). Although I am more closely aligned philosophically with the former position than the latter, I think it is useful for readers to know something about the background of those conducting the inquiry on which the book is based.

The core of the research team consisted of four individuals – the author of this book, who is a social psychologist; a postdoctoral fellow, who is an anthropologist; and two graduate students in social psychology. Three additional graduate students in anthropology participated either by conducting some of the student interviews or working on the content analysis of these interviews. In addition, over a dozen undergraduate students from various fields, supervised by the author and some of the graduate students just mentioned, assisted with the project primarily by working on

229

the analysis of the more than 200 student interviews conducted as part of this research.

Two members of the core team, the author and one of the graduate students, are women. The other two core members, the postdoctoral fellow and a graduate student, are men. The large majority of individuals involved in the conduct of this study are white. However, believing that it was especially important to have as diverse a group as possible working on a project conducted in a heterogeneous school like Whitmore, I also made strong efforts to recruit African American team members. Although it was not possible to balance the research team as well by race as by gender, one of the anthropologists who conducted many of the student interviews was African American, as were two of the undergraduates who contributed significantly to the analysis of these interviews.

I undertook this study because interest and opportunity coincided. For many years I have had a deep interest in issues related to race relations. For almost two decades that interest expressed itself in research on race relations in desegregated schools (e.g., Sagar & Schofield; 1979; Sagar, Schofield, & Snyder, 1983; Schofield, 1986a, 1986b, 1989a, 1991; Schofield & Sagar, 1979). Work on that topic focused my attention on the more general topic of educational change. Anyone thinking about educational change in the mid 1980s could hardly avoid issues relating to the likely impact of educational technology since computers were entering the schools at an astonishing pace to the accompaniment of often utopian predictions. Thus, questions concerning the potential role of computers in changing and improving education began to become a focus of my thinking. Learning about a possible funding opportunity for a qualitative study on this topic, I wrote the grant proposal that ultimately led to the research reported here.

Examination of that proposal suggests it foreshadowed quite well some of the issues discussed in this book. For example, it raised the possibility that the introduction of computers into classrooms might affect the nature of the relation between teachers and pupils, especially the nature of the authority relationship. It also argued that the use of computers was likely to have unintended side effects. However, other issues that emerged during the conduct of the research, especially the focus on gender, were not even referred to in that 50-page document and reflect a shift of attention that occurred during the course of the work. The proposal identified itself neither with the utopians who expected extraordinary change nor with the school of thought that viewed computers as just one more fad that would have no more effect in the schools than other once highly touted innovations such as film, radio, and television. In this it reflected the fact that I had no firm, well-articulated vision of what such technology was likely to accomplish, although I did have both a keen interest in its possibilities and an awareness of difficulties inherent in trying to achieve educational change.

Data-Gathering Techniques

As indicated in Chapter 1, the two major methods of data gathering used in this study were intensive qualitative classroom observations and repeated semistructured interviews. Observations were conducted using the "full field note" method of data collection (Olson, 1976), which involves taking extensive handwritten notes during the events being observed. Shortly thereafter these notes were audiotaped and transcribed. One major issue with the use of such notes as a database is what Smith and Geoffrey (1968) have termed the "two-realities problem" – the fact that field notes cannot possibly include everything that has transpired. Hence, a source of potential bias during subsequent analysis of these notes is the fact that the occurrences captured in them are only a part of the fuller set of behaviors that the researcher is trying to document and understand. Further, there is the possibility that selective recording of certain types of events means that the field notes may not only be incomplete but biased in some systematic way.

Although the two-realities problem is impossible to surmount completely in qualitative observation, there are some steps that can be taken to minimize its effects. For example, it was useful to have two researchers observe the same classroom. Although Scriven's (1972) argument that consensus does not guarantee accuracy is well taken, the discussion of differences between the two observers' notes helped to make research team members aware of individual biases, preconceptions, and note-taking practices. For example, very early on it became apparent that one observer was more likely to focus on the loudest or most talkative students, whereas another continually surveyed the class, paying roughly equal amounts of attention to both talkative and quiet students. Discussion of this difference in field notes taken in the same setting led to a change in the behavior of the observer who initially had focused his attention rather narrowly on the most active students.

Unwarranted inferences made by the observer can also be a potentially serious source of bias. To deal with this problem, care was taken to make the field notes as factual and as concretely descriptive as possible. For example, instead of or in addition to saying that a student is bored with a class, one can record behavioral manifestations of this internal state, such as sleeping, doodling, or looking at materials from other classes rather than at the teacher who is presenting the lesson. Transcribed field notes were monitored to keep observers aware of the importance of providing such information.

Another source of potential problems in research like that described here is that the people who are being observed will act differently because of an observer's presence. To minimize this problem, we paid careful attention to developing a role in the school's social system that caused as little disturbance as possible. We presented ourselves as individuals from a local university who were interested in observing if and how the presence of computer technology for instructional purposes changed the social processes occurring in classrooms. We took great pains not to be seen by the students as part of the school's authority structure because it was felt that this would inhibit their openness and spontaneity. Hence, we made it a rule never to interfere with students' behaviors. Similarly, we did not comment on students' or teachers' actions in an evaluative manner while at the school.

Although it seems likely that an observer's presence will make some changes in a classroom's functioning, our conscious efforts to minimize this problem seemed quite effective. Sometimes, in fact, it appeared as if individuals in classes we observed routinely literally failed to notice that we were there, as indicated by the following excerpts from field notes taken by two different observers:

> It is 10:07, about a half an hour into [geometry] class. . . . Alice sees me [an observer who has been in the class since before it began]. She looks a bit startled and says, "Oh! . . . I didn't know you were here."

> It's 20 minutes into the class [a business class] now, and the teacher is still collecting assignments. Students don't have any particular task. . . . Micky is busy at her desk brushing off some eraser crumbs. She hits me, apparently by accident, as she brushes the desk off and says, "I'm sorry. Did I hit you? I forgot you were there."

Very occasionally a teacher would try to use the fact that an observer was present to influence students' behavior, specifically to get them to work harder or to behave more in accordance with the teacher's idea of proper classroom demeanor and speech. Such efforts rarely appeared to be very successful:

> There are now four boys in the computer room [set aside for use by the gifted students]. . . . They are all just . . . horsing around, throwing paper, and the like. Ms. Prentiss says, "There's an observer here from the university." Two of the boys say, "Ah so," in funny voices with attempted Japanese accents and bow toward me. Then they immediately resume their horsing around just as before.

On one occasion a teacher tried to inhibit a discussion between a colleague and a student about their attempts to illegally copy software using various special programs developed for this purpose by pointing out the presence of an observer who was taking notes. Again, this effort was not successful and the conversation continued, implying either a high level of trust or the belief that such behavior was not likely to lead to trouble serious enough to be worth trying to avoid.

In spite of our efforts to influence the behavior of Whitmore's students and staff as little as possible, there were times, especially in the first months of the research, when it was clear that the presence of a researcher influenced or disrupted the normal flow of events in some significant way. Careful note was taken of such situations for three reasons. First, it was often possible to find ways to disrupt normal behavior patterns less. Second, such occasions suggested topics about which individuals or groups were especially sensitive and thus provided clues about issues that needed to be approached with special sensitivity and reassurances about confidentiality. Finally, noting that specific behaviors appeared to occur because of the observer's presence lessened the likelihood that such behaviors would be confused later in the data analysis phase of the research with behaviors that would most likely have occurred had the research not been conducted.

Observers, no matter how omnipresent and insightful, are at a great disadvantage if they do not test their emerging ideas through direct inquiry with those whom they are observing. Because interviews can be so useful in presenting participants' perspectives on events, both formal and informal interviews were used extensively, as indicated in Chapter 1. In constructing and conducting these interviews, strong efforts were made to procure valid and unbiased data. For example, questions were posed in a balanced manner so that leading questions were avoided, students were assured that their teachers would not have access to their interview transcripts, and the like.

We also made concerted efforts to build rapport with teachers and students so that they would share their thoughts and observations with us freely in interviews and in frequent informal conversations. Several factors seemed crucial to achieving this goal, including noninterference in events in the classroom, a nonjudgmental and sympathetic attitude, and careful guarding of the absolute confidentiality of information gathered during the observations and interviews. Perhaps the success of these efforts is best attested to by the kind of information made available to members of the research team. Individuals frequently shared information with us that could have caused them or those they cared for real problems had we not honored our pledges concerning confidentiality, thus demonstrating a substantial level of trust as is apparent from the following excerpts, first from project field notes and then from an interview:

> Jim [a student] says that I shouldn't tell anybody else [about this], that Don [another student] would get in a lot of trouble. He says that Don threw a stink bomb into the darkroom [an act for which he could be suspended] and that's why it smells so bad in there.

> Ms. Trexler:[1] . . . [She has said something extremely negative about her supervisor's work in a taped interview, after which she adds] If he knows I said that I'd be in a lot of trouble.

Formal interviews, which were routinely audiotaped, were generally quite structured. Interviewers worked from carefully designed sets of open-ended questions. However, interviewers were encouraged to probe respondent's replies extensively and to follow up on topics that interviewees suggested were important even if they were not part of the prepared set of questions. Interviews were conducted in private settings, such as a small conference room located in Whitmore's library, and respondents were assured that their comments would be treated as confidential and used only for research purposes.

Informal interviews ranged from extended conversations with teachers during free periods to short interchanges with teachers and students in the hallway. Notes on such conversations were recorded immediately after they occurred. However, since these interviews were not audiotaped, they were treated as field notes rather than as direct quotes.

Although observation and interviewing were the primary data gathering techniques used, other techniques were employed when appropriate. For example, archival material pertinent to the study, such as internal school memoranda, announcements, and copies of the student newspaper, were collected and analyzed. Again care was taken to procure data that was as representative and valid as

---

1 Although throughout this book pseudonyms are used consistently for all individuals, here I have used a special pseudonym that appears only this once so that information about this person's job responsibilities could not possibly be used to identify her by anyone familiar with the school.

possible. For example, early on in the study we left logs next to computers in many classrooms to gather information on who used computers and for what purposes. Both prior experience and the comments of some teachers suggested that this procedure might lead to underestimates of use. Being cognizant of the potential weakness of this approach, we supplemented it with interviews and direct observation. For example, we compared log entries with our observations of actual usage on randomly selected days to get some idea of the extent and type of misreporting that occurred (e.g., what proportion of the students working on the computers had failed to sign in, whether students frequently reported they were working on school assignments when they were actually playing games). In cases in which log estimates varied substantially from estimates based on more reliable approaches, we discontinued gathering logs. In cases in which they appeared to supply an accurate picture of usage, we continued to employ them.

Data Collection

Having described the general approach taken in this research and the kinds of methods employed, I shall now turn to a detailed description of the specific data-gathering activities. Since several of the chapters focus on specific milieus, it seems reasonable to organize the description of data-gathering activities by classroom type.

GPTutor Classrooms. A team of three researchers observed eight geometry classes taught utilizing the GPTutor. These classes were taught by the two teachers who participated in the field test of the GPTutor, Mr. Adams and Mr. Brice. Two of the classes observed were for gifted students (defined as those with an IQ near or above 130), two more were for "advanced track" classes (generally containing strong students with IQ's between 115 and 130), and four were for more average college-bound students. The academic performance of students in the regular college-bound track varied widely. Whereas some had solid math skills, others were prone to constant errors, even in simple addition and subtraction. The classes using the computer tutors ranged markedly in size (7–17 students) as did the control and comparison classes (6–25 students). Most were small enough so that each student had his or her own computer to work on. Alternatively, students worked in pairs on the 10 available machines. This occurred in two classes, in spite of the fact that the developers of the GPTutor were not enthusiastic about having their software, which was designed for individual use, be field-tested under these conditions. The impetus for this arrangement was interest on the part of one of the agencies that funded the development of the tutor in the question of whether the GPTutor could be productively used by pairs of students. The tutors' developers and the teachers involved concluded, generally speaking, that individual use was more effective than use by pairs (Wertheimer, 1990). I have chosen not to focus on this issue in this book, however, because the experiment with pairs was tried in only two classes. Furthermore, one of those classes was the only GPTutor class taught by Mr. Brice, making it difficult, if not impossible, to infer which aspects of that classroom's functioning were due to the fact that the GPTutor was used in pairs and which were due to other aspects of the situation, such as the teacher.

Observations in the GPTutor classes were made before, during, and after the part of the year in which the tutors were used so that the impact of the tutor could be assessed by comparing the way these classrooms functioned when the GPTutor was in use with when it was not. This was the heart of the observational work, since it provided an excellent set of comparisons for analyzing the impact of the GPTutor. The 183 periods during which these classrooms were observed were divided quite evenly between days when the GPTutor was in use and days when it was not. Of the 94 class periods in which the tutors were not used, the largest number, 39, were observed before the tutor was introduced in order to get a clear picture of how those classes functioned. The remaining observations were divided between days when the class did not utilize the tutors, even though the computers were available, and the period of the year after the class had completely finished working with the tutors.

In addition to observing the classes in which the GPTutor was used, we also observed in two "control" and three comparison classes. Students were assigned to the GPTutor control and comparison classrooms by the school, so self-selection into the different classes was not a problem. Students assigned to the GPTutor classes were allowed to transfer into a control or comparison classroom if they or their parents so desired. However, to the best of my knowledge, none did so. The two control classes were regular track classes taught *without* the GPTutor by Mr. Adams and Mr. Brice. These two classes were observed since there was the possibility that Mr. Adams and Mr. Brice would teach differently in these classes than they did in the equivalent GPTutor classes when the tutor was not in use. In addition, there was the possibility that the behavior of the students in the control classes would be markedly different from that of the students in the GPTutor classes before the computers were used. If this were the case, then analysis of the impact of the tutor based only on a comparison of the GPTutor classes when the tutor was being used and when it was not might well be misleading since the mere fact that the tutors were going to be or had been used might have changed classroom dynamics significantly.

Three comparison classes (one regular, one advanced, and one for gifted students) taught by the only two other geometry teachers at Whitmore High School, Mr. Tyrone and Mr. Carter, were also observed. The goal in observing these classes was to provide a context to which to compare whatever changes might occur in the classes using the GPTutor. For example, it seemed useful to have some way of judging if any changes we might observe in the GPTutor classrooms were changes in aspects of teacher or student behavior that were idiosyncratic to the teachers or classes using the GPTutor. If the GPTutor appeared to change widely shared instructional approaches or other common patterns in classroom life, the implications of that change would certainly be greater than if change was restricted to idiosyncratic aspects of classroom functioning. Mr. Tyrone's gifted student and advanced classes were selected for observation since they were the only non-GPTutor geometry classes offered to students in these tracks during the study. Mr. Carter's regular class was randomly selected for observation from the several regular geometry classes he taught.

In addition to all these classroom observations, further observations were made of staff meetings conducted by the developers of the GPTutor. This provided yet another rich source of information since such meetings revolved around reports from the staff members of the development team working at Whitmore in the GPTutor classrooms, discussion of problems made apparent in the tutor by the field-test, planning for the ongoing improvement of the tutor, and talk about teachers' and students' reactions to the GPTutor.

All of the students in the classes using the GPTutor were invited to participate in pre- and postuse interviews. Over 90% of these students ($N = 84$) and 82% of a group of control students ($N = 51$) randomly selected from other geometry classes actually participated. These 45-minute structured, open-ended interviews were audiotaped and transcribed. Both formal and informal interviews with the two teachers using the computer tutors, Mr. Adams and Mr. Brice, and the teachers of the comparison classes were conducted throughout the course of the research. To get yet an additional perspective on the computer tutors, interviews were also conducted with numerous individuals closely connected with the development of the tutor and its field test in the school setting, including the project leaders, programmers, and the individual whose job it was to oversee the field testing itself.

Computer Science Classes. Computer science classes were also observed intensively for a total of more than 100 hours, divided roughly evenly between Computer Science 1 and Computer Science 2 classes. During the study's first year, weekly observations were made in Computer Science 1 classes taught by Mr. Brice and Mr. Davidson, two of the three teachers who offered this course. Similarly, in the study's second year, we observed weekly in classes led by Mr. Brice, Ms. Brown, and Mr. Colgate, three of the four individuals teaching computer science that year. We also observed roughly every other week in Mr. Edward's classroom. In addition, in both years of the study we observed the one Computer Science 2 class offered. Mr. Brice taught both of these classes.

In addition to interviewing all of the computer science teachers, we conducted interviews with a randomly selected group of students enrolled in computer science during the study's second year. This group consisted of 29 students enrolled in Computer Science 1 and 7 enrolled in Computer Science 2. (The latter was a small class consisting of just 12 students.) Over 85% of the students asked to participate in the interview did so. The 45-minute interviews were semistructured, consisting almost exclusively of open-ended questions. The questions for both groups of students were very similar, although the interview for the more advanced students contained some extra questions on topics such as why they had enrolled in a second computer science course.

Business Classes. During each of the 2 years of this study one class called Office Automation and another called Business Computer Applications were systematically observed. Over this 2-year period a total of four different classes taught by four different teachers, Ms. Spring, Ms. Parton, Ms. White, and Ms. Young, participated in this study. A total of over 35 hours were spent in these classes observing roughly 50 separate class sessions. The Office Automation classes covered basic material on secretarial and clerical work including how to operate common office machines such as dictaphones, adding machines, typewriters, word processors, and computers. The Business Computer Applications classes were intended to teach students how to compute payrolls, prepare taxes, and do accounts using computer software.

In the study's second year we formally interviewed both teachers and students from these business classes. Specifically, we interviewed Ms. White and Ms. Parton, as well as 28 randomly selected students. Again, the participation rate was excellent, with over 80% of those students being asked to participate in the interviews agreeing to do so. In these classes, as in other classes in which we observed, both teachers and students were also informally interviewed repeatedly during the entire course of the study.

Computer Room for Gifted Students. The computer room set aside for the use of gifted students was observed twice a week during the first year of the study and twice every other week in the second year. By far the most common usage of this room was during two consecutive lunch periods each school day when students were free to go to this room instead of the cafeteria if they wished. Thus, our observations were concentrated on these back-to-back 25-minute lunch periods. Over the 2-year period we observed students in the lab during almost 100 separate periods. In addition, we also observed, when possible, on the very infrequent occasions when an entire class came to this room at other times of the day to work on projects in biology, art, or other subjects.

Given the informal nature of lunchtime in the computer room, it was possible to talk to the students there as well as the two teachers who supervised it during virtually every observational period. We used this opportunity extensively. However, we also conducted formal interviews. Such interviews were conducted with both of the teachers, as well as with 13 students, 6 boys and 7 girls, selected because records showed they came to the room frequently. Sampling of the students to be interviewed was stratified by gender, since so few girls came frequently relative to boys, and it seemed important to get both boys' and girls' perceptions of their experiences in this milieu. Thus, all the girls who came at all frequently were interviewed, whereas this was not true for the boys. Only one African American, a girl, came to the computer room on more than rare occasions. She was interviewed, but obviously no general conclusions about how African American students' reactions differed from their white peers' reactions can be drawn on the basis of such slender evidence.

Other Data-Gathering Activities. The four kinds of sites already mentioned were selected for close study because they were the places in which computers were most readily available for use by a substantial number of students. However, to gain a more complete picture of how computers were used at Whitmore and what effects they might have on classroom social processes, a considerable amount of additional data were gathered. Specifically, observations were conducted in virtually all the other sites in which computers were available for use at the school. Thus, to illustrate, roughly 25 hours of observation was focused on a Visual Communication classroom that had one computer. Additional observations were carried out in the room of a biology teacher who had students use various pieces of software relating to topics they were studying. To gain a balanced picture of teachers' attitudes toward and experiences with computer use, it also seemed important to seek out teachers who were not using computers for instructional purposes, even though they could do so if they desired or had done so at some time in the past. Thus, a list of such teachers was constructed and an extended formal interview was conducted with the large majority of these individuals. In addition, informal interviews were frequently conducted with these and other teachers who did not use computers in their classrooms.

Data Analysis

Briefly describing data analysis procedures in qualitative research is extremely difficult since the process is so complex and iterative. To summarize, observational notes were coded as described in sources like Miles and Huberman (1984), Strauss (1987), and Strauss and Corbin (1990). This involves carefully reviewing field notes as they are collected, creating coding categories of various types, developing and refining coding systems, writing working memos, and then searching for ways to refute or refine the ideas emerging from the preceding activities. Formal interviews were analyzed using traditional content analysis procedures when more than 10 individuals had responded to a particular set of questions. Informal interviews and formal interviews administered to very small groups of people were coded in a fashion similar to the field notes.

Space constraints make it impossible to present fine details on the data analysis. For example over a dozen different formal interviews were constructed, each consisting of roughly 20 to 30 questions. Although some questions appeared in all or most of the interviews, many had to be specifically tailored to fit the situation in question. Presentation of the dozens of individual coding systems developed for the content analysis of this very large set of questions would serve little purpose. However, it does seem important to discuss the general principles that guided both the data-gathering and the data analysis phases of the research and to illustrate them briefly.

First, in both data gathering and analysis a concerted effort was made to be as rigorous and systematic as possible. For example, sampling techniques were employed where appropriate, trained personnel coded the open-ended interviews using systems specifically developed for this research, and field notes were transcribed and then carefully indexed so that all notes relevant to a given topic could be examined. (Coding of these notes was conducted using Ethnograph – software designed precisely for this kind of analysis.)

Second, we took the importance of triangulating the data seriously (Webb, Campbell, Schwartz, & Sechrest, 1966). Care was taken to gather many different types of information bearing on the same issue, to minimize the potential problems with each data source, and to be sensitive to biases that could not be completely eliminated in analyzing and interpreting the data. This principle was illustrated in the earlier discussion of our use of the student-generated logs of classroom computer use. Perhaps a better example was our practice of routinely asking students and teachers questions on topics related to our classroom observations. For example, as discussed in Chapter 2, we concluded, based on observational data such as the fact that students began to arrive at class earlier and to stay longer, that they became more motivated when their class started using the GPTutor. However, questions about the GPTutor's effect on students' level of motivation were included in both student and teacher interviews to see if this conclusion was consistent with teachers' observations and students' self-reports. In drawing conclusions from the data, care was taken to look at these varying sources of information to see if they led to similar conclusions. When they did not, further data-gathering or analysis efforts were undertaken to try to clarify the reason for the discrepancy.

The third general principle that we took seriously was that data analysis should be an ongoing and iterative process. Connected to this was an explicit commitment to use the flexibility of the qualitative approach to shift the focus of our interviews and observations in directions that the ongoing data analysis suggested would be fruitful. Thus, as the field notes and other data accumulated, they were indexed, read, and reread. Because the huge database generated by these activities created a situation in which there was danger of getting bogged down in a morass of detail, emphasis was placed on generating working memos about emerging ideas so that data relevant to these themes could be sought in planned and systematic ways. Care was taken to explore ways in which these ideas could be disconfirmed or refined, as well as supported.

The emergent focus on issues related to gender discussed in note 4 is an example of one shift stemming from data analysis efforts during the course of the data gathering. Also of significance is the fact that although my initial orientation to the research was characterized by a focus on the effects of computer use on classroom social processes, the issue of the impact of the existing social arrangements on computer usage quickly gained increasing importance as the research progressed.

REFERENCES

American Association of Colleges of Teacher Education Committee on Research and Information (1987). *Research about teacher education (RATE)1. Teaching teachers: Facts and figures.* Washington, DC: American Association of Colleges of Teacher Education.

Ames, C. A. (1990). Motivation: What teachers need to know. *Teachers College Record, 91*(3), 409–421.

Ames, C. A., & Archer, J. (1988). Achievement goals in the classroom: Students' learning strategies and motivation processes. *Journal of Educational Psychology, 80*(3), 260–267.

Ames, R., & Ames, C. (1989). Adolescent motivation and achievement. In J. Worell & F. Donner (Eds.), *The adolescent as decision-maker* (pp. 181–204). New York: Academic.

Anand, P. G., & Ross, S. M. (1987). Using computer-assisted instruction to personalize arithmetic materials for elementary school children. *Journal of Educational Psychology, 79*(1), 72–78.

Anderson, J. R. (1984). *Proposal to the Carnegie Corporation to support demonstration and development of a geometry tutor.* Unpublished manuscript. Carnegie Mellon University, Pittsburgh.

Anderson, J. R., Boyle, C. F., & Reiser, B. J. (1985). Intelligent tutoring systems. *Science, 228,* 456–462.

Anderson, J. R., Boyle, C. F., & Yost, G. (1985). The geometry tutor. *Journal of Mathematical Behavior, 5,* 5–19.

Anderson, R. C., Shirey, L. L., Wilson, P. T., & Fielding, L. G. (1987). Interestingness of children's reading material. In R. E. Snow & M. C. Farr (Eds.), *Aptitude, learning, and instruction: Vol. 3. Conative and affective process analyses* (pp. 297–337). Hillsdale, NJ: Erlbaum.

Anderson, R. E. (1993). The technology infrastructure of U.S. schools. *Communications of the Association for Computing Machinery, 36*(5), 72–73.

Anderson, R. E., Welch, W. W., & Harris, L. J. (1984). Inequities in opportunities for computer literacy. *Computing Teacher, 11,* 10–12.

Arnold, L. (1975). Florence Bascom and the exclusion of women from the earth science curriculum materials. *Journal of Geological Education, 23,* 110–113.

Asher, S. R. (1980). Topic interest and children's reading comprehension. In R. J. Spiro, B. C. Bruce, & W. F. Brewer (Eds.), *Theoretical issues in reading comprehension* (pp. 525–534). Hillsdale, NJ: Erlbaum.

Baker, E. L., Gearhart, M., & Herman, J. L. (1989). *The Apple classrooms of tomorrow: 1988 UCLA Evaluation Study* (Report to Apple Computer, Inc.). Los Angeles: UCLA Center for the Study of Evaluation.

Baker, E. L., Gearhart, M., & Herman, J. L. (1990). *The Apple classrooms of tomorrow: 1989 UCLA Evaluation Study* (Report to Apple Computer, Inc.). Los Angeles: UCLA Center for the Study of Evaluation.

Baker, E. L., Gearhart, M., & Herman, J. L. (1991). *The Apple classrooms of tomorrow: 1990 UCLA Evaluation Study* (Report to Apple Computer, Inc.). Los Angeles: UCLA Center for the Study of Evaluation.

Bazler, J. A. (1988). *A comparative gender analysis of high school chemistry textbooks*. Unpublished doctoral dissertation, University of Montana.

Beck, R. C. (1990). *Motivation: Theories and principles*. Englewood Cliffs, NJ: Prentice-Hall.

Becker, H. J. (1983). *School uses of microcomputers: Reports from a national survey* (Issue No. 1). Baltimore, MD: Johns Hopkins University, Center for Social Organization of Schools.

Becker, H. J. (1984). School uses of microcomputers: Reports from a National Survey. *Center for Social Organization of Schools Newsletter* (Issue No. 4). Baltimore, MD: Johns Hopkins University.

Becker, H. J. (1986, August). *Instructional uses of school computers: Reports from the 1985 national survey*. Baltimore, MD: Johns Hopkins University, Center for Social Organization of Schools.

Becker, H. J. (1987, April). *The impact of computer use on children's learning: What research has shown and what it has not*. Paper presented at the meeting of the American Educational Research Association, Washington, DC.

Becker, H. J. (1990, April). *Computer use in United States schools: 1989. An initial report of U.S. participation in the I.E.A. Computers in Education Survey*. Paper presented at the meeting of the American Educational Research Association, Boston, MA.

Becker, H. J. (1993). Teaching with and about computers in secondary schools. *Communications of the Association for Computing Machinery*, 36(5), 69–72.

Becker, H. J., & Sterling, C. W. (1987). Equity in school computer use: National data and neglected considerations. *Journal of Educational Computing Research*, 3, 289–311.

Benne, K. D. (1970). Authority in education. *Harvard Educational Review*, *40*(3), 385–410.

Best, R. (1983). *We've all got scars: What boys and girls learn in elementary school*. Bloomington: Indiana University Press.

Bialo, E., & Sivin, J. (1990). *Report on the effectiveness of microcomputers in schools*. Washington, DC: Software Publishers Association.

Bierman, D., Breuker, J., & Sandberg, J. (Eds.). (1989). *Artificial intelligence and education*. Amsterdam: IOS Press.

Bierstedt, R. (1970). *The social order*. New York: McGraw-Hill.

Bikson, T., Gutek, B. A., & Mankin, D. A. (1981). *The office of the future* (Tech. Rep.). Santa Monica, CA: Rand Corporation.

Birmaimah, K. (1989, February). *Inequalities in classroom computer software*. Paper presented at the meeting of the Eastern Educational Research Association, Savannah, GA.

Blanton, W. E., & Zimmerman, S. (1994, April). *The effects of participation in a mixed activity system on the achievement of at-risk and special education students: A case study*. Paper presented at the meeting of the American Educational Research Association, New Orleans.

Bossert, S. T. (1979). *Tasks and social relationships in the classroom*. Cambridge University Press.

Bossert, W. H. (1988). The use of technology to improve two key classroom relationships. In R. S. Nickerson & P. P. Zodhiates (Eds.), *Technology in education: Looking toward 2020* (pp. 275–284). Hillsdale, NJ: Erlbaum.

Bowers, C. A. (1988). *The cultural dimensions of educational computing: Understanding the non-neutrality of technology*. New York: Teachers College Press.

Bracey, G. W. (1988). Computers in class: Some social and psychological consequences. *Electronic Learning*, *7*(8), 28.

Brady, H. (1986). Artificial intelligence: What's in it for educators? *Classroom Computer Learning*, *6*(4), 26–29.

Brady, H., & Slesnick, T. (1985, April–May). Girls don't like fluffware either. *Classroom Computer Learning*, *6*, 23–26.

Braverman, H. (1974). *Labor and monopoly capital: The degradation of work in the twentieth century*. New York: Monthly Review Press.

Britt, C. L., Eurich-Fulcer, R., & Schofield, J. W. (1991, May). *Gender role stereotyping in high school computer science materials*. Paper presented at the meeting of the Mid-Western Psychological Association, Chicago.

Brod, R. L. (1972). *The computer as an authority figure: Some effects of CAI on student perception of teacher authority* (Tech. Rep. No. 29). Stanford, CA: Stanford Center for Research and Development in Teaching.

Brown, J. S. (1985). Process versus product – A perspective on tools for communal and informal electronic learning. *Journal of Educational Computing Research, 1,* 179–201.

Buesmans, J., & Wieckert, K. (1989). Computing, research and war: If knowledge is power, where is responsibility? *Communications of the Association for Computing Machinery, 32*(1), 939–951.

Bulkeley, W. M. (1988, June 6). Computers failing as teaching aids: Heralded revolution falls short due to lack of machines, training. *The Wall Street Journal,* p. 17.

Burnham, D. (1983). *The rise of the computer state.* New York: Pantheon.

Buss, D. M. (1988). The evolution of human intrasexual competition: Tactics of mate attraction. *Journal of Personality and Social Psychology, 54,* 616–628.

Caldwell, J. H., Huitt, W. G., & Graeber, A. O. (1982). Time spent in learning: Implications from research. *Elementary School Journal, 82*(5), 471–480.

Campbell, L. P. (1984). On the horizon: A computer in every classroom. *Education, 104*(3), 332–334.

Carney, C. C. (1986). Teacher + computer = More learning. *Computing Teacher, 13*(6), 12–15.

Carroll, J. B. (1963). A model of school learning. *Teachers College Record, 64*(8), 723–733.

Chen, M. (1986). Gender and computers: The beneficial effects of experience on attitudes. *Journal of Educational Computing Research, 2*(3), 265–282.

Chipman, S. F., & Thomas, V. G. (1987). The participation of women and minorities in mathematical, scientific, and technical fields. In E. Z. Rothkopf (Ed.), *Review of research in education* (Vol. 14, pp. 387–430). Washington, DC: American Educational Research Association.

Clements, D. H. (1987). Computers and young children: A review of research. *Young Children, 43*(1), 34–44.

Cohen, D. K. (1988). Educational technology and school organization. In R. S. Nickerson & P. P. Zodhiates (Eds.), *Technology in education: Looking toward 2020* (pp. 231–264). Hillsdale, NJ: Erlbaum.

Cole, M., & Griffin, P. (1987). Computers' impact on the context of instruction. In M. Cole & P. Griffin (Eds.), *Contextual factors in education: Improving science and mathematics education for minorities and women* (pp. 43–69). Madison: University of Wisconsin, Wisconsin Center for Education Research, School of Education.

Cole, M., & Laboratory of Comparative Human Cognition (1990). Computers and the organization of new forms of educational activity: A socio-historical perspective. *Golem*, 2, 6–13.

Coleman, J. C. (1980). Friendship and the peer group in adolescence. In J. Adelson (Ed.), *Handbook of adolescent psychology* (pp. 408–431). New York: Wiley.

Collins, A. (1991). The role of computer technology in restructuring schools. *Phi Delta Kappan*, 73(1), 28–36.

Collins, A. (in press). The role of computer technology in restructuring schools. In K. Sheingold & M. Tucker (Eds.), *Restructuring for learning with technology*.

Crandall, D. P., & Loucks, S. F. (1983). *People, policies and practices: Examining the chain of school improvement* (Vol. 10). Andover, MA: The Network.

Cuban, L. (1986). *Teachers and machines: The classroom use of technology since 1920*. New York: Teachers College Press.

Deci, E. L., & Ryan, R. M. (1992). The initiation and regulation of intrinsically motivated learning and achievement. In A. K. Boggiano & T. S. Pittman (Eds.), *Achievement and motivation: A social-developmental perspective* (pp. 9–36). Cambridge University Press.

Demetrulias, D. M., & Rosenthal, N. R. (1985). Discrimination against females and minorities in microcomputer advertising. *Computers and the Social Sciences*, 1, 91–95.

Derfler, F., Jr. (1989). Imposing efficiency: Workgroup productivity software. *PC Magazine*, 8(16), 247–269.

DeSola Poole, I. (1977). *The social impact of the telephone*. Cambridge, MA: MIT Press.

Dickinson, D. K. (1986). Cooperation, collaboration, and a computer: Integrating a computer into a first-second grade writing program. *Research in the Teaching of English*, 20(4), 357–378.

Dunlop, C., & Kling, R. (1991). (Eds.). *Computerization and controversy: Value conflicts and social choices*. Boston: Academic.

Educational Testing Service (1988). *The nation's report card*. Princeton, NJ: Educational Testing Service.

Egbert, R. L., & Kluender, M. M. (1984). Time as an element of school success. In R. L. Egbert & M. M. Kluender (Eds.), *Using research to improve teacher education: The Nebraska consortium. Teacher Education*

Monograph No. 1 (pp. 89–107). Washington, DC: Clearinghouse on Teacher Education.

Elkind, D. (1978). Understanding the young adolescent. *Adolescence, 13,* 127–134.

Eurich-Fulcer, R., & Britt, C. (1990). *Computers and gender: Content analysis of a computer textbook.* Unpublished manuscript, University of Pittsburgh.

Eurich-Fulcer, R., & Schofield, J. W. (in press). Wide-area networking in K–12 education: Issues shaping implementation and use. *Computers and Education.*

Feigenbaum, E., & McCorduck, P. (1983). *Fifth generation: Artificial intelligence and Japan's computer challenge to the world.* Reading, MA: Addison-Wesley.

Ferrell, B. G. (1986). Evaluating the impact of CAI on mathematics learning: Computer immersion project. *Journal of Educational Computing Research, 2*(3), 327–336.

Feurzeig, W. (1988). Apprentice tools: Students as practitioners. In R. S. Nickerson & P. P. Zodhiates (Eds.), *Technology in education: Looking toward 2020* (pp. 97–120). Hillsdale, NJ: Erlbaum.

Fiske, S. T., Bersoff, D. N., Borgida, E., Deaux, K., & Heilman, M. E. (1991). Social science research on trial: Use of sex stereotyping research in *Price Waterhouse vs. Hopkins. American Psychologist, 46*(10), 1049–1060.

Fiske, S. T., & Taylor, S. E. (1978). Salience, attention, and attribution: Top of the head phenomena. In L. Berkowitz (Ed.), *Advances in experimental social psychology* (Vol. 11, pp. 249–288). New York: Academic.

Folk, H. (1977). The impact of computers on book and journal publication. In J. L. Divilbiss (Ed.), *Proceedings of the 1976 Clinic on Library Applications of Data Processing* (pp. 72–82). Urbana: University of Illinois Press.

Fredrick, W. C., & Walberg, H. J. (1980). Learning as a function of time. *Journal of Educational Research, 73,* 183–194.

Fullan, M. (1982). *The meaning of educational change.* New York: Teachers College Press.

Futoran, G., Schofield, J. W., & Eurich-Fulcer, R. (1994). *Eastman High: First year case study.* Unpublished manuscript, University of Pittsburgh, Pittsburgh.

Gallagher, V. G. (1980). *A comparative study of the female image in selected elementary school science textbooks.* Unpublished doctoral dissertation, University of the Pacific, Stockton, CA.

Garber, J., & Seligman, M. E. P. (Eds.). (1980). *Human helplessness.* New York: Academic.

Garfinkel, S. L. (1989, September). Videodiscs liven up learning. *Christian Science Monitor*, pp. 12–13.

Gearhart, M., Herman, J. L., Baker, E. L., Novak, J. R., & Whittaker, A. K. (1994). A new mirror for the classroom: A technology-based tool for documenting the impact of technology on instruction. In E. L. Baker & H. F. O'Neil Jr. (Eds.), *Technology assessment in education and training* (pp. 153–197). Hillsdale, NJ: Erlbaum.

Goodlad, J. I. (1984). *A place called school: Prospects for the future.* New York: McGraw-Hill.

Goodwin, M. H. (1990). *He-said-she-said: Talk as social organization among black children.* Bloomington: Indiana University Press.

Grant, L., & Fine, G. A. (1992). Sociology unleashed: Creative directions in classical ethnography. In M. LeCompte, W. Millroy, & J. Preissle (Eds.), *The handbook of qualitative research in education* (pp. 405–446). New York: Academic.

Groen, G. J. (1985). The epistemics of computer-based microworlds. *Proceedings from the Second International Conference on Artificial Intelligence and Education.* Exeter, United Kingdom: University of Exeter.

Gross, N., Giaquinta, J., & Bernstein, M. (1971). *Implementing organizational innovations: A sociological analysis of planned educational change.* New York: Basic.

Hartup, W. W. (1985). The peer system. In P. H. Mussen (Ed.), *Handbook of child psychology* (Vol. 4, pp. 104–172). New York: Wiley.

Hativa, N., Swisa, S., & Lesgold, A. (1989, March). Competition in traditional CAI: Motivational, sociological and instructional-design issues. In A. di Sessa (Chair), *Computers and classroom social processes* (pp. 201–237). Symposium conducted at the meeting of the American Educational Research Association, San Francisco.

Hativa, N., Swisa, S., & Lesgold, A. (1992). Competition in individualized CAI. *Instructional Science, 21,* 393–428.

Hawkins, J., & Sheingold, K. (1986). The beginning of a story: Computers and the organization of learning in classrooms. In J. A. Culbertson & L. L. Cunningham (Eds.), *Microcomputers and education* (pp. 40–58). Chicago: University of Chicago Press.

Hawkins, J., Sheingold, K., Gearhart, M., & Berger, C. (1982). Microcomputers in schools: Impact on the social life of elementary classrooms. *Journal of Applied Developmental Psychology, 3,* 361–373.

Heikkinen, H. (1978). Sex bias in chemistry texts: Where is a woman's place. *Science Teacher, 45,* 16–21.

Henderson, V. L., & Dweck, C. S. (1990). Motivation and achievement. In

S. S. Feldman & G. R. Elliott (Eds.), *At the threshold: The developing adolescent* (pp. 308–329). Cambridge, MA: Harvard University Press.

Hess, R. D., & Miura, I. T. (1985). Gender differences in enrollment in computer camps and classes. *Sex Roles, 13,* 193–203.

Hiltz, S. R. (1982). *On line scientific communities: A case study of the office of the future.* Norwood, NJ: Ablex.

Hiltz, S. R. (1988). Productivity enhancement from computer mediated communication: A systems contingency approach. *Communications of the Association for Computing Machinery, 13*(12), 1438–1454.

Hiltz, S. R., & Turoff, M. (1978). *The network nation: Human communication via computer.* Reading, MA: Addison-Wesley.

Holsti, O. R. (1968). Content analysis. In G. Lindzey & E. Aronson (Eds.), *The handbook of social psychology* (Vol. 2, pp. 596–692). Reading, MA: Addison-Wesley.

Honey, M., & Moeller, B. (1990). *Teachers' beliefs and technology integration: Different values, different understandings* (Tech. Rep. No. 6). New York: Bank Street College of Education, Center for Technology in Education.

Horowitz, J. M. (1992, October). Crippled by computers. *Time,* pp. 70–72.

Huberman, M., & Miles, M. (1984). *Innovation up close: How school improvement works.* New York: Plenum.

Hughes, M. (1959). *Development of the means for the assessment of the quality of teaching in elementary schools.* Salt Lake City: University of Utah Press.

Hunter, B. (1992). Linking for learning: Computer-and-communications network support for nationwide innovation in education. *Journal of Science Education and Technology, 1*(1), 23–34.

Igbaria, M., & Chakrabarti, A. (1990). Computer anxiety and attitudes toward microcomputer use. *Behavior and Information Technology, 9*(3), 229–241.

Jagacinski, C. M., & Nicholls, J. G. (1987). Competence and affect in task involvement and ego involvement: The impact of social comparison information. *Journal of Educational Psychology, 79,* 107–114.

Johnson, D. W., & Johnson, R. T. (1974). Instructional structure: Cooperative, competitive or individualistic. *Review of Educational Research, 44,* 213–240.

Johnson, D. W., & Johnson, R. T. (1992). Positive interdependence: Key to effective cooperation. In R. Hertz-Lazarowitz & N. Miller (Eds.), *Interaction in cooperative groups* (pp. 174–199). Cambridge University Press.

Johnson, D. W., Maruyama, G., Johnson, R., Nelson, D., & Skon, L. (1981). Effects of cooperative, competitive, and individualistic goal structures on achievement: A meta-analysis. *Psychological Bulletin, 89,* 47–62.

Johnston, V. M. (1987). Attitudes towards microcomputers in learning: 1. Pupils and software for language development. *Educational Research*, *29*(1), 47–55.

Kerr, S. T. (1991). Lever and fulcrum: Educational technology in teachers' thought and practice. *Teachers College Record*, *93*(1), 114–136.

King, C., McNamee, G., Schustack, M., Swaine, K., Willett, E., & Worden, P. E. (1994, April). *Assessing the impact of after-school computer activity on children's computer knowledge*. Paper presented at the meeting of the American Educational Research Association, New Orleans.

Kinney, D. A. (1993). From nerds to normals: The recovery of identity among adolescents from middle school to high school. *Sociology of Education*, *66*, 21–40.

Kleiman, G. M. (1984). *Brave new schools: How computers can change education*. Reston, VA: Reston.

Kling, R. (1987). Defining the boundaries of computing across complex organizations. In R. J. Boland Jr., & R. A. Hirschheim (Eds.), *Critical issues in information systems research* (pp. 307–362). Chichester: Wiley.

Kling, R. (1990). Reading "all about" computerization: How genre conventions shape social analyses. In D. Schuler (Ed.), *Directions and implications of advanced computing* (pp. 26–47). Norwood, NJ: Ablex.

Kling, R. (1991). Computerization and social transformations. *Science, Technology and Human Values*, *16*(3), 342–367.

Komoski, K. P. (1984). Educational computing: The burden of insuring quality. *Phi Delta Kappan*, *66*(4), 244–248.

Kramer, P., & Lehman, S. (1990). Mismeasuring women: A critique of research on computer ability and avoidance. *Signs: Journal of Women and Culture in Society*, *16*(1), 158–172.

Kuhn, S. (1989). The limits to industrialization: Computer software development in a large commercial bank. In S. Wood (Ed.), *The transformation of work: Skill, flexibility and the labor process* (pp. 266–278). London: Unwin Hyman.

Laboratory of Comparative Human Cognition (1989). Kids and computers: A positive vision of the future. *Harvard Educational Review*, *59*, 73–86.

Lawler, B. (1984). Designing computer-based microworlds. In M. Yazdani (Ed.), *New horizons in educational computing* (pp. 40–53). Chichester: Harwood.

Lawler, R. W., & Yazdani, M. (Eds.). (1987). *Artificial intelligence and education* (Vol. 1). Norwood, NJ: Ablex.

Lepper, M. R. (1985). Microcomputers in education: Motivational and social issues. *American Psychologist, 40*(1), 1–18.

Lepper, M. R., & Chabay, R. W. (1985). Intrinsic motivation and instruction: Conflicting views on the role of motivational processes in computer-based education. *Educational Psychology, 20*(4), 217–230.

Lepper, M. R., & Gurtner, J. L. (1989). Children and computers: Approaching the twenty-first century. *American Psychologist, 44*(2), 170–178.

Lepper, M. R., & Malone, T. W. (1987). Intrinsic motivation and instructional effectiveness in computer-based education. In R. E. Snow & M. J. Farr (Eds.), *Aptitude, learning, and instruction: Vol. 3. Conative and affective process analyses* (pp. 255–296). Hillsdale, NJ: Erlbaum.

Lepper, M. R., Woolverton, M., Mumme, D. L., & Gurtner, J. L. (1993). Motivational techniques of expert human tutors: Lessons for the design of computer-based tutors. In S. P. Lajoie & S. J. Derry (Eds.), *Computers as cognitive tools* (pp. 75–105). Hillsdale, NJ: Erlbaum.

Lerner, R. M. (1982). Children and adolescents as producers of their own development. *Developmental Review, 2*, 342–370.

Lesgold, A. M., & Lesgold, S. B. (1984). *Classroom computers and state curriculum policy.* Unpublished manuscript, University of Pittsburgh, Pittsburgh.

Lesgold, A. M., & Reif, F. (1983). *Computers in education: Realizing the potential* (Chairmen's Report of a Research Conference). Washington, DC: U.S. Government Printing Office.

Lever, J. (1976). Sex differences in the games children play. *Social Problems, 23*, 478–487.

Levin, H. M., & Meister, G. R. (1984). *Computers in the balance: Weighing costs and effectiveness.* Unpublished manuscript, Stanford University, Institute for Research on Educational Finance and Governance, Stanford, CA:

Levin, J. A., & Kareev, Y. (1980). *Problem solving in everyday situations.* Unpublished manuscript, University of California, Laboratory of Comparative Human Cognition, San Diego, CA.

Levin, J. A., Riel, M., Miyake, N., & Cohen, M. (1987). Education on the electronic frontier: Teleapprentices in globally distributed educational contexts. *Contemporary Educational Psychology, 12*, 254–260.

Linn, M. C. (1985). Gender equity in computer learning environments. *Computers and the Social Sciences, 1*, 19–27.

Linn, M. C. (1992). The computer as learning partner: Can computer tools teach science? In K. Sheingold, L. G. Roberts, & S. M. Malcolm (Eds.), *This year in school science 1991: Technology for teaching and learning* (pp. 31–69). Washington, DC: American Association for the Advancement of Science.

Lipinski, A. S., Lipinski, H. M., & Randolph, R. H. (1972, October). Computer-assisted expert interrogation: A report on current methods development. In S. Winkler (Ed.), *Computer communication: Impacts and implications* (pp. 147–154). New York: Association for Computing Machinery.

Lockheed, M. E. (1985). Women, girls, and computers: A first look at the evidence. *Sex Roles, 13*(3–4), 115–121.

MacGregor, S. K. (1985, March). *Research issues in computer-assisted learning environments.* Paper presented at the meeting of the American Educational Research Association, Chicago.

McGuire, W. J., McGuire, C. V., Child, R., & Fujioka, T. (1978). Salience of ethnicity in the spontaneous self-concept as a function of one's ethnic distinctiveness in the social environment. *Journal of Personality and Social Policy, 36,* 511–520.

Mageau, T. (1991, Spring). Computer using teachers. *Agenda, 1,* 51.

Malone, T. W., & Lepper, M. R. (1987). Making learning fun: A taxonomy of intrinsic motivation for learning. In R. E. Snow & M. C. Farr (Eds.), *Aptitude, learning, and instruction: Vol. 3. Conative and affective process analyses* (pp. 223–253). Hillsdale, NJ: Erlbaum.

Martin, S. E. (1978). Sexual politics in the workplace: The international world of policewomen. *Symbolic Interaction, 1*(2), 44–60.

Means, B., Blando, J., Olson, K., Middleton, T., Morocco, C. C., Remz, A. R., & Zorfass, J. (1993). *Using technology to support education reform.* Washington, DC: U.S. Government Printing Office.

Melmed, A. (1993). *A learning infrastructure for all Americans: Summary of a report to the National Science Foundation.* Unpublished manuscript, George Mason University, Institute of Public Policy, Fairfax, VA.

Mevarech, Z. R., & Rich, Y. (1985). Effects of computer-assisted mathematics instruction on disadvantaged pupils' cognitive and affective development. *Journal of Educational Research, 79*(1), 5–11.

Miles, M., & Huberman, M. (1984). *Qualitative data analysis: A sourcebook of new methods.* Beverly Hills, CA: Sage.

Mitchell, E. (1981, April). *Children's uses and perceptions of friendship.* Paper presented at the meeting of the American Educational Research Association, Los Angeles.

Miura, I. (1986, April). *Understanding gender differences in middle school computer interest and use.* Paper presented at the meeting of the American Educational Research Association, San Francisco.

255

Mowshowitz, A. (1986). The social dimensions of office automation. *Advances in computers, 25*, 335–404.

National Assessment of Educational Progress. (1985). *The reading report card: Progress towards excellence in our schools: Trends in reading over four national assessments, 1971–1984.* Princeton, NJ: Educational Testing Service.

National Science Foundation (1978). *Report of the 1977 National Survey of Science, Mathematics, and Social Studies Education.* Washington, DC: National Science Foundation.

Newman, D. (1990). Opportunities for research on the organizational impact of school computers. *Educational Researcher, 19*(3), 8–13.

Newman, D. (1992). Technology as support for school structure and school restructuring. *Phi Delta Kappan, 74*, 308–315.

Nicholls, J. G., Patashnick, M., Cheung, P. C., Thorkildsen, T. A., & Lauer, J. M. (1989). Can achievement motivation theory succeed with only one conception of success? In F. Halisch & J. H. L. van den Bercken (Eds.), *International perspectives on achievement and task motivation* (pp. 187–208). Amsterdam: Swets & Zeitlinger.

Oakes, J. (1990). Opportunities, achievement, and choice: Women and minority students in science and mathematics. In C. B. Cazden (Ed.), *Review of research in education* (Vol. 16, pp. 3–56). Washington, DC: American Educational Research Association.

Oettinger, A. B. (1969). *Run computer run: The mythology of educational innovation.* New York: Collier.

Office of Technology Assessment (1988). *Power on! New tools for teaching and learning.* Washington, DC: U.S. Government Printing Office.

Olson, S. (1976). *Ideas and data: Process and practice of social research.* Homewood, IL: Dorsey.

Omark, R. R., Omark, M., & Edelman, M. (1975). Formation of dominance hierarchies in young children. In T. R. Williams (Ed.), *Psychological anthropology* (pp. 289–315). Paris: Mouton.

Papert, S. (1980). *Mindstorms: Children, computers, and powerful ideas.* New York: Basic.

Paris, C. L., & Morris, S. K. (1985). *The computer in the early childhood classroom: Peer helping and peer teaching.* Paper presented at the Microworld for Young Children Conference, College Park, MD.

Phillips, D. C. (1990). Subjectivity and objectivity: An objective inquiry. In E. W. Eisner & A. Peshkin (Eds.), *Qualitative inquiry in education: The continuing debate* (pp. 19–37). New York: Teachers College Press.

Piller, C. (1992, September). Separate realities: The creation of the technological underclass in America's public schools. *Macworld*, pp. 218–230.

Podmore, V. N. (1991). 4-year-olds, 6-year-olds, and microcomputers: A study of perceptions and social behaviors. *Journal of Applied Developmental Psychology, 12*, 87–101.

Quality Education Data (1992). *Ed tech trends*. Denver, CO: Quality Education Data.

Ratcliffe, J. (1983). Notion of validity in qualitative research methodology. *Knowledge Creation, Diffusion, Utilization, 5*(2), 147–167.

Reeve, J. (1992). *Understanding motivation and emotion*. Fort Worth, TX: Harcourt, Brace, Jovanovich.

Reinecke, I. (1984). *Electronic illusions: A skeptic's view of our high tech future*. New York: Penguin.

Reinharz, S. (1992). *Feminist methods in social research*. New York: Oxford University Press.

Riel, M. M., & Levin, J. A. (1990). Building electronic communities: Success and failure in electronic networking. *Instructional Science, 19*, 145–169.

Ringstaff, C., Sandholtz, J. H., & Dwyer, D. C. (1991). *Trading places: When teachers utilize student expertise in technology-intensive classrooms*. Paper presented at the meeting of the American Educational Research Association, Chicago.

Ritter, D. E. (1988). *Curriculum content today and tomorrow: Will students be motivated to learn?* Bowling Green, KY: Western Kentucky University. (ERIC Document Reproduction Service No. ED 303 443)

Roman, L. G., & Apple, M. W. (1990). Is naturalism a move away from positivism? Materialist and feminist approaches to subjectivity in ethnographic research. In E. W. Eisner & A. Peshkin (Eds.), *Qualitative inquiry in education: The continuing debate* (pp. 38–73). New York: Teachers College Press.

Rubin, Z. (1980). *Children's friendships*. Cambridge, MA: Harvard University Press.

Sagar, H. A., & Schofield, J. W. (1979). Racial and behavioral cues in black and white children's perceptions of ambiguously aggressive acts. *Journal of Personality and Social Psychology, 39*, 590–598.

Sagar, H. A., Schofield, J. W., & Snyder, H. N. (1983). Race and gender barriers: Preadolescent peer behavior in academic classrooms. *Child Development, 54*, 1032–1040.

Salomon, G. (1991). Transcending the qualitative-quantitative debate: The analytic and systemic approaches to educational research. *Educational Researcher, 20*(6), 10–18.

Sanders, J. S. (1984). The computer: Male, female, or androgynous. *Computing Teacher, 11*, 32–34.

Sandholtz, J. H., Ringstaff, C., & Dwyer, D. C. (1990, April). *Teaching in high-tech environments: Classroom management revisited.* Paper presented at the meeting of the American Educational Research Association, Boston.

Sarason, S. (1971). *The culture of the school and the problem of change.* Boston: Allyn & Bacon.

Scardina, F. (1972). *Sexism in textbooks in Pittsburgh public schools.* Pittsburgh, PA: University of Pittsburgh. (ERIC Document Reproduction Service No. ED 096224)

Schank, R. (1984). *The cognitive computer: On language, learning, and artificial intelligence.* Menlo Park, CA: Addison-Wesley.

Schofield, J. W. (1981). Complementary and conflicting identities: Images and interaction in an interracial school. In S. R. Asher & J. M. Gottman (Eds.), *The development of children's friendships* (pp. 53–90). Cambridge University Press.

Schofield, J. (1982). *Black and white in school: Trust, tension or tolerance?* New York: Praeger.

Schofield, J. W. (1985). *The impact of an intelligent computer-based tutor on classroom social processes: An ethnographic study.* Unpublished research proposal, University of Pittsburgh.

Schofield, J. W. (1986a). Black–white contact in desegregated schools. In M. Hewstone & R. Brown (Eds.), *Contact and conflict in intergroup encounters* (pp. 79–92). Oxford: Basil Blackwell.

Schofield, J. W. (1986b). Causes and consequences of the colorblind perspective. In S. Gaertner & J. Dovidio (Eds.), *Prejudice, discrimination and racism: Theory and practice* (pp. 231–253). New York: Academic.

Schofield, J. W. (1989a). *Black and white in school: Trust, tension or tolerance?* (rev. ed.). New York: Teachers College Press.

Schofield, J. W. (1989b, March). *Computers and classroom social processes.* Paper presented at the conference on Intelligent Computer-Assisted Instruction, Orlando, FL.

Schofield, J. W. (1991). School desegregation and intergroup relations: A review of the research. In G. Grant (Ed.), *Review of research in education* (Vol. 17, pp. 335–409). Washington, DC: American Educational Research Association.

Schofield, J. W., Eurich-Fulcer, R., & Britt, C. L. (1994). Teachers, computer tutors, and teaching: The artificially intelligent tutor as an agent for classroom change. *American Educational Research Journal, 31*(3), 69–97.

Schofield, J. W., Futoran, G. C., & Eurich-Fulcer, R. (1994a). *Common Knowledge: Pittsburgh – Implementing network connectivity in the Pittsburgh public schools.* Paper presented at the annual meeting of the American Educational Research Association, New Orleans.

Schofield, J. W., Futoran, G. C., & Eurich-Fulcer, R. (1994b). *The Internet in school: Lessons learned from the first year of a national test-bed.* Paper presented at the Network Services Conference, London.

Schofield, J. W., & Sagar, H. A. (1979). The social context of learning in an interracial school. In R. Rist (Ed.), *Inside desegregated schools: Appraisals of an American experiment* (pp. 155–199). San Francisco: Academic.

Schofield, J. W., & Verban, D. (1988). Computer usage in the teaching of mathematics: Issues which need answers. In D. Grouws & T. Cooney (Eds.), *Effective mathematics teaching* (pp. 169–193). Hillsdale, NJ: Erlbaum.

Schulz, E. (1992, January 8). Learning a hard lesson on the introduction of technology. *Education Week*, pp. 18–20.

Scriven, M. (1972). Objectivity and subjectivity in educational research. In L. Thomas (Ed.), *Philosophical redirection of educational research* (pp. 94–142). Chicago: National Society for the Study of Education.

Shade, D. D., Nida, R., Lipinski, J., & Watson, J. A. (1986). Microcomputers and pre-schoolers: Working together in a classroom setting. *Computers in the Schools, 3*(2), 53–61.

Shaiken, H. (1986). *Work transformed: Automation and labor in the computer age.* Lexington, MA: Lexington Books.

Sheingold, K., Hawkins, J., & Char, C. (1984). "I'm the thinkest, you're the typist": The interaction of technology and the social life of classrooms. *Journal of Social Issues, 40*(3), 49–62.

Sheingold, K., Kane, J. H., & Endreweit, M. E. (1983). Microcomputer use in schools: Developing a research agenda. *Harvard Educational Review, 53*, 412–432.

Sheingold, K., & Tucker, M. S. (1990). *Restructuring for learning with technology.* New York: Center for Technology in Education, Bank Street College of Education.

Shelly, G. B., & Cashman, T. J. (1980). *Introduction to computers and data processing.* Fullerton, CA: Anaheim Publishing Company.

Shrock, S. A., & Stepp, S. L. (1991). The role of the child microcomputer expert in an elementary classroom: A theme emerging from a naturalistic study. *Journal of Research on Computing in Education, 23*(4), 545–559.

Sills, T. M. (1992, April). *Analysis of student/teacher interactions in an urban middle school computer laboratory*. Paper presented at the meeting of the American Educational Research Association, San Francisco.

Simon, M. A. (1993). *The impact of constructivism on mathematics teacher education*. Unpublished manuscript, Penn State University, University Park, PA.

Sirotnik, K. (1981). *What you see is what you get: A summary of observations in over 1,000 elementary and secondary classrooms* (Technical Report No. 29). Los Angeles: University of California, Graduate School of Education.

Sjogren, D. D. (1967). Achievement as a function of study time. *American Educational Research Journal, 4,* 337–343.

Smith, C. P. (1969). Introduction. In C. P. Smith (Ed.), *Achievement-related motives in children* (pp. 1–10). New York: Russell Sage.

Smith, L. M., & Geoffrey, W. (1968). *The complexities of an urban classroom.* New York: Holt, Rinehart, & Winston.

Smith, L. M., & Keith, P. (1971). *The anatomy of educational innovation.* New York: Wiley.

Soloway, E. (1991). How the Nintendo generation learns. *Communications of the Association for Computing Machinery, 34*(9), 23–26, 95.

Staff. (1985, September). A status report on computers in schools. *Personal Computing,* p. 88.

Staff. (1989). Teachers feel computer gap with students. *Post Gazette,* p. 11.

Steffe, L. P., von Glasersfeld, E., Richards, J., & Cobb, P. (1983). *Children's counting types: Philosophy, theory, and application.* New York: Praeger.

Steinberg, L. (1985). *Adolescence.* New York: Knopf.

Strassman, P. (1985). *Information payoff: The transformation of work in the electronic age.* New York: Basic.

Straub, D. W., & Wetherbe, C. (1989). Information technologies for the 1990s: An organizational impact perspective. *Communications of the Association for Computing Machinery, 32*(11), 1329–1339.

Strauss, A. (1987). *Qualitative analysis for social scientists.* Cambridge University Press.

Strauss, A., & Corbin, J. (1990). *Basics of qualitative research.* Newbury Park, CA: Sage.

Sussman, L. (1977). *Tales out of school: Implementing organizational change in the elementary grades.* Philadelphia, PA: Temple University Press.

Sutton, R. E. (1991). Equity and computers in the schools: A decade of research. *Review of Educational Research, 61*(4), 475–503.

Taylor, J. (1979). Sexist bias in physics textbooks. *Physics Education, 14,* 277–280.

Taylor, S. E., Fiske, S. T., Etcoff, N. L., & Ruderman, A. J. (1978). Categorical and contextual bases of person memory and stereotyping. *Journal of Personality and Social Psychology, 36*(7), 778–793.

Toffler, A. (1980). *The third wave*. New York: Bantam.

Turkle, S., & Papert, S. (1990). Epistemological pluralism: Styles and voices within the computer culture. *Signs: Journal of Women and Culture in Society, 16*(1), 128–157.

U.S. Department of Labor (1991). *What work requires of schools: A Scans report for America 2000*. Washington, DC: Secretary's Commission on Achieving Necessary Skills, U.S. Department of Labor.

Van den Berg, W., Van Velzen, W. G., Miles, M. B., Ekholm, M., & Hameyer, U. (1986). *Making school improvement work*. Heverlee, Belgium: Acco.

von Glasersfeld, E. (1989). Constructivism. In T. Husen & T. N. Postlethwaite (Eds.), *The international encyclopedia of education* (Vol. 1, pp. 162–163). Oxford: Pergamon Press.

von Glasersfeld, E. (1992). Constructivism reconstructed: A reply to Suchting. *Science and Education, 1*, 379–384.

Walford, G. (1981). Tracking down sexism in physics textbooks. *Physics Education, 16*(5), 261–265.

Walker, D. (1984). Promise, potential, and pragmatism: Computers in high school. *Institute for Research in Educational Finance and Governance Policy Notes, 5*(3), 3–4.

Ware, C. W., & Stuck, M. F. (1985). Sex-role messages vis-a-vis microcomputer use: A look at the pictures. *Sex Roles, 13*, 205–214.

Waugh, M., & Levin, J. A. (1989). TeleScience activities: Educational uses of electronic networks. *Journal of Computers in Mathematics and Science Teaching, 8*, 29–33.

Webb, N. W. (1982). Student interaction and learning in small groups. *Review of Educational Research, 52*(3), 421–445.

Webb, N. W. (1987). Peer interaction and learning with computers in small groups. *Computers in Human Behavior, 3*, 193–209.

Weitzman, L., & Rizzo, D. (1974). *Biased textbooks: Images of males and females in elementary school textbooks*. Washington, DC: National Foundation for the Improvement of Education.

Weizenbaum, J. (1976). *Computer power and human reason*. San Francisco: Freeman.

Wertheimer, R. (1990). The geometry proof tutor: An "intelligent" computer-based tutor in the classroom. *Mathematics Teacher, 83*, 308–317.

Wellesley College Center for Research on Women (1992). *The AAUW Report: How schools shortchange girls*. Washington, DC: American Association of University Women Educational Foundation.

Wilder, G., Mackie, D., & Cooper, J. (1985). Gender and computers: Two surveys of computer-related attitudes. *Sex Roles, 13*, 215–228.

Wilson, K. S., & Tally, W. J. (1991). *Designing for discovery: Interactive multimedia learning environments at Bank Street College* (Tech. Rep. No. 15). New York: Bank Street College of Education, Center for Technology in Education.

Wood, S. (1989). The transformation of work. In S. Wood (Ed.), *The transformation of work: Skill, flexibility and the labor process* (pp. 1–43). London: Unwin Hyman.

Youniss, J., & Smollar, J. (1985). *Adolescent relations with mothers, fathers, and friends*. Chicago: University of Chicago Press.

Zorfass, J. M. (1991, April). *Promoting successful technology integration through active teaching practices*. Paper presented at the meeting of the American Educational Research Association, Chicago.

Zorfass, J., Morocco, C. C., Russell, S. J., & Zuman, J. (1989). *Evaluation of the integration of technology for instructing handicapped children (middle school level) (Phase I final report)*. Newton, MA: Education Development Center.

Zuboff, S. (1988). *In the age of the smart machine: The future of work and power*. New York: Basic.

AUTHOR INDEX

263

SUBJECT INDEX